Eurofutures
Five scenarios for the next millenium

David Smith

CAPSTONE

Copyright © David Smith 1997

The right of David Smith to be identified as the author of this work has been asserted in accordance with the Copyright, Designs and Patents Act 1988.

This edition first published 1997
Capstone Publishing Limited
Oxford Centre for Innovation
Mill Street
Oxford OX2 0JX
United Kingdom

All rights reserved. Except for the quotation of short passages for the purposes of criticism and review, no part of this publication may be reproduced, stored in a retrieval system, or transmitted, in any form or by any means, electronic, mechanical, photocopying, recording or otherwise, without the prior permission of the publisher.

British Library Cataloguing in Publication Data
A CIP catalogue record for this book is available from the British Library

ISBN 1-900961-16-4

Designed and typeset by Forewords, Oxford
Printed and bound by T.J. Press Ltd, Padstow, Cornwall

This book is printed on acid-free paper

Contents

Introduction	1
The story so far	5
Part I	11
A 50-year journey	13
At the crossroads	37
Part II	61
Scenario 1: The renaissance	63
Scenario 2: Plus ça change	95
Scenario 3: Les Etrangers	123
Scenario 4: The dark ages	151
Scenario 5: The apocalypse	181
Probabilities	213
Part III	222
The players	223
Conclusion	247
References	249
Index	255

Acknowledgements

My grateful thanks to Mark Allin at Capstone, for initiating and seeing this project through to completion. Also to Jane, my wife, and Richard, Thomas, Emily and Elizabeth, my children, for their forbearance. This book has benefited from the observations and expertise of many people, too numerous to mention. My thanks to them all.

Introduction

Europe at the end of the 20th century is at a fascinating juncture, a crossroads. This book is an attempt to peer ahead into the 21st century. What will happen to Europe as a whole, and your part of it, and how will that affect business, goverment and individuals? Is Europe coming together or on the brink of a painful schism? Will Europe be a good place to live, work and do business in? Are our politicians thinking seriously enough about the challenges and dangers that lie ahead, or are they obsessed only with the short-term, with winning the next election? These are not just questions of academic interest. They will determine Europe's prospects, and its role in the world and are central for anyone with an interest, and a stake, in the continent's future. For business based in, or reliant upon, European markets, for policy-makers attempting to develop strategies and contingency plans, and for the interested citizens of Europe, it is hoped that this book will be both thought provoking and prove to be of significant practical use. Everyone has their own thoughts about Europe's future course. The virtue of setting out a range of possibilities, and incorporating them in a set of scenarios, is that it provides a more disciplined framework for such thoughts, and a spur for further ideas.

Is Europe in a period of terminal decline, painfully losing its economic faculties, or about to spring up again, revitalised? Is the future of a wider Europe, taking in the former communist countries of eastern Europe in a powerful cohesive whole, or will the narrow self-interests of a small core of countries come to dominate, to the detriment of the entire continent? What are the prospects for Europe's immediate, and perhaps boldest, exercise in integration, monetary union? As this book was being written, the tensions between the political will driving monetary union forward and the underlying economic realities were increasingly exposed. One of the key questions, therefore, is whether, and in what form, it goes ahead. Crucially, can Europe, as it has more or less done for the past 50 years, continue to live at peace with itself? These and many other questions deserve addressing, and this book attempts to do so.

Anyone attempting futurology invites criticism. Henry Ford's most famous observation was that 'history is bunk'. His comments on futurology would probably have been unprintable. Nevertheless, there is widespread, often intense, interest in Europe's future, not least among modern-day businessmen. In the course of writing this book I have discovered that many companies have been carrying out their own internal exercises along similar lines. This book will, I hope, provide both a supplement to these, and an encouragement to others.

A word about the scenario approach used in this exercise. Why not, some will say, take one view on the future and explore it in greater depth, whether it be optimistic, pessimistic or somewhere in between? Is not the use of scenarios something of a cop-out? Perhaps, but the single-scenario approach was rejected because it would have been too limiting. The book's intention is to provide the intelligent reader with a choice, it is for him or her, ultimately, to decide on the plausibility of the scenarios set out here. Even restricting it to five scenarios is quite limiting – the number of cross scenarios, in which aspects from one are combined with those of others, is infinite.

Scenarios also offer the advantage of being able to compartmentalise the forces that will affect Europe in the next century, some good, some bad, some known and some yet to emerge as shocks on the horizon. It is the interplay of these forces that will determine whether Europe has an optimistic or pessimistic future, and the kind of response policy-makers should now be confronting to the challenges that lie ahead. If, for example, a pessimistic economic scenario for Europe is based on poorly functioning markets, particularly labour markets, and the rising welfare burdens arising from ageing populations, the time to tackle them is now, not when they have pushed Europe to a position from which it cannot recover.

This is not a book about Europe's political institutions. The precise way in which the European Commission, European Parliament and European Council, together with other institutions such as the European Court of Justice, will develop in the 21st century deserves a study of its own. Conducting such a study ahead of the completion of the intergovernmental conference (IGC) on European institutions offers too many hostages to fortune. The different scenarios sketched out in this book carry clear implications for the institutions but, as I say, they are not the focus of this exercise.

The structure of the book is straightforward. I begin with a brief history of Europe's post-war progress, with a particular focus on integration, moving on to an assessment of where Europe stands today. Part II contains the five scenarios, and is thus the nub of the book. Their titles, The Renaissance, *Plus ça Change*, Les Etrangers, The Dark Ages and The Apocalypse, should be self-explanatory – they range from the very optimistic to the extremely pessimistic. At the end of Part II I attach probabilities to the five different visions of Europe in the 21st century, before, in Part III, looking at how the 'players' in Europe and beyond are likely to fare under the various scenarios.

Inevitably, the tone of this kind of exercise is conditioned by the mood of the time in which it is carried out. Pessimism about Europe has been much more widespread in the 1990s than, for example, in the 1980s. It may be that this is a symptom of chickens coming home to roost but it could also be just a temporary phenomenon. I have tried, as much as possible, to look beyond these inevitable short-term influences. The reader will judge whether I have succeeded.

The story so far

1950   May 9: Robert Schuman, the French foreign minister, proposes that France, Germany and other countries that wish to join pool their coal and steel resources.

1951   April 18: The Treaty of Paris, establishing the European Coal and Steel Community (ECSC), is signed by the Six – France, Germany, Belgium, the Netherlands, Luxembourg and Italy.

1952   May 27: A treaty to establish a European Defence Community is signed in Paris.

1954   August 30: The European Defence Community is rejected by the French Parliament.
October 20–3: The Western European Union (WEU) is established, with an agreement in Paris.

1955   June 1–2: Foreign ministers of the Six, meeting in Messina, decide to move forward to an economic community.

1957   March 25: The treaties establishing the European Economic Community (EEC) and the European Atomic Energy Community (Euratom) are signed in Rome.

1958   January 1: Both treaties come into force. Commissions, for the EEC and Euratom, are set up in Brussels.

1960   January 4: The Stockholm Convention, establishing the European Free Trade Association (Efta), is signed by Austria, Denmark, Norway, Portugal, Sweden, Switzerland and the UK.

1962   July 30: The Common Agricultural Policy (Cap) is introduced.

1963   January 14: After Britain has applied for membership of the EEC, General de Gaulle announces in Paris that France will veto UK membership.

July 20: The Yaoundé Association Agreement, between the EEC and 18 African countries, is signed.

1965 April 8: An agreement to merge the executives of all three communities (the ECSC, the EEC and Euratom) is signed in Brussels. The European Communities (EC) becomes their joint name.

1966 January 29: After de Gaulle pursued his 'empty chair' policy from July to December 1965 – in protest at majority voting and a perceived loss of national power to the EC's supranational institutions – the Luxembourg compromise is agreed, under which unanimity is required for decisions where important national interests are at stake.

1968 July 1: The remaining customs duties on trade in manufactured goods within Europe are removed, 18 months ahead of schedule, and the common external tariff etablished.

1969 December 1–2: Meeting at The Hague, EC leaders agree definitive arrangements for the operation of the CAP, thus bringing transitional arrangements to an end and agreeing to an 'own resources' budget for the Community.

1970 April 22: A treaty providing for a gradual introduction of own resources is signed in Luxembourg, which also gives the European Parliament greater budgetary powers (both were bones of contention for de Gaulle during the empty chair crisis – he died in 1970).
June 30: Negotiations begin for the accession of Denmark, Ireland, Norway and the UK.

1972 January 22: The Treaty of Accession for Denmark, Ireland, Norway and the UK is signed in Brussels.
April 24: As the Bretton Woods system of fixed-but-adjustable exchange rates collapses, the 'snake' is set up, with the Six agreeing to limit fluctuations between their currencies to 2.25%. The snake had a chequered history, the UK joining but only briefly, some non-EC countries joining (e.g. Sweden) but not all of the Six (e.g. France and Italy) remaining part of it.

1973 January 1: Denmark, Ireland and the UK join the EC but not Norway, after membership is rejected in a referendum.

1974	December 9–10: Meeting in Paris, EC leaders agree direct elections to the European Parliament and the setting up of the European Regional Development Fund.
1975	February 28: The Lomé Convention, between the EC and 46 countries in Africa, the Caribbean and the Pacific, is signed. July 22: Agreement is reached on wider budgetary powers for the Parliament and the establishment of a Court of Auditors (on June 1, 1977).
1978	July 6–7: At Bremen, France and Germany jointly present plans for closer monetary co-operation – the European Monetary System.
1979	March 13: The EMS begins. May 28: Greece's Treaty of Accession is signed. June 7 and 10: First direct elections to the Parliament. October 31: A second Lomé convention, involving 58 states, is signed.
1981	January 1: Greece joins the EC.
1984	February 28: The Esprit programme for research and development in information technology is signed. June 14 and 17: Second direct elections to the Parliament. December 8: A third Lomé convention, with 66 states, is signed.
1985	January 1: Jacques Delors becomes Commission president. December 2–4: Meeting in Luxembourg, EC leaders agree to step up the integration process by drawing up a Single European Act.
1986	January 1: Spain and Portugal join the EC. February 17 and 28: The Single European Act is signed in Luxembourg and The Hague.
1987	April 14: Turkey applies for EC membership. July 1: The Single European Act comes into force. October 27: The WEU, meeting in The Hague, adopts a joint security platform.
1988	February: Reform of EC financing is announced, with multi-annual programme of expenditure for 1988–92 and reform of the structural funds.
1989	January: Delors is reappointed Commission president for a further four years.

June 15 and 18: Third direct elections to the Parliament.
July 17: Austria applies for EC membership.
November 9: The Berlin Wall collapses.
December 9: Strasbourg European Council agrees to convene inter-governmental conferences (IGCs) on economic and monetary union (Emu) and political union.
December 15: Fourth Lomé convention is signed.

1990 May 29: An agreement to establish the European Bank for Reconstruction and Development is signed in Paris.
June 19: The Schengen Agreement, for the removal of border controls between participating countries, is signed by France, Germany and the Benelux countries.
July 4 and 16: Cyprus and Malta, respectively, apply for EC membership.
October 3: Germany is unified.
October 8: Sterling joins the exchange rate mechanism (ERM) of the EMS.
December 14: The two IGCs, agreed at Strasbourg, begin in Rome.

1991 July 1: Sweden applies for EC membership.
October 21: Agreement is reached on establishing a European Economic Area (EEA) comprising the EC and remaining Efta states.
December 9–10: Meeting in Maastricht, the European Council agrees the Treaty on European Union, paving the way for Emu by 1999.

1992 February 7: The Treaty on European Union is signed in Maastricht.
March 18 and 25: Finland and Norway, respectively, apply to join the EC.
April 6: The Portuguese escudo enters the ERM.
May 2: The EEA agreement is signed in Oporto.
June 2: Denmark rejects the Maastricht treaty in a referendum.
September 16: 'Black' Wednesday – a fierce speculative attack on the ERM forces the suspension of the membership of sterling and the Italian lira. Months of turbulence, characterised by devaluations of the minor currencies, follow.
September 20: France narrowly approves the Maastricht treaty, with 51.05% in favour.

	December 11–12: The European Council, meeting in Edinburgh, reaffirms the Maastricht treaty.
1993	January 1: The Single Market begins. May 18: After concessions, the Maastricht treaty is approved in a second Danish referendum. August 1–2: EC finance ministers and central bankers, meeting in emergency session in Brussels, agree to 'emergency' wider ERM bands of 15% on either side of central parities (from 2.25% or 6%). The Deutschmark and Dutch guilder will be maintained in 2.25% bands. November 1: The Maastricht treaty enters into force in all member states.
1994	January 1: Stage two of Emu begins, the European Monetary Institute begins to operate in Frankfurt. April 1: Hungary applies for EU membership. June 9 and 12: Fourth direct elections to the Parliament. June 24–5: Treaties of accession are signed by Austria, Finland, Norway and Sweden. November 27–8: Norway rejects EU membership in a referendum.
1995	January 1: Austria, Finland and Sweden join the EU. January 23: A new Commission begins work under the presidency of Jacques Santer. March 26: The Schengen Agreement enters into force with the original five signatory states plus Portugal and Spain. June 2: The Reflection Group for the 1996–7 IGC on EU institutions meets for the first time. December 15: The European Council approves January 1, 1999 as the starting date for the final stage of Emu.
1996	March 29: The 1996–7 IGC is launched at a special summit in Turin. May: The UK, in an echo of de Gaulle's empty chair policy, embarks on a short period of non-co-operation in EU matters over the issue of a ban on worldwide sales of British beef. It lasts until the following month's Florence summit. October 14: Finland joins the ERM (Austria had joined on January 8, 1995). November 24: Italy rejoins the ERM. December 13–14: Meeting in Dublin, the European Council

affirms January 1, 1999 as the start-date for Emu's final stage and agrees a 'stability pact' for Emu – a system of discipline for fiscal policy under Emu, including fines.

1997 March 25: Special summit of EU foreign ministers in Rome to commemorate 40th anniversary of the Treaty of Rome.

April 5–6: EU finance ministers, meeting in Noordwijk, the Netherlands, agree that a spring 1998 meeting, to be held in Brussels, will determine which countries are eligible for Emu.

June 16–17: Amsterdam EU summit and inter-governmental conference.

Part I

A 50-year journey

■ Founding fathers

Houjarray, a village in the Île de France, does not feature on many tourist itineraries, or even in the guide books. France's heritage tourism tends to focus on more distant historical figures than those concerned with late 20th-century European unity. It was there, however, in a modest thatched house, now preserved as a monument to him, that, in the immediate aftermath of the 1939–45 conflict, Jean Monnet, the father of the European Union, devised his vision and framework for the integration of the recently warring nations of Europe. Monnet, born into a well-to-do family of cognac producers in 1888, was a polymath: deputy director-general of the League of Nations from 1920 to 1923, after which he divided his time between the family business, international finance and international economic diplomacy. When the Second World War broke out and France was in full retreat, Monnet was the author, in 1940, of a bold plan, accepted by Winston Churchill, for an 'indissoluble union' between France and Britain. It was, however, overtaken by events. Albert Lebrun, the French president, appointed Phillippe Pétain as prime minister, Pétain sought an armistice with Germany, and the fascinating prospect of a single Franco-British union became a footnote of history. Monnet spent the remainder of the war as a British civil servant based in Washington.

Monnet may not have succeeded with his plan for Franco-British union but this did not deter him from pressing again in the immediate post-war period, this time with the arguably more difficult task of integrating the defeated and shattered German nation into a union with the countries over which, so recently, it had held sway. Monnet's philosophy in this was that integration had to proceed through practical actions (*réalisations concrètes*) rather than over-ambitious grand visions. The embodiment of this was the speech by Robert

Schuman, the French foreign minister, on May 9, 1950. Schuman, tutored by Monnet, counts as another of Europe's founding fathers although, as Roy Jenkins recounts in his *European Diary*, Monnet was later to observe that Schuman did not really understand the plan which carried his name. The Schuman plan, for a pooling of coal and steel production between France and Germany (German production then being controlled by the Allied International Ruhr Authority), was aimed at making another war between the two nations both 'unthinkable and materially impossible'. The plan was taken up, not only by the French and West German governments but also by Belgium, Italy, Luxembourg and the Netherlands (collectively, the Six), culminating in the Treaty of Paris of 1951, which brought the European Coal and Steel Community (ECSC) into being. From a modern perspective, coal and steel seem almost peripheral industries. At the time, however, they were dominant, both as employers and in respect of their central role in energy supply, for coal, and in Europe's industrial structure, in the case of steel. The integration of coal and steel in Europe was a bold and far-reaching step, without which further moves towards European Union would have been difficult, if not impossible.

Konrad Adenaeur, German chancellor from 1949 to 1963, was another key player. He proposed complete union between France and Germany in 1950 but, when this was rejected as too much too soon, channelled his energies into enthusiastic support for the ECSC and for subequent integration. He, like the other founding fathers of Europe, had no doubt about what the final destination of economic integration should be. 'From the personal conversations I have had with M. Monnet I have been confirmed that political elements weigh most heavily in the balance', Adenauer told the Bundestag in June 1950. 'The purpose of the French proposal is to create a European federation. On this I am in total agreement.'

Other key names include Paul-Henri Spaak, a passionate Belgian advocate of European integration, who chaired the committee which established the detailed framework for the European Economic Community, and for whom a bitter personal disappointment was Britain's refusal to join either the ECSC or the Common Market. Spaak was also, from 1957 to 1961, secretary-general of the North Atlantic Treaty Organisation (Nato).

Altiero Spinelli, who has become something of a bogeyman for modern British Eurosceptics, was another influential figure. Spinelli, a journalist, was imprisoned for opposition to Mussolini. While in prison in 1941, he and a group of fellow federalists wrote a manifesto for a federal Europe, which was adopted as the creed of his Movimento Federalista Europeo, founded in 1943. He and his followers were driven by a vision of creating a federal Europe out of the ruins of post-Second World War Europe. He was later a prominent member of the European Commission and European Parliament. In 1984 he was the principal author of a 'draft treaty establishing the European Union', adopted by the Parliament, which envisaged a new drive towards integration, and a pooling of national sovereignty, in economic and monetary affairs, social policy, including welfare and health, and in foreign policy, including security and disarmament.

■ Messina and the Common Market

It is easy to think of the progress towards European integration as being an uninterrupted journey, particularly in the heady days of the 1950s, when Europe was anxious to put the war behind it and remove the possibility of another. This, however, was far from the case. Despite the success of the ECSC, the next attempt at integration, the European Defence Community Treaty, ended in failure. Although the EDC treaty was signed in Paris by the Six in May 1952, and ratified by five national parliaments, it was rejected by the French National Assembly, on the grounds that it would mean an unacceptable loss of national sovereignty. This rejection also killed off the embryonic European Political Community, a draft treaty for which had been adopted in 1953. Instead, the Western European Union, a body to co-ordinate national action on defence and security matters was set up, which included Britain among its members, coming into force in 1955. In the same year West Germany was admitted to Nato, which had been established by 12 countries (Belgium, Britain, Canada, Denmark, France, Iceland, Italy, Luxembourg, the Netherlands, Norway, Portugal and the United States) in 1948–9. Neither the Western European Union (WEU) nor Nato had much to do with the vision of integration of Europe's founding fathers. Defence and political union, as was later to be confirmed, were difficult areas.

The question, then, was how to build on the success of the ECSC in the economic area. The significance of the earlier agreement on coal and steel was that it provided a common market for these products but also that it provided for co-operation in the production of coal, a key energy resource. In the 1950s, however, all the excitement was over another, newer, energy resource – atomic power. France, in particular, was keen to extend co-operation in this area, mindful of the fact that Britain had established a technological lead. France, too, was fully aware of the fact that Belgium had access to uranium reserves in the Congo, one of its dependencies. Thus, there was considerable French impetus for extending European co-operation in atomic energy. The Benelux countries, meanwhile, having established a customs union in 1948, were keen not only to extend this to other countries in Europe, but to make progress towards free movement in goods, services, people and capital – later to be the four pillars of the Single Market. They were supported by West Germany and Italy.

There were, thus, two substantial items on the agenda when foreign ministers of the Six met at Messina, Sicily, in June 1955. The first was a European Atomic Energy Community (Euratom), the prize that France sought. The second was a European Economic Community (EEC), which the others wanted but France had reservations about. Astonishing as it seems now, when even minor European decisions, and sometimes no decisions at all, require the full panoply of European Council meetings, or summits, with heads of state or government, foreign and finance ministers, countless officials and even more journalists in attendance – with communiqués prepared well in advance – this low-key, and relatively low-level meeting, marked the beginning of a period of intense European integration, and the establishment of the EEC or, as it was popularly known, the Common Market. Perhaps there was little awareness of the momentousness of the Messina deliberations – certainly the immediate press coverage, which was not extensive, devoted as much attention to Euratom, which now barely features in the European debate, as to the EEC. As Sir Roy Denman records in his book *Missed Chances*, Britain was invited to send a foreign minister to the meeting but, when a senior Quai d'Orsay official telephoned London to discuss the possibility of British attendance, he was told that Messina was 'a devilish awkward place to expect a minister to get to'.

The Messina conference agreed to the setting-up of an intergovernmental committee, mentioned above, under the chairmanship of Paul-Henri Spaak. The Spaak committee reported back to foreign ministers on two occasions in 1956, before being given the go-ahead to produce detailed drafts for treaties establishing the EEC, including a Common Agricultural Policy – the details of which, including the central element of price support, were worked out later at the Stresa conference of July 1958 – and Euratom. The two treaties were duly signed in Rome, hence the Treaty of Rome, on March 25, 1957 and, after ratification by the parliaments of the Six, came into effect on January 1, 1958. For the detailed treaty drafting, the Spaak committee had turned to Pierre Uri, the French economist who had been entrusted with a similiar task for the treaty establishing the ECSC. He, at least, had no doubt about the significance of the course that Europe had embarked upon:

> The free play of market forces in the simple abolition of tariffs and quotas was not acceptable to contemporary society. The state, or whatever economic authority held power, was expected to provide welfare, security and full employment and to increase prosperity for all its citizens. This meant that power over private enterprise and planning of development, previously the responsibility of individual states, could not simply lapse: it must instead be exercised by the wider European Community. This in the long run implied, and was meant to imply, fiscal, social, monetary, and ultimately, political union. (quoted in *Denman*, p. 200)

■ Britain and Europe: 'au revoir et bonne chance'

One of the great mistakes of history, according to the majority of those who believe that Britain's future lies, and back then lay, in closer relations with Europe, was the decision by British governments of the 1950s effectively to turn their back on the process of integration that was getting under way in the rest of Europe. Winston Churchill, in his Zurich speech of September 1946, had at least given a positive lead, talking of the need for partnership between a 'spiritually great' France and Germany. 'We must', he said resoundingly, 'build a kind of United States of Europe.' Churchill, despite revisionist attempts to portray him as the father of ever closer union between Britain and Europe, was careful to say that while Britain would be 'friend and sponsor' of this new United States of Europe, the pull of the Commonwealth, and of the special relationship with America, would prevent her from being part of it. Subsequent events, however, called into question even Britain's role as friend and sponsor.

The common theme in Britain's post-war relations with Europe has been that, whenever new proposals have come forward, British governments have contrived to be unprepared for them. The Attlee government was genuinely taken by surprise by the Schuman coal and steel proposals, although the characteristically blunt reaction of Herbert Morrison, the deputy prime minister – 'the Durham miners won't wear it' – was barely refined in the government's more considered response. 'We on this side are not prepared to accept the principle that the most vital economic forces of this country should be handed over to an authority that is utterly undemocratic and responsible to nobody', Attlee told the House of Commons.

Once Britain had opted not to take part in the ECSC (although in 1954 the Conservative government signed an association agreement with it), the chances of British participation in other aspects of European integration were clearly much slimmer. The failure of the European defence and political communities to get off the ground, and the subsequent strengthening of the WEU and Nato, appeared to suggest briefly that things were moving Britain's way, and thus against further integration. Messina was to change all that. Britain did not, as noted above, send a minister to the Messina meeting. Russell Bretherton, an Oxford economics don turned senior civil servant (under-secretary at the Board of Trade), did, however, become the eyes and ears of the British government in the initial negotiations over the establishment of the EEC. 'Pipe-smoking, spare and austere', according to Denman, 'with Americans and Commonwealth men he was relaxed. Apart from a few words of French, he spoke no foreign language; continentals, he believed, were unreliable fellows, apt to get up to mischief if not kept under control.'

Bretherton attended meetings of the Spaak committee, listened, said very little and was openly sceptical about the type of future for Europe being considered. Finally, in November 1955, after clearing his position with London, he was able to say that he had seen and heard enough, telling the committee:

> The future treaty which you are discussing has no chance of being agreed; if it was agreed, it would have no chance of being ratified; and if it were ratified, it would have no chance of being

applied. And if it was applied, it would be totally unacceptable to Britain. You speak of agriculture which we don't like, of power over customs, which we take exception to, and institutions, which frighten us. Monsieur le president, messieurs, au revoir et bonne chance. (quoted in Charles Grant, *Delors*, p. 62)

Twice within the space of five years, Britain had turned down the chance to be in on the ground floor of the development of a new, more integrated Europe. It was to be nearly 20 years before Britain acceded to a mature EEC, built around the Franco-German axis. Before then, Britain was to suffer the humiliation of two rejections, in January 1963 and November 1967, both largely at the hands of General de Gaulle. Britain was a maritime nation, with a tradition of free trade, and interests in the Commonwealth and the wider world, including the special relationship with America, said the general. Hence it was unsuitable for EEC membership. Curiously, 30 years on, these are the very arguments used by British Eurosceptics for loosening Britain's ties with Europe. Britain was also instrumental in the creation of the European Free Trade Area (Efta) in 1960, a system of mutually agreed tariff reductions for industrial goods – but most definitely not agriculture. Efta had seven members, Austria, Britain, Denmark, Norway, Portugal, Sweden and Switzerland. With the Six of the EEC in one grouping, and the seven of Efta in another, Europe was said, of course, 'to be at sixes and sevens'.

Only after de Gaulle had been replaced as French president by Georges Pompidou, in fact only after de Gaulle's death in 1970, was Britain finally admitted to the inner circle. Having applied in 1961, membership finally occurred, along with Ireland and Denmark (both of whose long-standing applications were scuppered by the de Gaulle veto of Britain), on January 1, 1973.

■ A Common Market

While Britain had been away, the Six got on with the task of creating a customs union, defined as the free movement of goods within an area bounded by a common external tariff. The notional free movement of goods was accomplished over a 10-year period, with roughly 10% cut annually from tariffs on trade between the member states of the EEC. Removing non-tariff barriers was a little more problematical, indeed some persist to this day. The common external tariff, like the removal of internal tariff barriers, was harmonised by July 1968, slightly ahead of schedule. In that year too, the Common Agricultural Policy (Cap), in which France had so much at stake, entered an important second phase, with the Mansholt plan (after Sicco Mansholt, former Dutch minister of agriculture, later president of the Commission), which proposed a move beyond initial agricultural co-operation between member states to a radical restructuring of European agriculture, including job losses, for which compensation would be offered.

In the 13 years from Messina, the Six had gone a long way towards creating a common market in goods. It had not been without its difficulties or dramas, notably de Gaulle's petulant empty chair strategy of 1965 when, in protest over what he saw as an unacceptable loss of national sovereignty to Brussels (majority voting and the introduction of the Community's 'own resources'), the French president boycotted meetings of the council of ministers and withdrew France's permanent representative from Brussels. The crisis was resolved by the Luxembourg compromise of January 1966, which allowed individual countries the power of veto over matters that otherwise could be decided by majority voting, and so calmed French fears.

The EEC, despite these bouts of awkwardness, usually emanating from de Gaulle – other members were rather more keen on British entry than the doughty French president – had been an outstanding political success. Britain's blatant attempt to scupper the EEC, by setting up the 'alternative common market' of Efta, had failed to divert the Six from their path. Efta was a poor relation to the EEC, a fact made obvious by Britain's intense efforts during the 1960s to join the inner circle occupied by the Six.

But was the EEC, in those early years, an economic success? The difficulty for the economist in making such an assessment is that, unlike the scientist, it is impossible to monitor the alternative in the form of a 'control'. In other words, it is impossible to know, with any certainty, what would have happened in the absence of the Common Market. One clear result is that every member state increased trade with the others markedly. In the 15 years from 1958, the share of gross domestic product (GDP) accounted for by intra-EEC exports increased, on average, from under 5% of Community GDP to 10%. For

Belgium and Luxembourg, with exports to other EEC countries up from 15% to 35% of GDP, there was an obvious benefit, as there was for France, up from 2.5% to 8%, and Italy, 2.7% to 7%. For Germany, however, arguably the main intended beneficiary of the Common Market, the effect was less pronounced – with intra-EEC exports rising from 5.4% to 9%, a smaller increase, in relative terms, than that enjoyed by Britain, with exports to the EEC up from 2.8% to 6% of GDP, despite being outside the system until 1973, and then only joining with a lengthy transitional period.

Other measures are little more conclusive. Total factor productivity, the weighted average of the growth in capital and labour productivity, is probably the best overall measure of economic performance. According to OECD figures, Europe's record on this score over the 1960–73 period, when the Common Market was coming to fruition, was impressive, with annual average growth of 3.3%, compared with 2.5% for North America and, admittedly, a far superior record – 5.4% a year – from the then emerging Japanese economy. Some EEC countries turned in sparkling performances – Italy 4.4%, Belgium 3.8%, France 3.7% – but then so did some Efta countries – Portugal 5.4%, Austria 3.1%. Britain, curiously in what was still the time of the German economic miracle or *Wirtschaftswunder*, had exactly the same record as Germany, 2.6%.

Free trade is, of course, a good thing, and free trade within Europe was welcome. But this was a time of trade liberalisation worldwide when, thanks to the Dillon and Kennedy rounds under the auspices of the General Agreement on Tariffs and Trade (Gatt), tariff barriers were coming down everywhere, and world trade was growing rapidly. The Common Market had the effect of diverting trade from outside the Community to other member states. It coincided with a period of notable European economic success. The extent of its contribution to that success remains, however, a matter of debate.

■ *Emu, mark I*

Another debate, one of the oldest in economics, is over the virtues of fixed versus floating exchange rates. Advocates of fixed rates argue that they provide the necessary stability and certainty for business, and protection against the vagaries of currency speculation, thus generating faster growth in trade. Floating rate supporters dismiss these arguments – apart from the fact that businesses can protect themselves against currency swings, they argue for the theory of 'one price', that it is better for an economy to change that one price, the exchange rate, frequently if necessary, than struggle to maintain an unrealistic fixed parity. Fixed exchange rates, on this view, inhibit growth rather than facilitate it. If there is a European, or at least a continental European, view on this matter it is on the side of fixed exchange rates. European politicians rail at 'Anglo-Saxon speculators' who undermine their best endeavours. As for the Anglo-Saxon view, it was best summed up by Margaret Thatcher when, alarmed that Nigel Lawson was trying to stabilise sterling's value against the Deutschmark, she said: 'There is no way in which one can buck the market.'

European economic and monetary union, which I prefer to call European monetary union (Emu) – economic union progressing along its own well-defined path from the creation of the EEC in 1958 – was not mentioned in the Treaty of Rome. At the time, with the Bretton Woods system of international fixed-but-adjustable exchange rates in operation, it perhaps did not need to be. Given the sensitivity of France, in particular, to surrendering too much sovereignty, hence the rejection of the European Defence and Political Communities, the treaty-drafters were probably wise to keep their powder dry. Bretton Woods did not involve, however, any notion of progress towards a world single currency. Nor was it a guarantee against exchange-rate shifts. November 1967, for example, was a humiliating month for the Wilson government in Britain. Not only did de Gaulle reject British entry into the EEC for a second time but in the same month sterling was devalued by 14% against other currencies.

Within the developing EEC, two specific exchange-rate problems were perceived. The first was that the mere existence of different currencies within the Community denoted an important barrier to trade, even as other internal barriers were being dismantled. The second was that even very small shifts of Community currencies against each other posed problems for the Cap, and necessitated the creation of special 'shadow' exchange rates, the green franc, the green Deutschmark, etc., specifically for the purpose of calculating the monetary compensatory amounts used for farm support purposes. From the mid-1960s onwards, Commission officials, notably those from DG2, the Brussels directorate responsible for economic and monetary affairs, had begun to raise, discreetly, the topic of Emu. One prominent Commission advocate, Frédéric Boyer de la Giroday, a Frenchman, argued strongly that separate currencies were a significant barrier to intra-European trade. As the Bretton Woods system moved towards inevitable collapse towards the end of the 1960s, such talk grew louder.

Another Frenchman, Raymond Barre, later prime minister, was the author of a plan to protect Europe from the vicissitudes of unstable world markets. The Barre plan envisaged closer co-ordination of economic policies within the EEC, a system of short-term credits to maintain fixed exchange rates against market pressure and the creation of a European Reserve Fund (ERF). Several aspects of the plan, although not the ERF, were adoped by the Six at a summit meeting at The Hague in December 1969. More significantly, the summit adopted the goal of achieving Emu and gave the task of examining the practicalities of it to a committee chaired by Pierre Werner, the prime minister of Luxembourg. The Werner committee, which reported in 1970, envisaged the achievement of Emu by 1980, with Community currencies irrevocably fixed against one another and preferably replaced by a single currency. Like its successor in the 1990s, the Werner plan saw a three-stage process leading to monetary union. Monetary policy would be co-ordinated by a Community system of central banks, fiscal policy by a beefed-up Ecofin (the Council of finance ministers of the member states).

It was a hugely ambitious plan and one which, even without the economic turbulence created by the first Opec (Organisation of Petroleum Exporting Countries) crisis of 1973, would have struggled to get off the ground. France, again, was concerned about the supra-national basis of the plan. Tentative agreement was reached to proceed with the first stage of Emu, mainly the relatively safe option of co-operating more closely on economic policy. In 1974, with Opec's oil price hike wreaking havoc on Europe's economies, and amid turbulence in international financial markets, the plan, and hence the goal of Emu by 1980, was quietly shelved. As for currency co-operation within Europe, all that was left to show for it was the 'snake', a system of narrow currency fluctuations, originally within the Bretton Woods limits, later, when Bretton Woods collapsed, on its own. The Six established the snake in March 1972, and were joined by Britain, Ireland and Denmark two months later. Britain, and with it Ireland, dropped out after six weeks, Italy left in 1973, France left in 1974 and again, after rejoining in 1975, in 1976. Other smaller countries joined but, by 1978–9, the snake was a limited Deutschmark zone, consisting of Germany, the Benelux countries, Denmark and Norway. And Emu looked like a pipe dream.

New Europeans

Despite this setback, the mere fact that Europe's leaders had been prepared to plan for monetary union by 1980 underlined the extent of their ambition. In the economic sphere, Europe was moving inexorably towards closer union. But was there also, socially and culturally, such a thing as a 'new' Europe developing? One of the first acts of European leaders in pursuit of their vision of a united Europe was the approval of the design of a European flag, the now familiar one of 12 gold stars, each with five points, on a blue background. This design, for which Paul Levy, director of information for the Council of Europe in the early 1950s, was largely responsible, beat off competition from others, including the European Movement's simple device of a large green 'E' on a white background. Contrary to popular impression, the number of stars on the European flag bears no relation to the number of member states. There were 12 stars when the EEC had six members, and there are 12 now that, at the time of writing, it has 15.

A flag is one symbol of cultural identity, another is an anthem. Seven years after adopting the 12-starred flag, Europe also acquired its own anthem, an arrangement by Herbert von Karajan of the 'Ode to Joy' from Beethoven's Ninth Symphony. There is also, in May each year, a 'Europe Day', although observance of it varies. Such symbols are important. Anyone who displays a European flag car-sticker or number-plate is either a Commission employee or a committed integrationist. There is, however, an inherent difficulty in the idea of too strong a European identity. Except for a minority, national symbols, and national identity, outweigh their European equivalents. The nation state comes first, Europe second. The French manage to be simultaneously chauvinist and enthusiastically European. The Germans, for good reasons, are wary of surrendering the Deutschmark in favour of the euro. Perhaps only in Belgium, perhaps the most confused nation-state of Europe, which also provides the Brussels home for the Commission and other European institutions, does Europe take precedence over country.

The creation of a European identity and culture has therefore proceeded with stealth, probably a wise strategy when even the introduction of a common passport design can provoke an outcry at loss of national sovereignty (the claret-coloured European design came into effect in 1985, much to the disgust of Britons unwilling to give up their larger, blue UK passports). For the Commission, in contrast, the common passport 'is for European citizens the symbol of European citizenship and of the freedom to go anywhere in the European Union'. On culture, although there is a treaty agreement to 'bring the common cultural heritage to the fore', diversity is recognised, even encouraged. According to the Commission's own guide, *European Integration*, written by Dr Klaus-Dieter Borchardt:

> One of Europe's most notable features is the cultural variety of countries and regions. Cultural assets such as the city of Venice, the paintings of Rembrandt, the music of Beethoven or the plays of Shakespeare are an integral part of a common cultural heritage and are regarded as common property by the citizens of Europe. (p. 73)

For Europe, the trouble has always been that cultural diversity and national pride mean that the idea of a European identity, or even a view of Europe, has been difficult to generate. Integration, too often, has been seen to favour the particular interests of big business, or of farmers, or of politicians and bureaucrats. Hence repeated attempts to create a 'People's Europe' – one in which the ordinary citizen had a direct interest. In 1975, a report drawn up by a committee under Leo Tindemans, then the Belgian prime minister, came up with a series of proposals, one of which came into vogue much later – the idea of a multi-speed Europe, in which countries could proceed towards integration at different paces. Nearly a decade later, the Committee for a People's Europe, the Adonnino committee, proposed among other things free movement of people within the Community (soon to form a central element of the Single Market programme). The committee also called for each member state to adopt similar election procedures, as well as unashamedly populist ideas such as a common European postage stamp and a Europe-wide lottery, which have remained on the shelf.

So has integration created a generation of new Europeans? To the extent that the majority of people, even in Britain, now accept the EU as a way of life, and any dismantling of it unthinkable, 'Europe' has entered the public consciousness. European Union is still in its infancy, the first serious steps towards the modern phase of integration were taken less than half a century ago. Even in America, with a head start of more than 150 years, many people still think of their state first, and the United States second. Europe has a long way to go.

▮ *From Common to Single Market*

The EEC had, as noted above, achieved tariff-free internal trade in goods before the end of the 1960s. In colloquial terms, the Common Market was in place. Economists would, however, give this achievement only five marks out of 10. Strictly speaking, the EEC had created a customs union rather than a common market. The Treaty of Rome envisaged a true common market as consisting not only of free movement of goods, but also in the factors of production – labour and capital. Even in the 1980s, Europe was a long way from achieving this, with many countries still operating both exchange controls, thus restricting the free movement of capital, and frontier controls, which prevented the free movement of people. Although workers had the right to take up jobs anywhere else in the Community, there remained serious barriers such as those arising from a lack of an agreement on recognition of common qualification standards. The Common Market needed new impetus, not least because the more that individuals moved and worked in different member countries, the more would the 'People's Europe' become a reality.

The new impetus was provided by the Single European Act, which came into effect in July 1987. Like the original Rome treaty, it had been prepared on the recommendations of a special committee, this time the Dooge committee (after its chairman, Irish senator James Dooge). And like that original treaty, it provided a huge step forward for European integration. The Single Market drive came at a time when many in Europe were fearful that the integration process was running out of steam. This was the context in which the European Parliament had published Spinelli's draft European Union treaty in 1984. The EEC was approaching its 30th birthday and, after striking progress in the first half of its existence, had become bogged down, partly because of international economic events, since.

The Commission, in the form of Lord Cockfield, the Commissioner responsible for Europe's internal trade, had drawn up a list of some 300 measures necessary for 'completion of the internal market'. They included the removal of physical trade barriers – controls at national borders – technical barriers, including different specification standards, and fiscal barriers, different tax regimes, particularly value-added tax (Vat), throughout the Community. Achieving implementation of these measures became known as the 1992 programme, with the aim being to have the 'single large market' in place by the end of 1992 (thus, '1992' was always '1993', in that the new market would not be effective until the start of the latter year). Cockfield also called for the removal of all remaining exchange controls within the Community to allow the free movement of capital, a measure that was the subject of a separate Commission directive in 1988, and achieved in line with the rest of the Single Market programme.

The Single European Act also gave new impetus to something that had been in abeyance since de Gaulle's empty chair crisis 20 years earlier – agreement on the widespread use of qualified majority voting (i.e. voting weighted to take account of the different size and population of member states). Apart from being considered essential in a larger Community (the Single European Act coincided with Spain and Portugal's accession), qualified majority voting would prevent countries with a particular interest in blocking a piece of liberalisation under the Single Market programme from halting progress – although the ultimate power of veto, under the so-called Luxembourg compromise, would remain. The drive to complete the Single Market did not, at first glance, have much to do with the idea of creating a true People's Europe. Most of the emphasis, indeed most of the publicity concerning the Act, was with the response of business. Even Britain, with the energetic Lord Young as trade and industry secretary, played its full part in the publicity drive to increase business awareness of '1992'. There were, however, two elements which would, in the future, have a profound impact on the lives of Europe's citizens.

The first was the agreement to protect poorer regions of Europe, notably Spain, Portugal, Greece and Ireland, sometimes known as the 'Club Med' countries, from the adverse effects of free movement of goods, people and capital by enhancing the Community's efforts to achieve economic and social 'cohesion', notably through expenditures from the budget on the structural funds – the European Structural Fund and the European Regional Development Fund. To have a true single market, in other words, the richer members would have to pay for it. The second was in the preamble to the Act, which recalled that Europe had, in 1972, committed itself to the achievement of full economic and monetary union. Emu was back on the agenda and, to the surprise of British ministers, Margaret Thatcher, while maintaining her strong opposition to British membership of the European exchange rate mechanism (ERM), had signed up. According to Nigel Lawson:

> She was able, with German support, to get the treaty reference to Emu watered down, and not removed altogether and, preferring the on-the-spot advice of the Foreign Office, who told her that what remained was little more than hot air, to the counsel I had offered in advance, she signed up. The great prize was allegedly the target of completing the Single Market by the end of 1992 and the facilitation of this by a large-scale move from unanimity to majority voting. I was sceptical about the wisdom of the deal she had struck. I felt that we had embarked on a dangerous slippery slope towards Emu. (*The View from No. 11*, p. 894)

■ *Emu, mark II*

We left monetary union and the single currency in the 1970s when, after the Werner timetable had been abandoned, Europe was left with the distinctly second-best solution of the currency snake, which provided limited exchange-rate stability within a small Deutschmark zone. Matters did not, however, rest there. Roy Jenkins, Britain's Chancellor of the Exchequer from 1967 to 1970, had taken on that post immediately after sterling's November 1967 devaluation. Whether because of this, or memories of Britain's humiliating rejections at the hands of de Gaulle, he was determined to prove his strong European credentials. He was appointed president of the Commission in 1976, Britain's first, and the following year, in a speech, revived the idea of Emu. Nor was this a voice in the wilderness. Helmut Schmidt, the

German chancellor, and Valéry Giscard D'Estaing, the French president, were increasingly concerned about the volatility of currency markets in what had become the floating rate era. They wanted to extend the process of monetary integration in Europe, as James Callaghan, then Britain's prime minister, later recalled. In April 1978, during a European Council meeting in Copenhagen, Giscard invited Callaghan to breakfast at the French embassy:

> The morning sun streamed into the breakfast-room and as we consumed our croissants and coffee, there evolved the idea of a European-type Bretton Woods, with a European exchange rate fixed against the dollar. Giscard's comments showed that he recognised that this would effectively mean Europe becoming a Deutschmark zone, but was nevertheless ready to go along. I was sympathetic with the general proposal, but had to make clear that as proposed, the effect of the scheme would be disadvantageous to Britain, for the strong Deutschmark would have the effect of tugging sterling upwards with deflationary consequences for the economy, unless long-term credit was absolutely unlimited. Helmut did his best to persuade us that membership of a monetary system would assist us, and I undertook to think the matter over. From the drift of Giscard's contributions there seemed little doubt that France and Germany would go ahead even of Britain did not join and their joint decision would almost certainly bring Belgium, Holland and Luxembourg into the scheme. (*Time and Chance*, pp. 492–3)

The European Monetary System (EMS), albeit not quite along the lines proposed by Schmidt and Giscard D'Estaing, was soon born. It had two main elements, a European Monetary Co-operation Fund (originally set up after Werner in 1973) in which each member would deposit 20% of gold and foreign currency reserves in exchange for Ecus (European currency units), the fund being used to co-ordinate joint intervention. The EMS is, of course, best known for the exchange rate mechanism (ERM). This was the European-style Bretton Woods system, in which most participating currencies were required to stay within a band, 2.25% on either side of a central rate. The central rate, just to demonstrate that, in design at least, this was not a Deutschmark zone, was specified against the Ecu.

The ERM story has been told often enough not to need repeating.

Suffice it to say that, in its early years – it began on March 13, 1979 without, as Callaghan had suggested, British participation – it was anything but a zone of monetary stability in Europe. There were 11 realignments of parities in its first eight years, the result of either a lack of convergence in economic performance, or President Mitterrand's attempt in the early 1980s to expand the French economy in the face of a world slowdown. Or perhaps it was the simple fact that, when it came to it, the currency markets expected the Deutschmark to rise against other European currencies, and nothing – certainly not an unproven exchange-rate framework – was going to persuade them otherwise. All this changed, at least for a while, with the French government's adoption of the *franc fort* strategy in the mid-1980s. After the 'final' realignment of January 1987, the ERM enjoyed more than five years of stability, bolstered by France's determination to be as tough on inflation as Germany. This lasted until September 1992, when the markets forced both the Italian lira (a founder member) and sterling, which had only entered in October 1990, out of the mechanism. From then until early August 1993, and the crisis that almost forced the collapse of the entire system, the ERM was wracked with turbulence. It held together, but only through the device of adopting very wide, 15%, fluctuation bands. The EMS was never explicitly a stepping-stone to monetary union, although, particularly during the 1987–92 period of stability (after the Emu goal had been reaffirmed), it was seen as part of the 'glidepath' to a single currency. Intriguingly, the subsequent near-collapse of the system merely hardened the attitudes of many in Europe towards the achievement of Emu.

Fortuitously, however, the period when the political goal of Emu was given fresh impetus coincided with a time when the ERM appeared to be working smoothly, so smoothly that, not for the first time, Britain began to feel like a poor relation in Europe and there was renewed, and ultimately successful, pressure for sterling's entry into the system. It was Roy Jenkins who, as Commission president in 1977, had revived monetary integration in Europe. And it was his successor but one, Jacques Delors, who was responsible for carrying it forward. (The president in the intervening period was Gaston Thorn of Luxembourg, whose tenure, from 1981–5, was remarkable for its lack of notable activity.) Delors, a French socialist, had been finance minister in the Mitterrand government in the early 1980s and therefore knew all about running the gauntlet of the financial markets.

Energetic, legendarily hard-working and driven by an intense commitment to the European ideal, Delors was the right president at the right time for the Commission. His 10 years at the helm in Brussels were extraordinarily productive. Even his enemies, and there was no greater one than Margaret Thatcher, had a grudging respect for him.

Delors, having been influential in having the goal of Emu inserted in the preamble to the Single European Act, seized upon it like a terrier. A committee, consisting of the central bank governors of member states, together with three independent experts, was convened to report on the practicalities of achieving monetary union. This was a shrewd move. Not only would the presence of central bankers provide the committee's deliberations with the imprimatur of solid practicability, but, as members of the central bankers' 'club', rather than ministers or government officials, they could be expected to reach broad agreement rather than descend into nationally driven squabbles. Thus, when the committee reported in June 1989, and set out a three-stage programme for the achievement of Emu, even Britain's representative, the then Bank of England governor Robin Leigh-Pemberton, admittedly something of a Euro-enthusiast, was able to sign up to it.

The three stages of Emu put forward by the Delors committee, and endorsed in the Maastricht amendments to the Treaty of Rome, agreed in December 1991, were:

1. All countries to be members of the European exchange rate mechanism, and be observing its normal fluctuation margins (then 2.25% either side of their central parity).
2. The European Central Bank (in the end, on German insistence, only its forerunner the European Monetary Institute) to come into being at the start of the second stage and oversee the process of preparation for Emu, including whether countries' economic performance was converging satisfactorily. Stage two began on January 1, 1994.
3. The final stage of Emu, to begin on January 1, 1997 if a majority of European Union (EU) – the usual post-Maastricht name for the Communities – members were then ready, or no later than January 1, 1999 with a minority of qualifying countries. The final stage would begin with irrevocable locking of exchange rates and the use of the single currency (which acquired its name, the euro, in 1995) to settle debts between them. The European central bank would

assume responsibility for monetary policy and gradually, the euro would come to replace national currencies, culminating in the calling-in of existing money in circulation and the changeover to euro notes and coin some three years after the beginning of the final stage. (When the January 1, 1997 start date was abandoned as too ambitious in favour of 1999, the date of the changeover to the new notes and coin was pushed out to the first half of 2002.)

A small town in Holland

Maastricht, the capital of Limburg province in the southern Netherlands, can truly claim to being at the heart of Europe. Quintessentially Dutch now, with more than its quota of bicycles, cheese shops and pleasant riverside walks, at one time or another in its history it has come under the control of most members of the EU. Its place in modern history was ensured by the decision of the Dutch government to hold the concluding European Council meeting of its 1991 presidency of the Community, not in Amsterdam, Rotterdam or The Hague but in Maastricht, symbolically regarded as at the crossroads of Europe. The Dutch pulled out all the stops at Maastricht. Not only was the level of hospitality high even by the standards of European gatherings (it is a rule of the game that each presidency attempts to outdo the preceding one), but Queen Beatrix was on hand to provide a personal welcome to the representatives and, as Sarah Hogg and Jonathan Hill record in their book *Too Close to Call*, there was even a special kite-flying contest. Nor was the December 1991 meeting any ordinary gathering of European leaders. It marked the conclusion of two inter-governmental conferences, one on Emu, set in train by the Madrid summit of June 1989 and the other on European Political Union, agreed at Dublin in June 1990. Delors was later to say that it was a mistake to run these two IGCs in parallel, and that it would have been better to have concentrated on securing agreement only on Emu.

From the point of view of Europe, the most significant thing about the Treaty on European Union agreed at Maastricht in December 1991 (and formally signed there on 7 February 1992) was that the Emu timetable, and the structure and status of the European central bank, were enshrined in a new formal agreement. In addition, the treaty provided for future co-operation on the two 'pillars' of foreign and security policy and justice and home affairs. The treaty also enhanced the powers of the European Parliament in its scrutiny of the Commission, introduced a Committee of the Regions and an Ombudsman, and endorsed the principles of European citizenship and subsidiarity (where decisions can be taken at local or national level, rather than at a European level, they should be). Maastricht was a decisive step forward to European union.

For Britain, the most notable aspect of the Maastricht negotiations was the successful securing by John Major and Norman Lamont, then the British chancellor, of two 'opt-outs' (or more correctly the freedom to opt in at a time of its choosing) on both Emu and the so-called social chapter. This, an agreement by the 11 other member states, pledging 'promotion of employment, improved living and working conditions, proper social protection, dialogue between management and labour, the development of human resources with a view of lasting high employment' was appended as a separate social protocol to the treaty. Major achieved his success (which was described by Gus O'Donnell, his then press secretary, as 'game, set and match for Britain' – a triumphalist verdict that Major was unhappy with) by dogged, grinding, negotiating determination, and by playing on the frailties of his fellow leaders. According to Hogg and Hill:

> The pressure was rising. As at all European Councils, there came a point when Chancellor Kohl began to get bored with sitting still and President Mitterrand began to think longingly of dinner in Paris. Their officials began to mutter portentously about cabinet meetings back home. The trick, John Major knew, was to engage these emotions for him rather than against him. . . .
>
> Shortly before 9 pm, the council reassembled. By now President Mitterrand looked very tired. Helmut Kohl was cheered up by the light at the end of the tunnel. The rest had plainly had enough. We were into what Tristan Garel-Jones [a British foreign office minister] called zimmer-frame time. But the prime minister had not given up. (pp. 154, 156)

Major won his opt-outs. But the treaty, as it remained, took the process of European integration into a new phase. It also ushered in a period of scepticism about such integration, throughout Europe.

■ Sceptical Europeans

One abiding characteristic of Europe's progress from the ruins of post-war Europe, through the creation of the Coal and Steel Community, the Common Market, the Single Market and an increasingly integrated set of nations, was the ability of the Community's leaders to carry the people with them. True, there were periods when some politicians appeared to want to move too quickly, as with the attempts to establish Defence and Political Communities in the 1950s. In the main, however, moves towards ever closer union chimed in with the prevailing sentiment among most Europeans. In this, Europe had succeeded where earlier efforts to achieve unity had failed. Europe after the First World War should, on the face of it, have provided a climate in which the people's anxiety to avoid further conflict would have spurred moves towards union. But, in spite of the efforts of some statesmen – such as Count Coudenhove Kalergi, Austrian leader of the Pan-European Movement, who in 1923 called for a United States of Europe, or Aristide Briand, the French foreign minister, who in 1929 proposed, with German backing, the creation of a European Union within the framework of the League of Nations – the forces of nationalism dominated.

A large part of the credit for Europe's modern success must go to Monnet, and his insistence that European union proceed through practical measures of obvious benefit, rather than grand visions. There was also an economic reason – Europe was seen to have delivered prosperity for its members. Living standards among the 'core' countries of Europe – France, Germany, Italy and the Benelux countries – were seen to be higher, and improving at a more rapid rate than those on the periphery, including Britain (although per capita national income levels in the Scandinavian countries were also high, raising doubts about whether the EEC was responsible for the core's success). For the period of the Cold War, too, European integration offered a cocoon against powerful, and in one case threatening, superpowers. The threat from the east encouraged western Europeans to huddle closer together.

Occasionally the degree of Euro-enthusiasm was put to the test. In Britain, a referendum on continued membership was held in June 1975 – the question was: 'Do you think that the United Kingdom should stay in the European Community (the Common Market)?' – and came out by more than two to one in favour (17m voted 'yes', 8m 'no'). Approval would have been higher in other member states. The Euroscepticism of the 1990s, and not just in Britain, therefore represented a distinct change in trend, which can be ascribed to the more difficult economic circumstances in which Europe found itself, the end of the Cold War, and concerns that supranationalism was proceeding too far and too fast.

On September 20, 1992, the French people voted in a referendum on the Maastricht treaty. After a vigorous campaign, in which the 'no' case was strongly put, the treaty was approved, but only by 51% to 49%, the narrowest of margins. Some pre-referendum opinion polls, indeed, had suggested that the 'no' camp would triumph. For France, whose politicians had provided the driving force behind European integration for more than 40 years, nearly to reject Maastricht was almost unthinkable and shook Europe's political establishment to the core. The French referendum knocked the cause of European unity in more ways than one. Market uncertainty leading up to the vote was a prime cause of the ERM crisis of September 16, 1992, when sterling and the Italian lira were forced out of the system.

Before the narrow French acceptance of Maastricht, a result which, equally narrowly, went the other way, had shown that the mood was shifting. The Danes rejected Maastricht by 50.7% to 49.3% in June 1992, a result only overturned nearly a year later, after Denmark was given a permanent opt-out from the final stage of Emu, together with additional assurances on defence and other matters. The people of Norway, who had rejected entering the EEC in 1972, when their country was due to join alongside Britain, Ireland and Denmark, did so again in 1994, when Austria, Finland and Sweden were accepted for entry. Switzerland applied for membership in 1992 but, after its citizens rejected participation in the wider European Economic Area (made up of the EU and Efta), its application was effectively shelved.

Most of all, there were the beginnings of serious protest about the direction of Europe. In Britain, where the Bill to approve Maastricht only made it through the House of Commons when the Conservative government turned it into the equivalent of a vote of confidence, the ruling party was split on Europe, with an energetic band of Eurosceptic MPs forcing the pace on the issue, making nonsense in the process of John Major's pledge, when he took office, to put Britain 'at the heart of Europe'. In France, there were public sector strikes about the sacrifices necessary to meet the conditions (notably a budget deficit of no more than 3% of GDP in normal circumstances) for participation in Emu. This pattern was repeated in other countries, including Germany. High unemployment, which reached post-war record levels in both France and Germany in the mid-1990s, added to the anger and frustration. Nationalist parties gained support. In Britain, the question of whether membership provided any benefits was, as in the period before the 1975 referendum, vigorously debated. The Referendum party, set up by Sir James Goldsmith, tapped in to this atmosphere of disquiet and damaged some Conservative candidates in the May 1997 general election which saw Labour sweep to power. Was the mood changing for good, or was this just the equivalent of temporary teething troubles on the road to the single currency? One thing was clear. After half a century in which Europe's politicians had generally succeeded in carrying the people with them, the century was ending on a sour note, with political leaders in danger of losing touch with their voters on the issues of integration and ever closer union.

At the crossroads

By the second half of the 1990s Europe, on the face of it, had come a long way. The original six signatories of the Treaty of Paris (establishing the European Coal and Steel Community) and the Treaties of Rome (establishing the EEC and Euratom) had become 15 with the accession of Britain, Ireland and Denmark (in 1973), Greece (in 1981), Spain and Portugal (in 1986), and Austria, Finland and Sweden (in 1995). The wider European Economic Area, which takes in Norway, Iceland and Liechtenstein, produces a free trade area of 380m people. In the late 1990s too, Europe was on the verge of its boldest integrationist step yet, the creation of a single currency and a European central bank. The creation of a true single market was well advanced.

Relations between member states have not always been smooth and untroubled but the central aim of modern Europe's founding fathers – enabling previously warring nations to live in peace – had been achieved. A unified Germany, of 81m people, has been politically directed towards the goal of European integration rather than, as at other times in its history, the domination of its neighbours. At each stage in the recent history of European integration, it has been the strength of political will of the leaders of France and Germany that has determined the pace of progress towards union. In this respect, modern-day Europe has been fortunate – the combination of Helmut Kohl as German chancellor, François Mitterrand as French president and Jacques Delors as Commission president ensured that the integrationist path would be pursued with vigour. Politics is all about the right people being in the right place at the right time. Under a different chancellor, Germany could have turned its back on Europe, devoting its full attention to consolidating the former East Germany within the Federal Republic. French presidents are always prone to what others would see as an excess of nationalism.

Compared with what might have been, therefore, Europe's progress has been considerable. In many respects, however, as a new century approaches the prospect is more uncertain than the extent of that progress would imply. The European model, of social protection, generous welfare provision and regulated markets, is seen to be under its severest economic threat from other regions of the world. The push to achieve monetary union, far from being a force to unite Europe, threatens to divide it. As in George Orwell's *Animal Farm*, in the European menagerie some are seen as inevitably more equal than others. The forces of nationalism, far from having been subsumed in the wider cause of a greater, more powerful, Europe, are reviving.

In the following chapters, Europe's medium- and long-term prospects in the light of these and other challenges will be examined in detail. First it is necessary to establish a starting-point. In other words, where Europe has got to now and where, in the short-term, it can be said with some certainty it is headed.

■ A single market?

At the end of 1996, the European Commission's directorate general with responsibility for the internal market, financial services, the free movement of people and direct taxation (DG15), produced the first comprehensive assessment of the impact, to date, of the Single Market. It was, perhaps unsurprisingly, very upbeat. The Single Market had, according to the Commission:

- Been responsible for between 300,000 and 900,000 jobs across the EU. These were not necessarily all new jobs, but they would, according to the assessment, not have been there without the Single Market.
- Boosted Community GDP by between 1.1% and 1.5% (Ecu 60–80 billion) by 1994.
- Reduced EU inflation by between 1% and 1.5% compared with what it would otherwise have been.
- Boosted trade in manufactured goods within the EU by between 20% and 30%.

These impressive figures were supplemented by, again according to the assessment, growing competition in both manufacturing and services; an accelerated pace of industrial restructuring; greater choice at lower prices to retail, public sector and industrial customers, particularly in transport, financial services, telecommunications and broadcasting; faster and cheaper cross-frontier deliveries, because of the absence of border controls on goods; greater mobility between member states, both for workers and the 'economically inactive', including students and the retired; growing economic convergence and 'cohesion', an increase in the EU's attractiveness for global foreign investment – by the mid-1990s Europe was attracting 44% of such direct investment compared with 28% in the mid-1980s, and greater convergence of production structures.

One of the difficulties with perceptions of the Single Market is that its introduction has coincided with a distinctly unimpressive period of European economic growth. In 1993, for example, the first year after the 'completion' of the Single Market, EU GDP *fell* by 0.6%, recovering to grow by 2.8% in 1994, 2.5% in 1995, before slowing again to around 1.5% in 1996. This does not mean that the Commission's estimates of the direct economic impact of the Single Market are wrong, but it does show that its effects have not been powerful enough to counteract other factors forcing growth lower – including attempts by member states to comply with the Maastricht convergence criteria, of which more below.

Nonetheless, it would be churlish to deny that some of the achievements of the Single Market programme have been impressive. In the mid-1980s there were some 100,000 sets of national technical specifications, most of which now abide by a common EU standard; the proportion of non-domestic goods and services now being purchased by public bodies has risen from 6% to 10%. Harmonised approval rules for cars have reduced the cost of developing a new model by 10% (although some of these gains have also accrued to non-EU manufacturers). The price of telecommunications equipment has dropped by 7%. Cross-border capital movements have risen by 25% with the elimination of capital controls. Road hauliers have benefited from a 5–6% saving on a typical 1,000km journey, largely due to the reduction in border delays, and the amount of haulage business carried out by hauliers from one member state in others has quadrupled. New airlines have emerged, economy fares in Europe have come down, and there has been a 20% increase in intra-EU passenger transport.

Some of these things might, of course, have happened without the Single Market. And there was, in addition, a sting in the tail of the

Commission's generally very upbeat analysis. This was that in certain countries implementation of Single Market directives had been slow; paradoxically Britain and Denmark – the two most Eurosceptical members of the EU – have tended to be the most diligent at implementing the Single Market. 'The Commission is urging that enforcement legislation and treaty rules be stepped up and more resources be committed to this task at national level', a statement from Mario Monti, the commissioner responsible for the internal market, said on October 30, 1996. 'In addition, the Commission calls for vigorous action to be taken to reduce excessive regulation at national level which inhibits both competition and competitiveness.'

The Commission's call for a new commitment to the Single Market on the part of member states underlines one of Europe's less attractive characteristics – a tendency towards protectionism and over-regulation among some member states. From the early days of European integration in the 1950s, France has always had a particular difficulty with the idea of unfettered trade, hence its demand then, of which there are echoes now, for a high tariff wall around the EEC and a lengthy transitional period for the removal of barriers. And, despite good progress in many areas, there remains a sense of frustration, among businesses, about the speed of implementation of the Single Market. According to the Confederation of British Industry:

> The Single Market is not yet complete and could work better in many areas. There are still gaps in the legal framework. Where EU directives have been agreed some member states are either slow to transpose them into national law or make them more costly to comply with than the original framework intended. Progress in achieving mutual recognition of standards has often been slow. The Single Market needs to be extended to major sectors in which competition remains underdeveloped and where, as a result, many European businesses fail to meet the global competitiveness test. Many member states have been reluctant to dismantle state owned and supported monopolies despite the benefits to consumers which would result. (National Conference Session Papers, November 1996, p. 11)

Of particular concern have been state aid to national airlines, which has slowed liberalisation, the absence of a single European market in energy and a begrudging attitude, in many countries, to giving foreign firms a fair opportunity when it comes to public procurement decisions. The Single Market is an evolutionary process. But evolution can be painfully slow.

A blackspot for jobs

The first two decades of European integration were either responsible for, or fortunate enough to be accompanied by, considerable economic success. Unemployment in the original six members of the ECSC and the EEC averaged between 2% and 4%, growth was strong and the region was internationally competitive. Since the early 1970s, however, Europe's record has been poor, with unemployment rising to 10% by the mid-1980s and 11.5% by the mid-1990s. Some of this, plainly, reflected international developments, such as the two Opec (Organisation of Petroleum Exporting Countries) oil crises, but this was far from the whole story. In the early 1970s, unemployment in the EEC was below that in the United States. By the 1980s Europe was consistently recording higher unemployment rates than America, and by the mid-1990s EU unemployment was roughly double that in the US. Japan, meanwhile, continued to run very low unemployment rates, typically 2–3% of the workforce.

Europe's modern-day problem has been a lack of private sector job creation. Between 1960 and 1995, according to the OECD *Jobs Study,* employment in Europe rose by less than 10%. In contrast, employment growth in North America over the same period exceeded 90%. Breaking this down for the period of Europe's employment 'failure' since about 1973, OECD figures show that while North America created over 30m jobs in the private sector, plus just over 5m in the public sector, Europe 'created' a similar 5m public sector jobs, but very few, around 3m, in the private sector. According to the *Jobs Study*:

> Weak employment growth in the European Community, most of it until the mid-1980s in the public sector, has been accompanied by strong productivity growth, achieved mostly through labour-shedding in traditional sectors rather than through shifts of production to high technology and skill-intensive activities. Unemployment has ratcheted up over successive cycles, resulting in rising long-term unemployment. Inflows into un-

employment have been relatively low but outflows even lower – suggesting poorly functioning labour markets. (p. 25)

Europe, in other words, has had to reduce employment, particularly in sectors exposed to tough international competition, in order to try to maintain its competitive position. Even in this, however, it appears to have failed.

■ Priced out of world markets

On most measures, including relative labour costs, Europe is not competitive. The World Economic Forum (WEF), in its 1996 'Global Competitiveness Report', named only one EU member state, Luxembourg, in its top 10 of nearly 50 countries ranked by overall competitiveness.

The WEF also plotted labour costs against productivity levels for 29 countries, including all EU members, Canada, the United States, Australia, New Zealand, Japan, and four Asian 'tiger' economies (Singapore, Hong Kong, Taiwan and Korea). The eight countries with the highest labour costs, adjusted for productivity, were Germany, Finland, the Netherlands, Belgium, Sweden, Austria, Norway and Denmark, all EU members except Norway. Unsurprisingly, the low labour cost countries were concentrated among the Asian tigers and the United States. Portugal was the only EU representative. According to Jeffrey Sachs, professor of economics at Harvard, who summarised the results:

> In part these high labour costs reflect the labour market consequences of the strong Deutschmark, which raises the dollar cost of labour. In addition, they reflect the structural inflexibilities of wage setting, and the very high social costs of labour (remember that social costs are included in the compensation measure). The evidence certainly supports the view that European Union policies, both monetary and structural, are pricing EU workers out of international labour markets. . . . The European Union, in comparison with the other major groupings of advanced economies, is suffering from the effects of heavy taxation, large

levels of government spending relative to GDP, inflexible labour markets and reduced savings rates. (pp. 25–6)

One of the strangest developments of the mid-1990s, indeed, was to hear Chancellor Kohl advancing an argument in favour of Emu to the effect that it would help constrain the Deutschmark and so prevent German workers from being priced out of world markets. Apart from the fact that this flies in the face of the Bundesbank's insistence that the euro should be at least as strong as the Deutschmark, it is an odd way of tackling a problem of uncompetitiveness. It also explains why the countries keenest to take part in Emu at the outset are also anxious to tie in non-participants into a formal exchange rate framework, usually known as 'ERM II', i.e. a successor to the present exchange rate mechanism, to prevent them from securing competitive advantage. Britain, which thanks to the Emu opt-out would not be required to enter any such arrangement, certainly acquired such an advantage, both as a result of sterling's post-ERM devaluation and the Thatcher government's labour market reforms of the 1980s. A 1994 comparison by the US Bureau of Labor Statistics showed that hourly compensation costs in manufacturing were $13.60 in Britain, $17 in France, $17.10 in the United States and $27.30 in Germany. To the extent that the German labour market model is seen in some quarters as also the model for Europe, these are disturbing comparisons.

In search of the euro

By the end of 1996, with the Dublin summit that marked the end of the Irish presidency of the EU, the parameters for monetary union were in place. Apart from meeting a set of five different 'convergence' criteria for entering Emu, countries would have to abide by a 'stability pact', intending to guarantee that, once part of the single currency area, individual member states would not become bad citizens of the Union by allowing their fiscal policy to run out of control. The stability pact would require countries to take action to reduce a budget deficit above 3% of GDP unless they were in a severe recession, defined as a decline in GDP of 2% or more measured over a four-quarter period. If the GDP decline was smaller than this – between 0.75% and 2% – they might be allowed special dispensation by the Council of finance ministers of participating Emu countries. In any other circumstances action would be expected, and could be enforced by fines up to an annual maximum of 0.5% of GDP.

Thus, monetary policy for participating Emu countries would be operated by the European Central Bank (organised, like the Bundesbank, with voting board members from individual states), while fiscal policy, while run nationally in terms of detailed decisions, would be subject to constraints set at European level. Emu, unsurprisingly, would represent a major transfer of economic decision-making from the national to the European level.

The convergence criteria, or gateways for initial participation in Emu, recommended by the Delors committee and enshrined in the Maastricht treaty, are by now familiar. The five criteria are as follows:

- An inflation rate of not more than 1.5 percentage points above the average of the three member states with the lowest inflation rates.
- A long-term interest rate within two percentage points of the average of the three members with the best inflation performance.
- A budget deficit, including central, regional, local government and social security funds, of 3% of GDP or less.
- A public debt ratio of less than 60% of GDP.
- A currency which for two years has observed the normal fluctuation bands of the exchange rate mechanism (ERM).

To this could be added one other economic policy condition – the requirement that countries have made their central banks independent, or are taking steps to do so. In addition, most countries would need to have secured the approval, either of their national parliaments, or the electorate, or both. Set out in this way, the criteria appear straightforward. The treaty, however, built in certain flexibilities. Both the fiscal criteria – debt and deficits – were known as 'reference values', rather than strict limits. Countries with debt ratios above 60% of GDP, for example, would be permitted to enter Emu provided they could demonstrate they were 'moving towards' the ceiling at a satisfactory pace. If countries could demonstrate that 'the ratio is sufficiently diminishing and approaching the reference value at a satisfactory pace' they would qualify. Similarly with the deficit 'ceiling' – the ratio would apply unless it has 'declined substantially and continuously and reached a level that comes close to the reference value', or that it exceeds it for 'exceptional and temporary' reasons. There has also been considerable debate over the application of the exchange rate condition – did it require formal membership of the ERM, or would countries like Britain, outside the ERM but with a relatively good recent record of currency stability, thus behaving 'as if' within the ERM's 15% fluctuation bands, be permitted to enter? Italy, which exited the ERM as the same time as Britain, was taking no chances, re-entering the ERM in November 1996 to ensure that this was not used as an excuse to exclude it from Emu.

■ Economists and monetarists disagree

Throughout the history of monetary integration in Europe, there has been a debate between the so-called economists and the monetarists (not, in this case, Chicago-type monetarists). The economists, among whom the Bundesbank is prominent, have always taken the view that economic convergence must precede monetary union. The monetarists argue that, while this may be true to a point, monetary union would itself be a force for convergence. Both views were accommodated in the Maastricht treaty. While the setting of the convergence criteria was, in one sense, a triumph for the economists, accompanying it with a timetable for Emu was a nod in the direction of the monetarists, by embodying in the treaty the idea that Emu, or at least its approach, would force countries to converge with one another. This debate has subsequently been taken on by the European Monetary Institute, the fledgling European Central Bank, and the European Commission.

In November 1996, the Commission produced its assessment of convergence within the EU. Had, at that stage, a majority of EU countries satisfied the criteria then, in theory, the final stage of Emu could have begun on January 1, 1997. In fact, 10 countries (Belgium, Denmark, Germany, France, Ireland, Luxembourg, the Netherlands, Austria, Finland and Germany) met the inflation condition, and 11 (Belgium, Denmark, Germany, France, Ireland, Luxembourg, the Netherlands, Austria, Finland, Sweden and the UK), the requirement on long-term interest rates. Eleven also satisfied the exchange-rate condition, or were on course to do so (a slightly different 11, including Spain and Portugal, but not Sweden or the UK). Only three countries –

Denmark, Ireland and Luxembourg – however, met the condition of having budget deficits of 3% or below, and two of these, Denmark and Ireland, had debt ratios of above 60%.

The Commission was still able to say, however, that most countries were on the road to achieving the budgetary criteria in 1997, in order to participate in the final stage of Emu at the beginning of 1999. Only Britain, Italy and Greece, on the basis of its forecasts, looked likely to miss these criteria, and two of these, Britain and Italy, could do so if they were to pursue appropriately tough fiscal policies. Thus, on the Commission's view, 12, and possibly 14, member countries could be in at the start of the final stage of monetary union. The EMI, which reported on the same day as the Commission, was not so sure, expressing concern at the pace of convergence, and implicitly suggesting that a smaller number of countries would genuinely qualify. Shortly after this, Eddie George, Governor of the Bank of England and therefore Britain's representative on the EMI's decision-making council, said what most European central bank governors believe, but few are able to say publicly. He doubted, he said in a speech to the Confederation of British Industry, that those who drew up the convergence criteria 'envisaged the present hectic dash for the line – the chosen calendar deadline. I doubt whether they envisaged either that some of the runners might be tempted to take artificial stimulants in order to get there.' This was a reference to what both central bankers and statisticians regarded as the use by some countries of suspect measures to reduce their budget deficits – exemplified by the French government's utilisation of a one-off payment of Fr37.5 billion from France Telecom's pension fund to reduce the country's budget deficit.

But Emu goes ahead anyway

For the purposes of the remainder of this book, however, it is assumed that Emu goes ahead on or soon after the January 1, 1999 target date for the start of the final stage, albeit as a triumph of politics over economics and other considerations. Thus, when the decision on participation in the final stage is taken in the early months of 1998, a smaller group of countries than the Commission's 12 or 14 go ahead. Britain and Denmark will, it is assumed, exclude themselves for domestic political reasons, while Italy, Spain, Portugal and Greece will be left out because they do not meet one or more of the criteria. This leaves a possible nine 'founder' members of Emu, of which Germany, France, Belgium, the Netherlands, Luxembourg and Austria are the most likely to go ahead, and Ireland, Finland and Sweden rather less likely. Thus, it is assumed that the core six are there at the outset of Emu, either on January 1, 1999, or within 12 months of it. Others may join later – in the case of Ireland, Italy, Spain, Portugal, Finland, Sweden and possibly Britain, one suggested entry window is between the formal start of the final stage on January 1, 1999, and the switchover from national currencies to euro notes and coins in the first half of 2002. Nothing, however, is guaranteed for these subsequent members, as we shall see later in the book.

Growing together?

There are two persistent criticisms of monetary union, and the design of the convergence programme leading up to it. The first is that there is an undue emphasis on financial criteria, rather than 'real' economic criteria such as growth rates and unemployment. The second is that countries which have a lot of ground to make up in terms of living standards in relation to the prosperous nations at the core of Europe will be constrained by Emu and thus less able to achieve that catch-up. The argument goes both ways. The strongest argument against the drive towards Emu imposing a 'deflationary bias' is that a good inflation performance and sound fiscal policy are prerequisites of growth and low unemployment for all countries. Once in Emu, it is also argued, there would be plenty of scope for differential growth rates in different regions or countries. Portugal, Spain and Ireland could still grow at rates far faster than Germany or France, and could be assisted in this process if Emu brings low, Europe-wide interest rates.

At the root of concerns over Emu is the fact that Europe is an economically diverse bloc. This comes out clearly from a comparison of economic performance. But it also shows clearly, and arguably more importantly, in the fact that there is no European consensus on underlying economic philosophy. To take these in turn.

The idea of economic union is one that suggests a grouping of broadly similar countries, subject to similar influences and moving boldly forward together. It is possible to suggest that, at least until the accession of East Germany through unification in 1990, that this was more or less what the original Treaty of Rome Six had achieved. True, there is the significant problem of southern Italy, much poorer than the north, as there is of other depressed regions even within the original Six. But, taking OECD data for 1995, the range of per capita national incomes was relatively small. At the then prevailing prices, but using purchasing power parity exchange rates (that is, assuming exchange rates reflect relative price levels) Luxembourg was the richest of the Six, with a per capita national income of $31,002 – the richest in the OECD – followed by Belgium on $20,987, Germany on $20,508 (the west dragged down by low income levels in the former East Germany), France $20,035, Italy $19,691 and the Netherlands $19,401.

When the later entrants are taken into account, however, Europe starts to look economically diverse. Portugal (per capita national income $12,994) is significantly poorer than the original Six, as are Spain ($14,312) and Ireland ($16,764). Sweden ($18,360) and Britain ($18,476) are a little behind the pack. Furthest behind of all, however, is Greece, with a per capita national income of just $11,761, after 15 years as a member state. Thus the richest member of the EU, Luxembourg, is nearly three times better off than the poorest. The richest part of the EU, Hamburg, has a per capita GDP more than four times that of the poorest, Ipeiros in Greece.

There are also huge variations in employment structure – the proportion of the workforce in permanent, salaried employment and in 'mature' occupations such as industry and financial services – between member states. Most clear of all are the differences in national unemployment rates. In mid-1996 for example, Luxembourg again drew first prize with an unemployment rate of 3.1%, followed by Austria, 4.1%, and Denmark, 5.9%. The Netherlands (7%), Portugal (7.5%) and Britain (8%) had higher rates, but not as high as Germany and Sweden, both just over 10%, or Italy, France and Ireland, all between 12% and 13%. Finland at 17% clearly had a huge unemployment problem, but Spain was worst off of all, on 21.5%. Thus, the highest national unemployment rate was seven times that of the lowest, a strange sort of convergence. Even bigger variations emerge, of course, if unemployment rates in the regions of individual member states are compared.

Wide apart

There is another sort of divergence which is particularly important for Emu. As a result both of variations in historical inflation experience and in the way banking systems developed in different European countries, there are important differences in interest-rate sensitivity between economies. As Christopher Taylor puts it in his paper 'Emu 2000?':

> A new type of asymmetry may develop under Emu with a single monetary policy, reflecting the differences between monetary transmission mechanisms of economies. . . . These arise from differences in financial structures and practices, for example levels of credit utilisation by the household sector, and shares of fixed and variable-rate borrowing in mortgage, company and government finance. Accordingly a given change in short-term interest rates will have larger effects in an economy like the UK's with deregulated and highly competitive financial markets than in continental economies, where the main lending rates are sluggish, there is more fixed-rate finance, and households are less heavily geared. (p. 56)

Simulations by economists at Sumitomo Finance International in London suggest, for example, that the British economy is five to six times more sensitive to a change in short-term interest rates than the 'core' or Schengen group of European economies (France, Germany and the Benelux countries, so-called because of an agreement they signed at the Luxembourg town of Schengen in 1985 to progressively remove frontier controls ahead of the Single European Act). Such differences could cut both ways. A modest rise in interest rates to correct an incipient inflation problem affecting the core economies could have the effect of plunging the British economy, assuming it is part of Emu, into recession. By the same token, too low a level of European interest rates could be highly inflationary in a highly interest-rate-sensitive economy such as Britain.

Banking systems can evolve over time, as can custom and practice among borrowers and lenders. But this could be expected to take decades. Christopher Johnson, in his pro-Emu book *In With the Euro, Out With the Pound*, suggests that this problem could be dealt with by giving a more active role to fiscal policy. 'Regional differences within one country have to be dealt with by changes in government spending and taxation', he writes. 'The same would be true over a wider monetary union including Britain and the continental countries. Fiscal policy has to take over some of the present functions of monetary policy' (p. 89). Apart from the important question of whether fiscal policy, constrained by an Emu stability pact, could actually do this, many would see this as a strange way to tackle the problem of divergent financial systems.

■ *Philosophically diverging*

Modern Europe represents a battle between at least two conflicting economic philosophies. The dominant force is the German model of capitalism, complemented by elements of French dirigism; the brash newcomer is the more red-blooded 'American-style' capitalism. Indeed, even this may not fully capture the different economic philosophies competing for supremacy. Michel Albert, in his book *Capitalism Against Capitalism*, identified four different models of capitalism within Europe:

- The German model, with its emphasis on mutuality and a community of interests, together with its practical expression, in industry, of a concentration on production techniques, training and high levels of research and development spending.
- The British approach, borrowing much from the American model, although with higher levels of welfare protection than in the United States.
- The Italian version, dominated by 'family capitalism', with a huge public sector deficit, high levels of unofficial or 'black economy' activity and, perhaps as a result, dynamic small and medium-sized businesses.
- The French–Spanish model, with a tradition of protectionism, state intervention and corporatism, lately prone to 'Americanisation', including increased speculative activity, and the rise of social tensions resulting from polarisation of incomes and opportunities.

Not everyone would agree with the details of Albert's four-part schema, still less with his conclusion that, so superior, both economically and socially, is the German or 'Rhine' model of capitalism, not just to anything else in Europe, but, with the possible exception of the similar Japanese model, to any of the alternatives elsewhere in the world, Europe must follow it to succeed. Europe, concludes Albert, has the choice between following the neo-American model, or:

> We will actually begin to build the United States of Europe: in which case, we will have all the means at our disposal to choose the best possible socio-economic system, that which has already proven its mettle within one part of the continent and which will become the European model of capitalism. The United States of Europe can do better than the United States of America, if we put our minds to it. (p. 260)

At a time when the Rhine model is showing signs of extreme strain and, as the comparisons earlier in this chapter showed, has turned the *Wirtschaftswunder* of the 1950s and 1960s into the worryingly uncompetitive economy of the late 20th century, this would seem to be a peculiar basis upon which Europe should chart its future. The difficulty, for Europe, is that so many member states are philosophically opposed to the proven alternative, or to the Asian models of small-state, low-tax, flexibility. The simple fact that, after nearly half a century, Europe has failed to settle on an all-encompassing economic and social model underlines, in stark terms, the limits of genuine integration.

How big a Europe?

The EU, as noted at the start of this chapter, had grown from six to 15 members by the mid-1990s. Part of the process of enlargement has been the recognition that it would, at least initially, bring greater diversity of economic performance and living standards into the Community. Britain, in 1973, was the last big, prosperous country to be admitted to membership. Subsequent members have either been smaller (Sweden, Austria, Finland), poorer (Greece, Spain and

Portugal), or both. Perhaps the most economically diverse country to be admitted to membership was the former German Democratic Republic, as a result of German unification in 1990. Enlargement clearly increases the potential size of the 'domestic' market for companies operating in Europe, and adds to the international weight of the EU. But it also creates potential problems, notably the greater demands for economic assistance, under the Cohesion and other funds. The more members, the greater the danger that decision-making at a European level, already cumbersome, becomes completely unwieldy. The EU operates on the basis of a revolving six-month presidency, with each member state assuming responsibility, in turn, for hosting European Council meetings and representing Europe in its dealings with other countries or groupings. When there were six member states, each country would hold the presidency every three years. The more members, particularly small members, the longer it takes for the presidency to come around to the larger countries, and the greater the danger of discontinuity and loss of momentum. Concern has rightly been expressed that two of the current applicants for membership, Cyprus and Malta, are far too small to take their turn at the presidency.

Notwithstanding this, it appears highly likely that Cyprus and Malta, who applied in 1990, will be in the next group of entrants, probably around the turn of the century. Either then or a little later, the EU can be expected to continue the process begun with the accession of the former East Germany, by beginning to admit some of the other former Communist states of eastern Europe, in line with a European Council commitment made in Copenhagen in 1993. Hungary and Poland applied for membership in 1994. The Czech Republic has already become a member of the OECD, often a prelude, where appropriate, to EU membership. Slovakia, Bulgaria and Romania are the other relevant countries. Norway and Switzerland could return to the question of membership, despite the rejection by their people of entry, twice over a 20-year period in the case of Norway. The Swiss have yet to permit their country entry into the looser European Economic Area.

Enlargement in other directions is problematical. Although in the past, countries with previously unacceptable regimes have been subsequently admitted, almost as a reward for good political behaviour – Greece and Spain are examples – the accession of Turkey, which applied in 1987, appears to be indefinitely delayed because of the country's human rights record. Morocco was rejected in the 1980s for the good reason of not being a European country. Finding new members out of the wreckage of the former Yugoslavia will be possible, but difficult. In the next 5–10 years, the EU should be able to acquire up to eight new members – Malta, Cyprus, Bulgaria, the Czech Republic, Hungary, Poland, Romania and Slovakia. Going beyond that will take rather longer.

Europe as political heavyweight?

Europe has matured economically during nearly half a century of integration. One frequent criticism, however, is of the EU's failure to develop and sustain a powerful and effective political voice in the world. Thus, six-monthly European Council meetings typically end with long political declarations, solemnly read out by whichever national leader happens to be holding the presidency at the time. Most of the time, however, they sound like platitudes, probably because most of the time they are. Europe's political ineffectiveness came to a head over the break-up of the former Yugoslavia. According to two of the strongest British critics of the EU:

> As Communism crumbled, the peoples of Slovenia, Croatia and Bosnia grimly prepared to break loose from the Belgrade government, to set up free, independent, democratic states on what they imagined was the western European model. Nothing better symbolised these yearnings than the rash of EC 'ring of stars' flags suddenly flying everywhere in Slovenia and Croatia, alongside their new national flags. But slowly a terrible realisation dawned. Far from championing the rights of free peoples to assert their own independence, the EC was encouraging the old Communist tyranny in Belgrade to take tough action to hold its federation together. In the summer of 1991 the Italian foreign minister Signor de Michelis said the Community could not accept the disintegration of Yugoslavia. . . .
>
> Over the next three years nothing was to be a more pitiful reflection of the Community's dream of a common foreign policy than the utter futility of all its efforts to intervene in the Yugoslav catastrophe. The successive Carrington, Owen and Bildt peace

> missions, the peace conferences summoned by EC countries including Britain, the endlessly self-deluded, self-important waffling of every EC statesman involved, the constant appeasement of Milosevic and the Serbs, comprised as dismal and humiliating a chapter in Europe's history as anything since the days of the late 1930s. (Christopher Booker and Richard North, *The Castle of Lies*, pp. 212–13)

The failure over Yugoslavia was doubly damaging. Not only was the crisis on Europe's doorstep, but early in the crisis EU leaders had made clear to the United States that Europe had both the experience and proximity necessary to handle it. Nor was this an isolated event. Europe has rarely responded with alacrity to the great international crises or developments of the day, such as the Gulf war or the collapse of communism in eastern Europe. In the case of the United Nations sponsored war against Iraq in 1991, following the invasion of Kuwait, Europe could not muster a united response, either for or against, a situation replicated when the United States launched further air raids against Iraq in 1996. Such problems and divisions are, to an extent, inevitable in a grouping of countries with very different historical alliances and interests. There is, in addition, sometimes an element of 'passing the buck' to Europe, when national governments are themselves uncertain of how to respond. Thus, Keith Middlemas, in his book *Orchestrating Europe*:

> The Community is at best slow moving and liable to protectionism, rarely more than a sum of its members' interests; but it has so far been a reasonably efficient vehicle for the things its members require – which is itself a characteristic of successful states. There is already a danger, however, in that member states (and the national media that reflect their preconceptions) tend more than in the past to blame it for what are at best joint failures: the Gulf war, the Yugoslav civil wars, high unemployment. The scapegoat function is a useful tool in the game, but since member states' own networks and responsibilities extend to the heart of it, their fault remains, and in the long run may discredit them and increase disillusion with all political enterprises. (p. 697)

Be that as it may, Europe's problem in framing a confident, coherent and effective strategy on most foreign policy issues begs the question of how it will be possible to develop a common foreign and security policy. National differences will not go away, neither will they easily be subsumed in a common European position.

Democratic deficits

The difficulties over common foreign policy are symptomatic of a wider European problem, that of democratic legitimacy. The 'democratic deficit' – there is no European parallel to the scrutiny of domestic decisions by national parliaments – appears to be a permanent feature, despite repeated attempts to bridge it, including the 1996–7 intergovernmental conference (IGC). The European Parliament, while slowly achieving a greater role in the legislative process ('co-decision'), is widely perceived as of limited influence and relevance. Elections to it are characterised by low turnouts and become referenda on the performance of individual national governments. Barely a third of the electorate voted in the 1994 European Parliament elections in the Netherlands, Portugal and Britain, while in all member countries apart from Belgium and Luxembourg, the turnout in European elections was well below that in national elections (in Luxembourg it actually exceeded it). 'Most important of all', writes David McKay in his book, *Rush to Union: Understanding the European Federal Bargain*, 'European elections do not result in a change of government or even in a meaningful change in European Parliament policy. If the socialist grouping were to be replaced as the single largest party by the conservatives, it is unlikely that this would *in terms of voters' perceptions* be seen to herald significant changes in policy.' McKay argues that the emphasis on reducing the democratic deficit through institutional change at a time when the public is uncertain and apathetic about the role of the Parliament, raises many difficulties. More typically, it could be expected that the demand to give the Parliament greater powers, and make the Council of Ministers more democratically accountable, would follow from any greater centralisation of tax-raising, and therefore redistributive, powers:

> A democratic deficit may exist, but for the vast majority of EU citizens, it is a deficit limited to just a small part of the total government activity affecting their daily lives. Should the

activities of the Union expand to include redistributive income transfers of a magnitude necessary to cushion regions and countries against the effects of negative economic shocks, then the pressure for institutional reform will be greatly increased. . . . As with so many aspects of the European Union, these events would follow a sequence which is quite different from those which, historically, have characterised federations elsewhere. In other federations the building of democratic institutions preceded policy; in the EU, policy has typically preceded institution-building. Put another way, in such countries as the United States, the enhancement of the federal government's powers resulted from popular pressure for centralised redistributive measures which could be accommodated within an existing constitutional and institutional structure. (p. 151)

Europe, therefore, has put the policy cart before the institutional horse, a strategy which at times has had its advantages, but which may have run up against a brick wall of opposition. If people have no respect for, or belief in, European institutions, they will resist further transfers of powers to what they perceive to be a mysterious and shadowy centre.

■ *Brotherly tensions*

During 1996, the European Monetary Institute (EMI), the embryo central bank, ran a competition for the design of the banknotes for the euro, the single currency. The brief was extraordinarily difficult. Competitors, professional currency designers from each member state, could either submit abstract designs, intended to convey an image of modern Europe, or they could submit design ideas based on 'ages and styles of Europe'. The problem with the latter was that it was required to be representative, not of any single country, or group of countries but, somehow, the whole of Europe. As it turned out, although this was not discovered until later, the winning design broke the rules by copying actual bridges in Europe (and one outside Europe) and attempting then to disguise them, to the embarrassment of the EMI.

For what is the smallest of the continents except for Australasia/Oceania, Europe has an extraordinary range of peoples, languages and cultures, reflecting the patterns of its original colonisation, large climatic variations and the rise and fall of empires within Europe. Europe is not even easy to define as a geographical entity. According to Felipe Fernández-Armesto:

> There is no geographical logic in distinguishing Europe as a continent at all. Thus 'Europe' is left as a term of convenience hard to match to any objective reality. Its landward extent can be made to vary according to the perspective of the beholder. Herodotus despised the Scythians who, he claimed, never washed and drank their enemies' blood; so he fixed the frontier of Europe at the Don; Strabo, who thought of the Scythians as a useful buffer for Rome, drew the line at the Dnieper. The elastic nature of Europe's landward frontiers has been illustrated in recent times by the temporarily successful attempt of Soviet geographers, for political reasons, to supplant the conspicuous Caucasus by the unhappily-named Manych Depression as the boundary in the southeast. People inside the European Union today have developed the misleading habit of speaking of Europe when they mean only themselves. Even on the seaward side, it is not clear which Atlantic islands to include in Europe, except by convention, and while the Canaries and Azores, for instance, get reckoned European for historical reasons, Iceland is sometimes left out of the account. (*The Times Illustrated History of Europe*, p. 9)

If defining Europe is tricky enough, defining what it is to be a European is even harder. A 'European', according to anthropological definitions, can be of Mediterranean type, with dark skin, black hair, dark eyes and long heads; Alpine, with light brown skin, brown hair and eyes and round heads; or Nordic, with blonde hair, very fair skin, blue eyes and, again, long heads. More likely than any one of these types, a European is likely to be a mélange of them, although with huge variations. European languages, with minor exceptions such as Finnish, have an Indo-European base. The religious tradition is predominantly Christian although plainly reflecting different branches of Christianity. There is, then, perhaps something that can, at best, be only very broadly defined as European, even though the construct is a modern one. Within it, there are tribes, and tribes-within-tribes, as fiercely individual as anything to be found in more primitive societies.

The essential question is whether, in the late 20th century, European unity, pursued through an economic route, with the goal of securing peaceful coexistence – through demonstrating that the economic sum of the whole is greater than that of the parts – can permanently overcome the forces of nationalism and tribalism. There is a tendency, bordering on complacency, to assume that, as far as conflicts within Europe were concerned, the latter part of the 20th century marked the 'end of history'. Thus, the Second World War marked the last great clash between the great powers of western Europe, and the collapse of communism the end of the conflict between the philosophies of western and eastern Europe; the European continent has entered the sunny uplands of that peaceful coexistence. The war in former Yugoslavia – which arose ultimately out of the tensions that built up in what was an artificial 20th-century creation – was a powerful shock to that mood of complacency. At the very least, the idea that Europe can avoid serious internal conflict in the future, particularly if serious economic tensions re-emerge, is not proven. This is not the place to revisit European history. Suffice it to say that there have been plenty of occasions in the past when alliances between nations apparently guaranteed permanent peace. The EU may be more sophisticated but it is not, pun intended, bomb-proof.

■ EU for ever?

As Europe has added layers of economic co-operation, and the EU has gained new members, the impression has been conveyed of an irreversible process, both for the continent as a whole, and for individual participants. The latter, as a simple fact, is untrue. Greenland, a vast country but with a tiny population, joined the EEC as part of Denmark in 1973 but withdrew less than a decade later, in 1982, after being given the right, under the Danish constitution, to hold a referendum on continued membership. Norway has twice come within a whisker of membership but, on each occasion, the Norwegian people have rejected it. Switzerland, as already noted, did not even make it into the European Economic Area, thanks to the caution of its electorate.

The examples of Greenland, Norway and Switzerland, indeed, have been employed by British Eurosceptics as 'options' for Britain. Thus, according to Brian Burkitt, Mark Baimbridge and Philip Whyman, in their Campaign for an Independent Britain pamphlet, 'There *is* an Alternative', the Greenland option for Britain would be complete withdrawal from the EU, with new trading relationships established either with the former Commonwealth, or the North American Free Trade Agreement (Nafta) countries – the United States, Canada and Mexico – or both. The Norwegian option would be to withdraw from the EU but remain part of the EEA, while the Swiss option would be to seek free trade in industrial and financial commodities with the EU but otherwise for Britain to be independent.

The crunch for Britain, according to Burkitt, Baimbridge and Whyman, would come with the creation of Emu. Without it, the status quo of gradual but manageable integration seems more attractive than the cold, unprotected world of independence. But with it:

> Emu threatens not only living standards but also the right of people to govern themselves. The changes it generates will mean that, whenever the House of Commons fulfils its constitutional role of bringing citizens' complaints to the attention of executive authority, no effective response is possible since power has moved to EU institutions. Britain must, therefore, make a clear statement expressing its opposition to any future erosion of the ability of its people to govern themselves and to rebuild its industrial strength. This would uncouple the UK from damaging integrationist trends, whilst allowing it to seize the global opportunities open to it as an internationally competitive but independent country. (pp. 106–7)

I shall return later to the question of Britain and Europe. The key point about Emu, however, is that for the first time in the history of European integration it offers the possibility, indeed the likelihood, of different member states proceeding towards integration at different paces, of a multi-speed Europe. And, while the parallel is often drawn with the enlargement process, this is clearly different in character. Then, countries made a decision on membership of the Community but all insiders were given the opportunity, indeed were expected, to proceed towards integration at a similar pace. Emu is different. There may be an optimist somewhere in the Commission who expects all 15 member states to enter the final stage of Emu at the same time, although it is difficult to see the single currency accommodating the

Greek drachma at any time in the foreseeable future. Thus, Emu will create, at least for a time, insiders and outsiders *from among* the member states. According to David McKay:

> Survey evidence tends to confirm a weak loyalty on the part of most of the citizens of the EU to European institutions. Such loyalty cannot somehow be created through education and information. It will follow only if governments and citizens see in a united Europe benefits which are unavailable through national action alone. If the cost of price stability which it is widely accepted would result from monetary union is further unemployment and deflation im some countries without compensating income equalisation, the whole project may fail. As of the mid-1990s all the evidence points to the creation of a smaller, more cohesive union based on a core of states dominated by the German economy . . . and is extremely unlikely to include the high-inflation peripheral states such as Britain, Italy and Spain. (*Rush to Union*, p. 177)

The risk, therefore, is that the core of first wave Emu states becomes *the* EU, with other members stranded at an earlier stage of integration. Emu becomes the catalyst, not for closer union, but for disunion.

■ *Many directions*

There are those who are so certain of where they are headed that uncertainty never enters the frame, on the old and confusing adage that: 'When he saw a fork in the road he took it.' For some in Europe, among them many of the current generation of political leaders, such certainty exists. Looked at dispassionately, however, the fork in the road Europe has reached offers a choice of directions, some appealing, and some downright alarming. The story of Europe could be poised on the brink of its greatest chapter, or its grimmest. It is to the varying prospects for Europe's future I now turn for the remainder of this book.

Part II

SCENARIO

1

The renaissance

Summary

European economic growth accelerates to a sustainable rate of between 3.5% and 4% a year, as a series of favourable factors come into play – the opening-up of eastern Europe, the completion of the Single Market and the single currency, which lowers average European interest rates significantly. Faster growth provides an environment in which Europe tackles its competitiveness problems, including inflexible labour markets. The euro overtakes the dollar as the world's major currency. Europe is a stable, high-growth region, while Asia becomes turbulent and unstable. Economically, culturally and politically, the 21st century is a time of sustained European revival.

Scenario 1: The renaissance

■ Renaissance then

The first European Renaissance, the intellectual rebirth of a continent, the wave of ideas and energy originating in 14th-century Italy, marked the transition from the middle ages to a new and exciting era. Though most obviously a cultural and social phenomenon, it was underpinned by economic change, notably technical progress – such as the invention of printing – and outward expansion, in the form of colonisation of other continents. The Renaissance marked the beginning of a long period of European intellectual and economic hegemony, which lasted until well into the 20th century. Is it fanciful, when the fashionable view is one in which Europe's continued relative economic decline is seen as a certainty, when the centre of world economic gravity is seen as shifting from west to east, when the European ideal is struggling against a rising tide of nationalism, and when the well of intellectual and creative ideas appears in danger of drying up, to talk of a second European renaissance for the new millennium? Not at all. There are many who believe that, far from fading into the economic sunset, Europe is on the brink of just such a revival.

■ Europe as Rip van Winkle

Europe starts with one significant advantage – the sheer size of its combined economy. Currently, according to the Organisation for Economic Co-operation and Development, the EU has a weighting of 36.6% in the global economy (as defined by the combined output of the Western industrialised countries, itself the lion's share of overall world output). This is similar to the weight of the United States, 36.8%, and well in excess of that of Japan, the second largest economy in the world, which is only 14.9%. The EU, unlike the United States or Japan, is expanding in size – in under 40 years it has grown from six to 15 members. Add in potential EU members, notably in central eastern Europe, and the EU's combined weight, other things being equal, could easily exceed 40% of world economic output in the early part of the 21st century.

Other things have not, however, been equal, and the EU's size and economic firepower are counterbalanced by what many would see as a crushing disadvantage, the fact that it is an economy which has been growing only slowly for two decades or more. Eurosclerosis, once it has set in, is a difficult condition to cure. But is Eurosclerosis a condition that has only been diagnosed by quack doctors? The evidence for it, certainly, is weaker than is often suggested. Over the period 1979–96, for example, EU economic growth averaged 2.1% a year. This was unimpressive. In the 1960s, the six founder members of the European Community had grown by an average of 4.8% a year. But look what has been happening elsewhere in the world in recent times. Set against an average growth rate for the United States of only 2.4% over the same 1979–96 period, the difference is hardly enough to justify labelling the EU as a plodding economic has-been and America as the very model of a modern, free enterprise economy. The growth slowdown was a world-wide phenomenon, for familiar reasons – the two Opec (Organisation of Petroleum Exporting Countries) oil price crises, currency market instability, and the loss of the old controls and mechanisms, some formal, some voluntary, that enabled low inflation to co-exist with negligible unemployment. Japan, it is true, managed a much faster pace of expansion, 3.2% a year, but this, for Japan, was very much a 1980s phenomenon. The bursting of the 'bubble economy' has given way to a period of near-stagnation, with average growth from 1992 of under 1% a year. I shall return to the issue of rapid growth in the Asian 'tiger' economies later in this chapter.

Where Europe's record has undeniably been poor, in a way that has been obvious to the public, is in its record in creating jobs. In 1979, EU unemployment, at 5% of the workforce, was below that of the United States, with 5.8%. By 1996 the position had been dramatically reversed, with the EU on 11.5% and the US 5.5%. Employment growth in the EU over the period 1979–96 averaged a paltry 0.2% a year, compared with an annual 1.5% for the US. Crucially, Europe created no net new private sector jobs over the period.

Thus, while the growth record has not been as poor as is sometimes suggested, a second European renaissance would require it to be far better, and for stronger growth to be translated into jobs. Europe had one 20th-century economic miracle – the continent's recovery, helped it should be said by the Marshall aid programme, from the devastation of the Second World War. Indeed, Europe's survival and prosperity through two world wars underlines the ability of its people to bounce back from adversity. Is it now time to look, not merely to survival, but for a performance as startling as that of the 1950s and 1960s, when Germany's *Wirtschaftswunder*, or economic miracle, set the tone for an entire continent, and gave the EU's founding fathers confidence to look forward to a united, successful and peaceful Europe?

Eastern illusion

When the Berlin Wall came down in 1989, and communist regimes collapsed throughout the old eastern bloc, there was a brief wave of optimism that this, together with the market reforms introduced by Mikhail Gorbachev in Russia, would result in an immediate economic bonanza for western Europe. European companies and financial institutions were urged to move in quickly, for fear that Japan and the United States would snap up the richest pickings. The big management consultancies, never ones to miss a business trick, established representative offices throughout the old Comecon states. Investment banks recruited specialists with detailed knowledge of the region for the lucrative task of setting up local stock exchanges and bringing former state corporations to these and other markets via large-scale privatisation programmes. For companies, the prospect of tens of millions of new consumers, and the pent-up demand that would be unleashed after half a century of effective rationing and grey conformity, was mouth-watering.

The reality, however, was somewhat different. In the special case of German unification, where the citizens of East Germany were provided, courtesy of the politicians and people of the former west Germany, with an immediate income boost, there was a short-lived boom. Bright new BMWs and VW Golfs replaced smoky, obsolete

Trabants. Nearly 16.5m east Germans, starved of western consumer products, provided a hungry market. But this could only be a nine-day wonder. For the iron curtain, once drawn back, was shown to have been concealing as many problems as opportunities. According to Brian Reading, in *The Fourth Reich*:

> Prior to unification, both east and west Germans harboured illusions about the efficiency of east German industry and the productivity of east German labour. . . . East Germany had been held up as the jewel of the Communist system and was thought to have performed rather well. . . . The reality was that East Germany was a place of despair and decay, with an economic system in the final stages of collapse. The roads were full of pot-holes. Houses and flats were ancient and decaying. Over 70% of the housing stock was pre-war. Factories were full of rusting pipes and aged machines. Temporary sheds on the point of collapse contained stores. Even new factories were full of technologically old plant and equipment. The shops, such as there were of them, had mainly empty shelves. Banks were nearly non-existent and restaurants and theatres rare. (p. 123)

The Communist system had, it appeared, perpetrated a huge confidence trick on the west. Many western economists who were supposedly experts on the eastern bloc and the Soviet Union regularly talked in glowing terms about the economic achievements there. There was, after all, no unemployment. All those gold medals in Olympic competition surely told us that these were efficiently run societies. As for consumer goods which the east used to try to sell in western markets, usually at very low prices because of their need for hard currency, they were for the most part poorly made and of obsolete design, but was not this because industrial effort was directed towards high-technology defence and capital equipment, and not to trying to satisfy the fickle whims of consumers? In fact, the backwardness of eastern European consumer products was a fair reflection of the backwardness of the economies from whence they came. Western Europe did not so much have competitors on its doorstep as a bunch of geriatric economies badly in need of care and attention. The newly industrialising countries of the Far East, rather than the tired industrial countries of eastern Europe, became the magnet for international investment.

■ Eastern promise

The mistake, however, would be to conclude that, just because the benefits to western Europe of unleashing the economic potential of eastern Europe and the former Soviet Union did not come through quickly, they will not come through at all. Indeed, it can be argued that the benefits for the EU of assimilating eastern Europe into a European market economy will be all the greater for the fact that these economies start from a very low base. Compared with the one-off boom that would have resulted from allowing eastern consumers access to western consumer goods (in which Europe would have to compete against Japan and other Far Eastern countries), there is the prospect of a more sustained growth boost from rebuilding and investing in these economies. Some of this is already happening. Skoda cars, long regarded as a low-quality joke in western markets, have been transformed by the firm's acquisition by Volkswagen. Motoring writer Ray Hutton, describing the Skoda Octavia, referred to the use, in the car, of platforms, engine technology and other equipment common to other vehicles in the VW-Audi range:

> The result of all this mixing and matching is that Skoda has the best car it has ever made; a solid, well-equipped, five-door hatchback that is as big as a Mondeo, drives well, and provides Volkswagen qualities at lower-than-Golf prices. (*The Sunday Times*, September 22, 1996)

More significantly, the exploitation by western European countries of the lower cost base and skilled industrial tradition of eastern Europe allows direct competition, on price, with imports from the tiger economies of the Far East. Skodas, for example, will compete head-to-head with Far Eastern marques such as Daewoo and Hyundai. Western Europe therefore has an answer, on its own doorstep, to the route used successfully by Japan to gain market share in western Europe – compete initially by selling at low prices and then, when a significant position has been established, sell on quality. If quality, low-priced products are available, backed by established names, from eastern Europe, why buy unproven Far Eastern products? Fiat, which has a long history of licensing its vehicle designs, usually elderly ones, to eastern Europe and the former Soviet Union, is following a similar route of basing the production of new models behind the old iron curtain.

Over the next quarter of a century, the EU is likely to gain at least 10 new members from central and eastern Europe and the former Soviet Union. They include Bulgaria, the Czech Republic, Estonia, Hungary, Latvia, Lithuania, Poland, Romania, Slovakia and Slovenia. Again, too much attention has been focused on the problems of assimilation, for example integrating the agricultural sectors of these economies into the Common Agricultural Policy. But again, the potential is enormous. Almost unnoticed, some of the old Comecon countries have been turning in growth performances which, if not quite matching those of the Asian tigers, are extremely impressive. Poland's growth rate over the 1994–7 period, for example, is put by the OECD at an average of 6% a year, as is the Slovak Republic. Romania, Slovenia and the Czech Republic were growing by 5% a year over the same period. The Czech Republic was the first former Comecon country to join the OECD, which it did in December 1995, closely followed by Hungary. The OECD, in its June 1996 Economic Outlook, was glowing about both the transformation and prospects for the Czech Republic which, as recently as 1990, was entirely subject to state ownership and control:

> Average real incomes have been growing rapidly as the economy begins to reap the benefits of liberalisation. . . . About two-thirds of GDP is now generated by the private sector and practically all prices are liberalised. The ratio of gross fixed investment to GDP is the highest among OECD members and the unemployment rate is among the lowest. The Czech economy is very open. (p. 104)

Not all eastern European economies have matched the Czech Republic's model reforms. But a distinct pattern is emerging. After an economic earthquake of enormous proportions, including the loss of guaranteed markets elsewhere in eastern Europe and the former Soviet Union, the loss of cheap energy supplies from Russia, and the abandonment of a familiar, if grossly inefficient, system of state ownership and control, they are starting to find their feet. Even the old East Germany, a neglected shell of an economy when the former West Germany 'acquired' it, has displayed formidable powers of recovery. More importantly, the story of revival for central and eastern Europe is being spread around the globe, proving an additional spur for foreign investors. Richard Kornik, in a *Time* magazine special report on the region, was enthusiastic:

> The Slovak capital of Bratislava is busily restoring the Baroque beauty of the old town, but just a few metres away in the city centre is a Tesco superstore that attracts shoppers from Austria. In rural Poland formerly ramshackle houses and public buildings gleam with new paint, the proud emblem of private ownership. In western Hungary hundreds of previously state-owned factories now carry the names of multinational giants like Volkswagen, General Electric and Philips Electronics. The future looks bright for central Europe. Seven years after the collapse of communism, even the atmosphere in the major countries of the former Warsaw Pact has been overhauled by the restoration of capitalism. The clouds of sulphurous pollution that used to hang over the region have thinned out palpably as inefficient state factories that relied on subsidised energy and raw materials to produce inferior goods have been driven out of business. After more than four decades of communism, central Europe is enjoying a breath of fresh air. (pp. 33–4, November 25, 1996)

■ Russian boom

One could be even more confident that western Europe's eastern front will provide a building block for a new European renaissance, if there was greater certainty about the economic re-emergence of Russia. Popular wisdom has it that the Russian economy is a basket-case, propped up by the International Monetary Fund and the European Bank for Reconstruction and Development, prone to runaway inflation, and controlled, in place of the old party apparatchiks, by an even more sinister local mafia. Economic reforms, again according to the conventional view, have failed and the country is ready to slip back into its old Communist ways at the first opportunity. But this, while it may chime in with too many newspaper headlines, is far too gloomy a view. Richard Layard and John Parker, in their book *The Coming Russian Boom*, argue strongly and persuasively that private property and free markets have taken root in Russia, and that there will be no turning back:

> Russia has a lot going for it. As in all of eastern Europe, the workforce is highly educated. On top of that Russia has natural

resources unparalleled on a per capita basis except in the oil states. As a large country of 150m people (plus 100m more in its surrounding sphere of influence) Russia will exert a special appeal to foreign capital. And it has a new dynamism, based on rapid privatisation and substantial concentration of wealth. Given all this, Russia is likely to experience growth averaging at least 4% a year for a decade or more. In living standards Russia by 2020 may well have outstripped countries like Poland, Hungary, Brazil and Mexico, with China far behind. (pp. 147–8)

Layard and Parker argue that Russia's economic re-emergence, based on private enterprise, will occur 'whatever happens to the politics'. Indeed, their prediction that the Russian economy is headed for growth of some 4% a year for a decade or more is not based on a rose-tinted forecast for the reform process. A Russian government that could go further than currently seems likely, and force through further, full-blooded market reforms would, they say, be rewarded with annual growth rates of 6% or more. Certainly, the evidence is that western business is responding to the potential, rather than the negative propaganda, surrounding the former Soviet Union. Foreign direct investment rose by 111% to $12.7 billion in 1995, and seems certain to continue to rise rapidly in the future.

The flowering of the economic potential of eastern Europe, the former Soviet states and Russia itself would be a powerful force for accelerated growth within the existing EU. By the end of the first quarter of the 21st century, it is thus perfectly possible to envisage a rapidly growing economic region, with the enlarged Germany at its hub, taking in areas as diverse as Scandinavia, the Mediterranean, the mature economies at the EU's core which came to prominence as a result of the first Renaissance, the USSR's former Comecon satellites in eastern and central Europe, and large parts of the former Soviet Union itself. Diversity, seen in this way, is no disadvantage. After all, many of the economies of this enlarged Europe have a lot of catching up to do.

■ *Wider and deeper*

When the Berlin Wall came down in 1989, and the integration of one eastern European country – the German Democratic Republic – into western Europe speedily became a reality, the timing was far from ideal for proponents of the European federal vision. The drive to 'deepen' integration was in full swing, with the single market programme well under way, the Delors report on European monetary union pointing to a new and determined push to create a single currency before the end of the century, and, a momentum for political union having been re-established, there was a reluctance to throw it away. But for Jacques Delors and the European leaders of the time, notably François Mitterrand and Helmut Kohl, there was an impeccable logic in pursuing the deepening process, at a time when attention might been expected to switch to relations with eastern Europe in general, and questions of enlargement in particular.

On a political level, abandonment of deepening in favour of widening would have jeopardised one of the central aims of the Kohl–Mitterrand axis – ensuring that the newly unified Germany did not, as in the past, become too powerful for its own good. This could only be achieved by ensuring that the integration process continued. Anything less and Germany's attentions would be easily diverted towards the task of assimilating the eastern *Länder* into the capitalist economy of the existing Federal Republic. The momentum towards deepening would have been lost. There was also, for the proponents of this view, a powerful economic logic, along the following lines. Closer integration, and in particular the completion of the Single Market, would lead to stronger growth among the existing EU states. Thus the EU would be better able to take on and carry 'passengers' in the form of eastern European countries requiring help with their transition from centrally planned to market economies. Deepening did not mean closing the door on potential candidates from the east, instead it was essential to the widening process. As long as this logic is followed through, and the European Union's protectionist instincts do not display themselves, the potential is indeed very exciting.

■ *Europe's renaissance potential*

In 1987 the European Commission published a report, 'Efficiency, Stability and Equity', compiled by a team of experts under the chairmanship of Tommaso Padoa-Schioppa, then deputy director-general of the Banca d'Italia. Its task was to examine the consequences of enlargement (the entry of Spain and Portugal) and the completion of the Single Market. It noted the opportunities for achieving faster growth in the EU, firstly from the fact that high levels of unemployment signalled a degree of spare capacity that would safely permit an accelerated pace of expansion without seriously damaging price stability – at the time the Commission had put together a 'co-operative growth strategy' to raise Europe's annual trend growth rate from 2.5% to 3.5% a year.

Secondly, according to the Padoa-Schioppa report, the Single Market would in itself contribute to raising Europe's trend growth rate. 'The market opening process, by improving the efficiency of resource allocation, will permit a step up in the level of productivity and output in the economy. Implemented over a medium-term period, this translates into an increase in the annual potential growth rate for a number of years' (p. 109).

This opened up the possibility of a virtuous circle for Europe, in which the opening-up of markets, which itself stimulated growth, would also allow European governments to adopt more expansionary policies, without triggering inflation:

> The economic channels whereby market liberalisation should lead to faster economic growth are well established. With the elimination of trading barriers, competition is increased and prices fall towards the level of the most efficient producers. Prices are further reduced over a period of years as production is rationalised and economies of scale exploited in new investments. The lower prices lead to higher real disposable incomes. Wage inflationary pressures are dampened doubly, directly through the lower prices and indirectly through the sharper competitive pressures bearing upon enterprises. (p. 108)

A successful growth strategy, together with the successful completion of the Single Market, could raise the EU's annual growth rate to something approaching a sustainable 4% a year. This, as we have seen, would be nearly double the rate of the past two decades, and markedly faster than the recent growth performance of Japan and North America. It would also, however, represent a transformation in comparison with Europe's recent experience. The EU greeted the start of the Single Market (always called the '1992' programme, it did not take effect until the end of that year) with a recession in 1993. Since then, growth has been far from exceptional – the 1993–6 average was just over 1.5%. Were hopes of accelerated EU growth merely pie in the sky?

Again, as with the development of eastern Europe, it may not be so much that hopes were dashed, as deferred. The growth strategy was blown off course by the onset of a period of higher German interest rates, themselves directly attributable to the effects of unification. The scope for accelerated growth has, with unemployment and thus spare capacity higher than in the mid-1980s, increased. The benefits of the Single Market, in the form of much stronger growth in intra-European trade, have been partially but not fully realised. As Europe moves into the 21st century, they can be.

■ *One market, one money . . . fast growth*

Apart from unhelpful cyclical factors, the missing ingredient for accelerated growth in Europe may, in fact, be staring us in the face. Could the single currency, in fact, become the spur for an economic renaissance in Europe, a farewell to the sclerosis, evident in anaemic growth rates, to which the continent has fallen prey? The most straightforward argument that says it could is based on free trade. The fewer the barriers to trade, the greater, other things being equal, is likely to be the growth of trade. The Single Market, which began to come to fruition at the end of 1992, represented a major stride towards the realisation of free trade within Europe. But it remains unfulfilled because persisting with separate national currencies itself creates a formidable barrier to trade.

According to Christopher Johnson, in his pro-Emu book, *In With The Euro, Out With The Pound*:

> The absurdity of trying to run a Single Market in Europe without a single currency is becoming increasingly apparent to businesses, if not to politicians. . . . The advantages of the Single Market and single currency interact, so that their combined benefits are greater than the mere sum of each in isolation. The Single Market has reduced transactions costs by cutting down Customs delays, but separate exchange rates continue to make exports more costly than home sales. The single currency will slash transactions costs by eliminating exchange rates, but

Customs delays will continue to make exports dearer if the Single Market is not completed or goes into reverse. Only the combination of no Customs delays and no exchange rate barriers will put exports on a par with domestic goods. (pp. 46–7)

The Single Market programme dates back to December 1985 when European leaders, meeting in Luxembourg, 'decided to give new impetus to European integration' by drawing up a Single European Act, which was signed in February 1986 and came into force in all member states of July 1, 1987. A year later the European Commission published another report, put together by a team under Paolo Cecchini, a senior Commission official, which included 16 volumes of evidence and which went beyond the Padoa-Schioppa exercise in attempting to put figures on the impact of the Single Market on Europe's economies.

This impact, from economies of scale and increased competition, fell into two categories. There were the one-off effects from the introduction of the Single Market, broadly a boost to European GDP of 4.5% over the first five years (a third of which was expected to come from the liberalisation of financial services), creating two million extra jobs, and a fall in the price level of 5% or 6%, relative to what it would otherwise have been, over the same period. The second set of effects were those on Europe's growth potential over the longer term. Here the main impact was seen as reducing the constraints of macro-economic policy, partly because greater competition within Europe would act as a systematic restraint against inflation, and partly because the Single Market would act to synchronise economic cycles in Europe. The situation of balance of payments crises because one country in Europe was booming relative to the others would be far less likely.

Surely though, these effects of the Single Market are now behind us? Almost certainly not. The 1992 programme marked the beginning, not the end, of the task of creating the Single Market. According to European Commissioner Mario Monti, at a 1995 conference to assess the impact and effectiveness of the Single Market:

It is important to underline that the removal of legal barriers to market entry does not, in itself, create a Single Market. There is much more to be done, and not just by lawmakers, before a Single Market, in which business treats the entire territory of the Union in the same way as a 'national' market, can become a reality. In other words, we are not at the end of the road, although I would suggest that we are well on our way.

In addition, the period when the Single Market should have been beginning to exert a positive influence on Europe's economies was one of extreme financial turbulence in the European Monetary System, marked by the forced departure of sterling and the Italian lira from the exchange rate mechanism (ERM) on 'Black Wednesday', September 16, 1992. It was followed by a string of devaluations among the smaller European currencies, the Irish pound, Spanish peseta and Portuguese escudo, before what appeared to be a final bout of system-destroying pressure on the key French franc/Deutschmark rate in the summer of 1993. The ERM was saved, but only by the adoption of wide, 15% currency bands (most currencies had operated within 2.25% bands prior to the crisis). Sterling and the lira, now no longer within the ERM, traded well below even these new wide bands.

The effect of the ERM crisis was to give an immediate competitive advantage to the countries whose currencies had left the system, lock in the others to high interest rates – partly a function of the Bundesbank's efforts to deal with the monetary repercussions of German unification – and, eventually, bring conditions of near-recession to the core economies of Europe, notably France and Germany. These were not conditions where the benefits of the Single Market could easily be realised. In the case of financial services – a third of Cecchini's one-off benefits – progress towards liberalisation has been painfully slow. More generally, France and Germany have been more concerned about protecting their domestic industries from cheap currency exports from Italy and Britain than pushing forward unfettered trade within Europe.

If most of the benefits of the Single Market have yet to be realised, and will only occur when European monetary union is in place, to them can be added the potential benefits for growth of the single currency itself. The European Commission, in its report 'One Market, One Money', identified several classes of transactions savings from the abolition of separate currencies within the European Union. They would include the removal of direct currency commission charges (including the difference between buy and sell rates) for transactions in European currencies, the parallel removal of indirect charges, for example on credit card transactions in other European countries, and substantial savings on companies' in-house costs for currency dealing and managing exchange rate risk. Overall, these effects were estimated to produce a saving in transactions costs of 0.3–0.4% of European GDP, equivalent to Ecu20 billion to Ecu25 billion a year. They are not, however, the only possible growth benefits from monetary union.

■ *One currency, cheap money*

At any given time in Europe there is an array of interest rates, both short rates and long-term interest rates as measured, for example, by the yields on government bonds. Typically, the 'harder' the currency, and thus the smaller the exchange rate risk as perceived by international investors, the lower the level of interest rates. Put another way, the better the long-term inflation performance of a country, the more likely that country is to have both a strong currency and relatively low interest rates. In Europe this has tended to mean that, because the Deutschmark is traditionally the strongest currency, German interest rates have been both a benchmark and a base for the rest. A typical array of European interest rates in the autumn of 1996 had short rates ranging from 3% in Germany to 3.3% in France, 5.8% in Britain and 8.4% in Italy. Similarly, long rates ranged from 6.2% in Germany and France through 7.8% in Britain, 8.4% in Spain and 9% in Italy.

If monetary union is properly established, with a workable commitment to low, German-style inflation, and the Maastricht fiscal criteria properly observed – because the greater the control of budget deficits, the lower the bond yields that will result – the effect will be significant gains in the form of lower interest rates for all participating countries, simply through the process of exchanging their higher, risk-affected, national interest rates for a common, and lower, European rate. The size of the gain would depend on how far, for each country, rates are above existing German levels. Only Germany, it appears, would not register any direct gains on this score, but German industry would also share in the gains through the mechanism of the acceleration in economic growth in partner countries.

There is another potential benefit, beyond this 'averaging down' effect, however. This is that even the standard-setter in Europe has had abnormally high real interest rates, partly because the unification of

Germany led to a significant increase in Germany's budget deficit, and partly because, internationally, investors have demanded a higher real return, during the 1970s, 1980s and to a lesser extent the 1990s, compared with the low-inflation 'golden age' of the 1950s and 1960s, because there have been times when they have been caught out by unexpectedly high inflation. In the golden age, real interest rates, measured by bond yields relative to inflation, averaged under 3%. In the 1980s and 1990s they have more usually been 4% or above. Again, to the extent that monetary union is associated with low inflation and stronger growth in Europe, replicating the conditions of the golden age, the benefits could be self-feeding. Christopher Taylor, a former senior adviser to the Bank of England on Europe, has estimated that the combined impact of 'averaging down' and lower interest rates than current German benchmark levels could be to reduce real interest rates in Europe by between 1 and 1.5 percentage points, with consequent, and highly significant, growth benefits.

All these factors will help reduce what has become modern Europe's most intractable problem, high unemployment. In 1996, unemployment in the EU stood at 11.5%, or nearly 19m people. Unemployment in Europe has many causes, not least inflexible labour markets. The necessary reform of these markets could, however, be much more easily achieved in an environment of rapid economic expansion – converting growth into jobs. Faster growth in Europe would be the key to reducing unemployment, and offer the prospect of a return to the virtual full employment of the 'golden age' of the 1950s and 1960s.

■ One currency, biggest currency?

'A strong euro will make us less dependent on the whims of the dollar.' So said Jacques Santer, European Commission president, in April 1996. Is it possible that others, well beyond the confines of the Commission, could come to a similar conclusion, so that the euro would challenge the global hegemony of the dollar? Peter Kenen of Princeton University, in his book *Economic and Monetary Union in Europe: Moving Beyond Europe*, argues that monetary union would have a two-stage effect on the foreign exchange markets. Initially, there would be increased trading in Deutschmarks, as a proxy for the euro, at the expense of other European currencies. Later, this trading would switch to the euro, and the euro, as a 'vehicle currency', could begin to take on the dollar as the anchor currency of the international monetary system.

> It should diminish the basic advantage of using a single vehicle currency, challenging the pivotal role of the dollar in the foreign exchange market. . . . It will change the functioning of the foreign exchange market and remove one of the main institutional arrangements that has preserved the role of the dollar in the international monetary system. (p. 112)

The euro, on this view, would also become the natural currency for central and eastern Europe, the countries of which would see themselves as waiting in the wings for eventual Emu membership, and for whom it would be natural to peg their currencies to it, and conduct the bulk of their international transactions and hold most of their foreign exchange reserves in it. The same could be true of French-speaking countries in the developing world and, assuming sterling forms part of the single currency, significant parts of the British Commonwealth. Kenen raises the possibility of oil and other commodities being priced in euros rather than in dollars.

This is certainly a view which finds favour among Europe's strongest proponents of the single currency. 'We think that this currency is going to become as powerful as the dollar and that in future it will prevent the domination of the dollar, which over the past 50 years has become not only the world's leading currency but an irresponsible one, i.e. it can do what it wants since it is the world's sole major currency,' said Hervé de Charette, the French foreign minister in September 1996. 'Tomorrow, the euro will be the alternative major currency and will carry considerable weight in international financial and monetary debates' (interview with RTL, September 29, 1996).

The euro could not, of course, become the main international reserve currency overnight. Despite long-standing talk of diversification out of dollars, the US currency accounts for more than 60% of international reserve holdings, compared with under 20% for existing European Union currencies combined, of which the Deutschmark is the most important. The euro would, however, provide a viable alternative main reserve currency, in a way that the Deutschmark on its own, or the Japanese yen (around 10% of international reserves) have failed to do. It would also be poised to increase its share of international bank lending – currently the combined share of EU currencies is around a third, compared with 40% for the dollar – and international bond markets, where already, at a share of just under 40%, European currencies combined vie with the dollar in importance.

From G7 to G3

The euro's growing importance as a world currency would provide EU countries with significant seignorage gains – the income gained from currency issue. The emergence of the euro in this way would greatly enhance the weight of the EU in terms of international economic diplomacy. The Group of Seven (G7) – the United States, Japan, Germany, France, Britain, Italy and Canada – evolved in the 1980s into the key forum for economic decision-making. The G7 countries have, since 1975, been holding annual world economic summits. Their finance ministers and central bankers meet regularly to discuss matters such as the alignment of international exchange rates. In the mid-1980s, this role developed into one of central importance for the currency markets, with the Plaza agreement in New York in 1985, which set in motion moves to bring down the value of the dollar, followed by the Louvre accord in Paris in 1987, which aimed to stabilise the dollar at its new lower level, as well as usher in a new era of stability for other currencies.

Latterly, while the G7 remains important, and continues to hold its annual, largely ceremonial summits of world leaders, and regular meetings of finance ministers and central bankers, a more select Group of Three (G3), consisting of America, Japan and Germany, is regarded, for practical purposes, as the centre of power, although it never holds formal meetings. America's G3 role is because of the sheer size of the US economy and the importance of monetary policy decisions by the Federal Reserve Board. In the case of Japan it is because of economic size, together with the key role played by yen investors in world financial markets. Germany's pivotal role rises because the Bundesbank is seen as driving monetary policy in Europe – where it leads others follow. But, while this is true for the setting of interest rates in the core economies of Europe, those mostly closely tied to the

Deutschmark at the heart of the ERM, Germany's monetary policy hold on Europe has been far from complete. British interest rates, to give one example, were set independently of Bundesbank rates after sterling's departure from the ERM in September 1992. So too were those of Italy.

Under a European single currency, with a single central bank, Germany would be replaced by Europe within this informal G3 framework, which could then become formalised. Indeed, one of the central arguments of the pro-single currency school is that the international clout of Europe would be greater than the sum of its parts (currently, in the G7, Germany, France, Britain and Italy). According to Christopher Johnson again:

> From the point of view of a single country such as the UK, entry into a world currency such as the euro makes it possible to have more influence over world exchange rates and monetary policies than as a middle-ranking power with declining international financial influence. (p. 174)

Indeed, if Japan has now entered a phase of economic consolidation and much slower growth, preoccupied with retaining the country's existing power-base in the Far East, and if, at the same time, America continues on a path of relative insularity, Europe could then begin to take the lead on world economic issues, acting as a source of new ideas – which individual European countries such as Britain and France would say they have already been doing – and the driving force for putting them into practice. Europe led the world once, it could do so again.

■ Business bonanza

A European economic renaissance would offer a superb environment for business, a combination of strong growth, intra-European free trade and the extensive opportunities arising from the exploitation of eastern European markets. Opportunities for new business alliances will abound, as will those for creating vast operations built around liberalised telecommunications and transport systems. There will be widespread opportunities for exploiting economies of scale. Europe, having lagged behind America, will begin to develop fully its information technology potential. In a large, liberalised market, the forces of comparative advantage will exert themselves, leading to greater specialisation within countries. In some cases this will mean dropping out of certain industries altogether. Britain will be able to exploit its comparative advantage in financial services and pharmaceuticals, Germany in mechanical engineering and capital goods, Italy in designer luxury goods, and so on. The key point about this scenario is that specialisation and rationalisation will occur in an environment of expanding employment and opportunity, minimising any adverse consequences.

The development of a true, Europe-wide single currency will bring obvious advantages in terms of lower transaction costs and stability for business. But it will have other, equally profound, effects. Continental companies will have easier access to the most efficient capital-raising centres. London would become the stock market for Europe. At the same time, the type of specialist banking that has proved successful in financing Germany's *Mittelstand* will become available to small and medium-sized businesses across Europe.

■ And a new political mood

Nationalism, racism and a suspicion of the motives of neighbouring states are all products of economic adversity. In a Europe that works, where all are seen to benefit from the co-operative project, such forces will first diminish and then disappear. Political parties that have been encouraged by their electorates to adopt defensive, even hostile attitudes towards Europe and its institutions will be driven towards a belief in the greater good, in a way probably not seen since the 1950s and 1960s. Pooling of sovereignty will be seen as advantageous, not the creation of a distant, unresponsive United States of Europe run by unaccountable supranational institutions. The politicians who pushed through the integrationist agenda in the 1990s, against voter opposition, notably François Mitterrand and Helmut Kohl, will be seen in the 21st century as visionaries mentioned in the same breath as Jean Monnet. Europe's politics in this scenario will be outgoing and co-operative, as envisaged by the founding fathers.

■ Pricking the Asian bubble

If there is one piece of conventional wisdom about trends in the world economy over the next quarter of a century, it is that the centre of gravity is switching from the North America–Europe axis to a new hub of activity, encapsulating Asia, Australasia and the western United States. The Atlantic economies will be displaced by those of the Pacific rim. These newly industrialised countries of Asia, and some of them not so new, are recording growth rates of between three and six times those that are now the norm in the old industrial economies. With this kind of momentum, how long can it be before they overhaul the old, slow-growing economies of Europe?

Faced with numbers such as these, however, should not the economist's natural response be to conclude that there is a significant 'flash in the pan' aspect to them? Professor Paul Krugman of Stanford University puts the counter-argument forcefully, arguing that from the perspective of the year 2010, current projections of Asian supremacy extrapolated from recent trends may well look almost as silly as 1960s-vintage forecasts of Soviet industrial supremacy did from the perspective of the Brezhnev years. 'The idea that these high growth rates can be projected 30 years into the future is likely to be unrealistic', he maintains. 'Even China will run out of peasants to expand its workforce, and diminishing returns – for which there is already some evidence – will set in. The high performing Asian economies will not be able to grow over the next twenty years at the pace they have been growing' (*Centrepiece*, October 1996, p. 11).

Krugman's point is that growth in these economies will slow from its present breakneck pace and, perhaps more importantly, that there is nothing 'miraculous' about their current pace of development. It can be explained, he insists, with reference to known factors of production – investment and the rapid shift of labour from agriculture to industry. Today's mature industrial economies went through the same process. This emphatically does not mean they can be ignored but, as Dr Gerard Segal of the International Institute for Strategic Studies (IISS), director of the Economic and Social Research Council's Pacific Asia Research Programme notes, it should mean that Europe and its businesses break out of the '10-feet tall' mentality:

We are still at the stage where many businesses regard what is happening in these countries as a miracle – they believe the people there must be 10 feet tall. What we need to develop is a frame of mind which recognises that these countries have both strengths and weaknesses, that they represent market opportunities as well as competition, and that the economic potential of these markets is huge. Like all late developers, they have certain advantages over incumbent industrial powers, just as America in the early part of this century had an advantage over Britain. They can learn quickly and avoid mistakes. But Krugman is right to say there is no miracle – the recipe for the current success of countries in the Asia-Pacific regions is that of following a well-understood pattern. (conversation with the author, February 1996)

The east Asian economies have benefited from high levels of investment which takes advantage, typically of low labour costs, and productive workforces. 'Asian values', the peculiar brand of eastern capitalism in which the role of the family is paramount, appears to be conducive to rapid rates of economic development. But even in these economies, the price of such development is an erosion of the advantage of low labour costs. Industrialisation, which typically begins when national income per head is $500–1,000 (£300–600), begets consumerism as incomes rise to $3,000 a head, a demand for basic banking and financial services at $5,000 a head, an expanding market for luxuries at $10,000 a head, and so on. All economies grow rapidly during the initial phase of industrialisation, slowing to a more manageable pace as they mature, and the Asian economies will be no exception. Rapid growth rates merely tell us that these economies have a long way to go to catch up.

Surely, however, the most telling point about Asia is its sheer weight of population. China has a population of 1.2 billion, nearly double that of an enlarged 'Europe' which took in the existing EU and likely new members, plus much of the former Soviet Union. India has a population of 950m and a rapidly emerging middle-class. Between them China and India have more than 40% of the world's population and have been recording rapid rates of growth in the 1990s – with annual rates exceeding 10% and 5%, respectively. Europe, however, has as much to gain from rapid growth in Asia, and its contribution to world trade growth, as it has to lose. Economic development means, as well as the emergence of new competitors, the creation of new markets. European businesses have already done much to ensure that they will have a stake in the future of these 'new' economic powers.

More importantly, it would be unwise to base an entire belief about far-reaching shifts in the geographical balance of world economic power. It is easy to forget, in the context of 20% annual growth rates in Guangdong and other pseudo-capitalist regions of the country, that China is attempting something that has never been successfully achieved before, combining rapid, market-based economic development with politically repressive government. Can market freedoms be easily squared, and sustained, with a lack of personal and political freedom for the Chinese people? Tiananmen Square has been over-quoted as an example of that repressiveness, but it remains in the memory as an important, and unattractive, window on China. As the historian J. M. Roberts has written, China at the very least offers a different model of economic and political development from any seen elsewhere in the world:

> Transformed though so much of the world already was, China after Tiananmen Square still baffled observers and futurologists by its seemingly massive immunity to currents outside its borders. One of the traditional roles of its governments has always been to act as the guardian of Chinese values. If, anywhere, modernisation might not turn out to mean westernisation, it could be in China. (*The Penguin History of the World*, p. 1096).

The tensions between market-based economic development and the Communist political model could spill over, as in Russia and eastern Europe, into a powerful counter-revolutionary drive. If this culminates in the unwinding of the current economic reform programme, the experience of former Communist countries elsewhere in the world suggests, at the very least, a lacuna in the process of economic development. On the other hand, capitalist economic development may be allowed to go so far and no further – once 'westernisation' is seen to be a threat to existing political structures, it will be nipped in the bud. However bright China's economic prospects may look now, the hard part is yet to come. According to Jim Rohwer:

> Even if it enjoys more tolerance from ordinary Chinese than almost any westerner can imagine, China's Communist party still

faces a daunting second challenge: how to execute a modernisation of its authority in the radically changed China of the mid-1990s. It is clear to almost everybody that the old methods are rusted beyond rescue, but new ones capable of working in an economy equally balanced between state-run and free-market are hard to fashion. (*Asia Rising*, p. 161).

European stability . . .

The founding fathers of European Union were driven, not by the prospect of economic advantage derived from greater co-operation, although this was important, but by the prize of ensuring that Europe, ripped apart by two world wars, could enjoy a new era of peace and stability, in which former enemies would become partners. According to Dennis Swann:

> It was not until 1945 that there occurred a combination of new forces together with an intensification of old ones, compelling action. Europe had been the centre of yet another devastating war arising out of the unbridled ambitions of nation states. Those who sought, and still seek, a united Europe, have always had at the forefront of their minds a desire to prevent any further outbreak of war in Europe. By bringing the nations of Europe closer together it has always been hoped that such a contingency would be rendered unthinkable. (*The Economics of the Common Market*, p. 2)

The agenda, often unspoken, always clearly understood, was the containment of Germany. Twice, in the space of 30 years, German aggression had been the source of devastation. The approach followed after the First World War, of making Germany pay, had only fed that sense of national resentment that provided the breeding-ground for the rise of the Nazi party. This time, the approach had to be an inclusive one, with Germany a full member of the new club, and one which offered the German people the prospect of economic revival, partly arising from greater co-operation, rather than confrontation, with its neighbours. As Jean Monnet, describing the thinking behind the European Coal and Steel Community, recalled in his memoirs:

All successive attempts to keep Germany in check, mainly at French instigation, had come to nothing, because they had been based on the rights of conquest and temporary superiority. But if the problem of sovereignty were approached with no desire to dominate or take revenge – if on the contrary the victors and the vanquished agreed to exercise joint sovereignty over part of their joint resources – then a solid link would be forged between them, the way would be wide open for further collective action and a great example would be given to the other nations of Europe. (*Memoires*, p. 361)

It has worked every bit as well as its designers could have hoped. Western Europe has become a haven of peace and stability in the second half of the 20th century, in stunning contrast to the first 50 years. Successive post-war German politicians have not only acquiesced in the process of European integration but have become its most enthusiastic supporters. Helmut Kohl, German Chancellor since 1981, has become the key player in that process, and the driving force beind the move towards monetary union. The Franco-German axis, once a source of tension, division and war in Europe, has become the pivot upon which the new, united Europe rests. In this respect, European integration has been an unqualified success.

Asian turbulence

Europe's stability could become one of its key advantages in the 21st century, and is another reason to doubt the inevitability of Asian economic domination. Just as China's emergence raises all sorts of internal conflicts, so it raises important questions about whether the newly emerging economies of Asia will be able to live in harmony with the region's established economic leader, Japan. Tension between China and Japan is long-standing, from the latter's presence in Manchuria in 1905 through to the 1937–45 Sino-Japanese war, that tension was virtually continuous. Unlike in Europe, where the continent's economic heavyweights are bent on co-operation, the prospect of China and Japan jostling for position as number two economic power in the world, behind the United States, is a potential powder-keg. China's armed forces, totalling nearly 3m, are small in relation to the size of population but are nearly 15 times the size of those of Japan. Nor is this the only likely source of tension emanating from China.

Gerald Segal of the International Institute for Strategic Studies, again, cites Chinese attitudes to Taiwan as raising more general questions about the stability of a region with a resurgent China at its heart:

> Will China's nationalist instincts be constrained by economic interdependence? There are powerful conservative nationalist forces in Beijing, especially in the armed forces, which are convinced that the civilian leadership is already taking too soft a line on questions of national sovereignty. The continuing uncertainty in China about post-Deng Xiaoping policies has given such nationalists scope to demand tougher policies. Hence the ever-increasing military activity in the region. The debates in China are not just about personalities, they are about the tough choices China must make in domestic and foreign policy. Will China continue with economic reform when this means a continuing decentralisation of power? Will China continue to depend heavily on external investment and access to foreign fuel, food and markets? As China grows more dependent, nationalists will worry that China will abandon its territorial objectives and will be tied down by the international system. China is the only great power not to be content with its neighbours' existing borders. And with its rising economic power it has a sense that it can re-order the world. (*The World in 1996*, *The Economist*, pp. 71–2)

Europe's 'peace dividend', broadly defined, is potentially enormous. Two world wars robbed Europe of economic and political domination of the globe. A Europe that lives in harmony with itself, indeed co-operates ever more closely on defence and pools its foreign policy, is a completely different animal from the one that succumbed to division and conflict in the first half of the 20th century. Europe, however, has had peace for more than 50 years, why should this suddenly click now, to the continent's advantage? There are two reasons. The first is that European countries have had separate and distinct foreign policy agendas, particularly in response to American military action, of which varying degrees of willingness to co-operate with the US over the bombing of Libya was a classic example. A greater pooling of foreign policy will erode such differences. Second, peace in western Europe had, until 1989, to exist under the shadow of the threat from the Soviet Union and eastern Europe. A divided Europe could never be a truly stable Europe. No longer divided, it can be.

■ *A cultural renaissance?*

Bernard Connolly, in his book *The Rotten Heart of Europe*, describes how Jacques Delors, when Commission president in 1991, asked his staff for some summer holiday reading material on 'Europe's cultural identity'. They were unable to provide him with any. The first European Renaissance was associated with a flowering of creative energy in art, music, drama and literature. It provided the basis for Europe's cultural domination of the world until the 20th century. Since then, however, that domination has been lost to America, most notably in the popular cultures of film and television but also, to a lesser extent, music and literature. The basis of America's success has been cultural homogeneity. Where Europe is culturally diverse, and culturally protectionist – such as, for example, the activities of the Académie Française – America has been able to build on what is, on the face of it, a smaller home market than exists in Europe, to sell its brand of popular culture to the world. Hollywood has the big-budget, movie-house industry, Europe has the low-budget, art-house, poor relation.

Cultural diversity is potentially a huge advantage for Europe, but it has been turned into a disadvantage. Different parts of America retain their cultural identity but are also part of a larger whole. This cannot yet be said to be the case for Europe. There is no single market in European culture. Should the provisions of the wider Single Market come to fruition, however, it could very easily develop. In particular, geographical mobility is the key to America's greater homogeneity. When people live, and work, in different parts of the same large nation, they are more likely to respond, and appreciate, their cultural output. Europe needs, for economic reasons, greater geographical mobility than is currently the case. It also needs it for cultural reasons. In a thriving economy this would start to happen. A cultural renaissance also probably requires, more controversially, far greater emphasis on a common language, probably English. Europe starts with enormous cultural advantages; there is no reason why economic and cultural renaissance cannot, once again, be intertwined.

Fifty years on

Drawing these strands together, Europe's second renaissance has many facets. It begins with powerful economic revival, brought on by a range of factors – the completion of the Single Market, the single currency, and the opening-up of eastern Europe and Russia – to push economic growth in Europe onto a decisively stronger trend. With this comes a new confidence in foreign policy, and an enhancement of Europe's place in the world. The squabbles of the 1990s, about who runs Europe, about loss of national sovereignty, and about the integrationist path the continent is pursuing, seem like an ancient relic.

In 50 years, Europe is the hub of the world economy – rich, politically stable and the largest and most vibrant single market in the world. The euro has long replaced the dollar as the world's leading currency and, as happened in the past, the world looks to Europe for its cultural and philosophical lead.

SCENARIO 2

Plus ça change

Summary

Europe gains from the growth of world trade, despite the gradual loss of market share to the emerging economies of Asia, this is not a zero-sum game. The growth of world trade is fast enough to compensate for Europe's gradually declining share. The Single Market is gradually completed and the single currency extends its reach, beyond the initial 'core' countries which join at the outset. Closer integration, and the absence of internal and external shocks, lifts sustainable European growth to 2.5% a year initially, rising to 2.75%. European integration continues to be economically driven, member states baulking at any attempt to force through 'big bang' moves towards political union.

Scenario 2: *Plus ça change*

■ *Fin de siècle?*

At the end of the 19th century, more so than at the end of the 20th, there was a *fin de siècle* spirit about Europe. Part of it reflected concern about the pace of progress – the motor car and automation promised a different but uncertain future. Part of it reflected worries, among the ruling class, about the sustainability of the existing social order. Revolution had already threatened most European countries during the century and in Germany Bismarck had already introduced the social security model that most others would follow. Some of this sense of an era approaching its natural finale was, however, based on economic concerns. On the face of it, Europe did not have much to worry about. Its combined population, 400m including Russia, was five times that of the United States. The New World was, however, like the economies of Asia today, developing at a far faster pace. America established a productivity lead over the Netherlands in the 1870s, Belgium in the 1880s and Britain in the 1890s. The output of the US chemicals industry had, by 1913, reached that of Britain and Germany combined. For late 19th-century Europeans, as much as for their late 20th-century equivalents, the prospect of economic decline was a real one.

It got worse. In the First World War, Europe wasted millions of lives and countless resources and surrendered its leadership in many other sectors. In the wreckage of the 1920s, few could be genuinely optimistic about Europe's future. The experience was repeated after the Second World War. The war effort had shown Europe to be innovative and highly productive, when its efforts were geared mainly towards destructive ends, but by its end the continent was emotionally, industrially and financially exhausted. Nor did the building of post-war integration lead to an immediate restoration of Europe's confidence. In 1963, Théo Lefèvre, the then Belgian prime minister, said: 'In western Europe there are now only small countries – those that know it and those that don't know it yet.' The Opec oil crisis of 1973–4 appeared to mark the beginnings of a fundamental shift in economic power away from the old, petroleum-poor industrial countries of western Europe, and towards the primary producers.

The central message about Europe in the 20th century has been its extraordinary powers of survival in the face of the most extreme adversity. Two world wars and the cold war have either originated, or been conducted in their entirety, on its territory. On several occasions, Europe's economy has been on its knees, its countries bitterly divided. Like all old stagers, however, Europe has learned a few tricks along the way, and the ability to recover and then thrive in the face of extreme adversity is one of them. This is the context in which to challenge the notion of Europe's inevitable decline in the 21st century.

■ Not a zero-sum game

Imagine there is a country which, alone in the world, has developed a manufacturing industry, while all others are still engaged in tilling the land, tending their animals, and trading in sacks of corn or cowrie shells. That country, which sells its products to these others, has 100% of world trade in manufactures. But then, as a result of imitation or initiative, another country develops its own industrial base, and begins to sell to the world. The first country's share drops to 80%. Does this then mean that the first country is worse off? Of course not. Although its share of world trade has declined, the amount of that trade has increased sharply, because of the second country's greater income and wealth – which boosts overall demand for industrial products. This, which is not far removed, as a caricature, of Britain's position in the 18th and early 19th centuries, should be an antidote to the idea that a decline in Europe's share of world trade means that the continent is in a period of absolute decline. World trade is not a zero-sum game. As long as Europe's share of trade is declining at a slower rate than the increase in the level of trade, Europe will be better off, year-in, year-out.

Europe's record, indeed, has been better than is generally believed, and more than bears out this general conclusion. Comparing 1977 and

1993 for example, using OECD data, the world trade share of the 'big four' EU countries – (west) Germany, France, Britain and Italy – declined, but only slightly, from 27.2% to 25.8%, and this in an environment in which cumulative world trade growth, in real terms, exceeded 125%. Looked at in a slightly different way, and over a longer time period, Europe's record looks even better. In 1962, imports from other industrial countries accounted for 6.06% of the combined GDP of OECD countries, while imports from non-OECD countries accounted for a further 2.39% of GDP. By 1994, these shares had risen to 10.72% and 3.73% respectively. Within this, imports from European countries accounted for 3.83% of GDP in 1962, rising to 6.7% in 1994. Disentangling these figures, Europe accounted for 45.3% of OECD imports in 1962, *rising* to 46.3% by 1994, hardly a picture of secular decline. Europe has not only at least maintained its share, but this in a context in which the denominator (the combined GDP of OECD countries) has increased severalfold in real terms.

Some of this success, plainly, reflects the development of trade within Europe. Indeed, the expansion of intra-European trade has been one of the key successes of the integration process. For European countries, imports from elsewhere in Europe increased from 8.6% to 14.6% of GDP, on average, from 1962 to 1994. The development of the EU into a thriving hub of trade, through good times and bad, has been the lasting achievement of Europe's founding fathers, and one that will be further enhanced by the completion of the Single Market. European consumers may have shifted a little towards goods from Japan and the newly industrialised countries of Asia, but they remain loyal to, and dependent upon, imports from elsewhere in Europe.

■ *Declining but prospering*

Europe's share of world trade and output will, in this scenario, decline as we move through the 21st century. The key point, however, is that this decline will be gradual, manageable and more than offset by the expansion in world trade. The best way of illustrating this is by reference to the so-called dynamic Asian economies (Hong Kong, Korea, Malaysia, Singapore, Taiwan and Thailand) and China. Their share of OECD imports (expressed as a percentage of GDP) has been doubling every decade since the early 1960s, from 0.18% in 1962, to 0.35% in 1972, 0.85% in 1982 and 1.62% in 1994. By 2020, the western industrial countries will be importing in vastly greater quantities from the Asian region (excluding Japan which, for these purposes, is regarded as 'western'). Imports from the dynamic Asian economies and China should exceed 5% of OECD GDP.

This will not, however, be one-way traffic. While OECD imports from non-Japanese Asia have been rising strongly, and are set to continue to do so, the same is true of flows in the opposite direction – exports from the western industrialised countries, of course including Europe, to these emerging economies. Again, taking the three-decade comparison, such exports have risen from 0.25% of OECD GDP in 1962 to 1.65% by 1994. Continued growth to perhaps 4–5% of OECD GDP by 2020 is likely. The emerging economies of Asia are highly competitive producers, but they are also consumers, and not just of the capital equipment needed to provide for their continued development. All the evidence is that rising prosperity brings with it demand for imported consumer goods, which are often seen as more exclusive and desirable than domestic products. In Japan, long the home of quality motor manufacturing, the demand for top-of-the-range imported Mercedes cars, with left-hand-drive to distinguish them from domestically produced vehicles, has been a source of frustration to Japanese car-makers, and of comfort to a government anxious to reduce the country's trade surplus with the rest of the world.

Japan, indeed, looks to be more vulnerable to the rise of the Asian tiger economies and China than does Europe. Over the past 30 years, Japanese exports to these economies have trebled as a proportion of the country's GDP, while imports into Japan from the rest of Asia have merely doubled. But now, reflecting the high cost of manufacturing in Japan and the overvalued yen, the effects of a shifting of production to other Asian locations by Japanese corporations will increasingly show through. This does not mean Japan has to be a net loser: the prospects of very strong growth in intra-Asian trade should ensure that. The biggest effects of the emergence of new, powerful Asian economic nations, however, will be on Japan and the United States, not Europe. Imports into America from the Asian tigers and China, indeed, are already rising at a far faster rate than into Europe, and far faster than exports from the United States to these countries. The rise of Asia in the 21st century, together with the emergence of other new economic powers such as India and the Latin American nations does not, on this view, pose a threat to Europe.

Competitiveness and other myths

Such a sanguine view of Europe's prospects is surely at odds with another, worrying development – Europe's high costs, particularly labour costs, and consequent lack of competitiveness. In an era where technology and capital are both much more footloose, and business will locate where the costs of production are lowest, surely Europe is in deep trouble? Again, this is too simplistic a view.

Europe has not suddenly become a high-cost region, nor have its governments recently introduced expensive social legislation. To the extent that Europe is uncompetitive it has been for most of this century. Simple comparisons of relative labour costs rarely provide much useful information about a country's prospects. Thus, Christopher Gentle, in his book *After Liberalisation*:

> Conventional economic theory has suggested that high wage economies, such as Germany, will be unable to compete in the merging global economy of the 21st century. The cost of labour, so existing theory goes, makes the European economy uncompetitive. It cannot be denied that there is a lag between the level of exports and international competitiveness of an economy. This is because structural changes have got to work through a country's economic system. Nonetheless, in the turbulence that swept through global currency markets in the spring of 1995, the hot money fled towards Europe and, in particular the Deutschmark: an indication that the markets believed that Germany would remain the strongest future economy in Europe, if not the world. Hardly a sign that the German economy is past its best. (p. 11)

Gentle argues persuasively that for any EU country to attempt to ape the low-wage, low-cost Asian economies, with a minimum of regulation and small government, would be to embark on a game they cannot possibly win, and that to attempt to do so would be economic suicide. Thus Europe's economic future lies in a continuation of existing patterns – with an emphasis on technological and product innovation, design and quality. The older industrial countries have the advantage of large, sophisticated home markets. They have a welter of experience. Capital may be mobile, but there is a limit to how much production can shift to faraway countries which may currently be the lowest-cost producers but will not necessarily retain that position. Relatively poor in natural resources, western Europe has long had to live on its skills and wits. It has done so successfully in the past, and can do so in the future.

■ *Europe's low-cost economies*

While a particular problem of competitiveness has been identified for the German economy, albeit one the country is living through in a way that would be the envy of many others, it would be wrong to tar the whole of Europe with the same brush. Ireland achieved the sobriquet of 'tiger economy of Europe' in the mid-1990s, with annual growth rates of 6% and 7% a year built on low labour costs and moderate inflation. Between 1979 and 1995, for example, Ireland's relative unit labour costs halved, adding to the country's attractiveness as a location for foreign investment. Brendan Walsh, writing in the *Oxford Review of Economic Policy* (Autumn 1996), charts the Irish economy's transformation from 'economic underachiever' to 'a model of successful macroeconomic stabilisation', with a growth rate of more than twice the OECD average, low inflation, declining external indebtedness and a strong exchange rate, but makes the key point that this has been achieved without the reforms of product and labour markets, or the reduction in the role of state enterprises, that characterised Margaret Thatcher's Britain. Ireland could do better, notably in terms of its unemployment record. But it is a success built on following the European model.

Nor is Ireland alone. The picture of a generalised loss of competitiveness for other European countries is not borne out by the facts. The OECD publishes data for relative unit labour costs. Compared with the base year (1991), their figures show that, while Germany had by 1995 lost competitiveness in relation to 21 out of 23 other countries – the two exceptions were Japan, and interestingly, Hong Kong – this was not true for the rest of Europe. Italy, Britain, Finland, Sweden and

Spain had all gained strongly in competitiveness relative to the four dynamic Asian economies monitored – Korea, Hong Kong, Taiwan and Singapore – in large part because of a fall in their currencies. Even countries at the core of the exchange rate mechanism such as France, Belgium, Luxembourg and the Netherlands had held their competitive positions relative to the tiger economies. Markets adjust, and so do wages. It is difficult for any country, tiger or otherwise, to hold its position as a permanent low-cost producer.

And Europe's even lower-cost producers

Another essential point about Europe's competitiveness is that the continent's average labour costs are being brought down by the gradual integration of the former centrally planned economies of eastern Europe into the trading and production system of western Europe. Even allowing for lower levels of productivity, wages in Poland, the Czech Republic, Hungary and the other former Soviet bloc countries are but a fraction of those in the EU. Gross domestic product per head, expressed in dollar terms, is typically 10–15% of the EU average. There is a thriving cross-border trade between Poland and Germany, some of it unofficial, with Germans crossing into Poland to buy petrol, clothes, food and, apparently, garden gnomes, the Polish variety of which are said to be both cheap and very popular. And then there is the tradition left over from the days of central planning, a thriving black market:

> Every morning, hordes of small traders from all over eastern Europe and Asia converge on a somewhat grim sports stadium in Warsaw to buy and sell a dazzling variety of consumer goods in the 'Europa Bazaar'. Occasionally braving bandit attacks by compatriots en route, individuals from the former Soviet Union arrive in special buses to purchase items that are pricey or scarce at home. Although Warsaw residents visit the stadium as well, two thirds of sales are exports, amounting to an estimated $350m in 1995. If the bazaar were a company rather than a collection of hawkers and stallholders, it would be Poland's fifth largest exporter. (*OECD Economic Survey of Poland*, 1997, p. 153)

The point about the low-cost producers of eastern Europe, together with those in the EU, is that Europe has plenty of scope to switch activity *within* the continent, rather than see it shipped halfway around the world to Asia. Indeed, one striking phenomenon, which is set to continue, is the ability of these lower-cost areas to attract activity from the United States, Japan and the tiger economies of Asia. Even Britain, for example, as a medium-cost European country, has attracted huge investment projects from Korea (Samsung, Daewoo, Lucky Goldstar, Halla, to name just a few of them), which contradicts the idea of an inexorable shift from west to east. Location remains a big advantage, particularly location within the Single Market.

■ *European restructuring*

There are, as set out above, many reasons to question the caricature of Europe as a high-cost, sclerotic region, sailing blithely on towards economic oblivion. The most important reason, however, is that Europe itself is changing. According to Francis Fukuyama, author of the books *The End of History* and *Trust*, Europe has little choice in this:

> The European model is at a dead end. This high labour cost, large social welfare state model has priced European firms out of global competition and is not conducive to the technological innovation that would help them move into higher value niches. I have absolutely no complaint with the agenda of corporate restructuring that has to begin with a political restructuring of priorities and a scaling back of welfare state guarantees. (Merrill Lynch seminar on European Restructuring, November 15, 1996)

The restructuring, as Fukuyama says, is taking two forms. Partly under the influence of programmes designed to meet the convergence criteria for monetary union, action is being taken to rein back the rising cost of welfare provision. Alongside this, at a corporate level, management is taking steps to ensure Europe is competitive as we move into the next century. Neither presents an easy task. Part of the problem with restructuring welfare is that Europe has a strong tradition of generous provision in this area, dating back to the 19th-century Bismarckian welfare state. A bigger difficulty, however, is that politicians have allowed the quest for monetary union to become, in the public mind, the only reason for reducing the oversized state sector when, in fact, there were sound reasons for embarking on radical surgery, with or without the imminence of the single currency. Thus, social discontent has been widespread, and monetary union widely seen as the scapegoat for the pain being endured by Europe's citizens. In 1996, general government spending in Europe averaged 49.9% of GDP, with Italy, the Netherlands and Germany clustered around this level, Belgium and France at 54–55% of GDP and the Scandinavian countries significantly higher than this, with Denmark and Sweden at 63% and 66%, respectively. At the other end of the scale, Ireland, Britain, Portugal and Spain all have government spending to GDP ratios of 40–45%. For the purposes of this scenario it is assumed that government action to cut the size of the state is successful, with the EU average dropping to 45% of GDP by about 2015, and settling in the 40–45% range from about 2030 onwards. This fall requires tough measures, in the absence of which the pressure from ageing populations would result in a rising burden of government spending, and therefore taxation.

Corporate restructuring in Europe is proceeding along several different pathways, all of which involve, in countries such as Germany, some sacrifice of the traditional consensus model. Costs are being reduced by new production methods, a relocation of activity, as noted above, to cheaper production areas within Europe, disposal of poorly performing assets, even those that are associated with the tradition of the business, and privatisation. Bill Trent of McKinsey, at the same Merrill Lynch seminar, distinguished between the urgency of restructuring activity in Germany, and the much slower pace in France and Italy. In the case of Germany, management has recognised a problem and acted, in a planned way, to tackle it. Restructuring in France and Italy, in contrast, tends to be done in response to crises. But there has also been a wider difference, and this will continue, between 'Anglo-Saxon' restructuring, for which read downsizing, and the European approach. Anglo-Saxon restructuring is 'raider-driven' – the impetus coming from the threat of hostile takeover – while European firms, much more protected in this regard, respond to other stimuli. Trent characterises the former as focused on raising labour productivity (by cutting the number of workers for a given amount of output), and the latter on strategies for raising capital productivity and long-term growth:

The classic Anglo-Saxon model is predicated on the power of improving labour productivity and in continental Europe that's quite difficult. It is very expensive to lose labour, there are lots of constraints. So we would expect a lot of restructuring to focus on growth strategies and capital productivity improvements. There will be efforts to improve labour productivity but in many situations this will be a long, hard and painful process and won't actually generate rapid returns. (Merrill Lynch seminar)

Whether voluntary or forced, European business is taking action to ensure it remains big in the 21st century. The idea of European corporations as sitting ducks, waiting to be picked off, is not tenable. Efficiency gains are being sought, and achieved. The tougher the environment in the home market, as it has been in Europe in recent years, the more competitive will European corporations be at the end of the day.

■ *European specialisation*

The logic of genuinely free trade within Europe is that comparative advantage will be able to shine through. As we shall see below, genuinely free trade is perhaps too strong a term to describe the present and prospective position in Europe. Even so, a trend that is already emerging – greater specialisation by region and by dominant company – will develop to a much greater extent in the 21st century. Without internal barriers to trade, locations which combine high levels of labour productivity, relatively low costs, available skills and good transport links to markets, will gain at the expense of others. The idea of an area of Europe which is particularly blessed relative to the rest goes back a long way – at the time of British accession in 1973 the talk was of the development of a golden triangle, the points of which were Milan, Hamburg and Birmingham, within which activity and prosperity would be concentrated. European regional policy, and the Commission's ambitious trans-European networks (TENs) are deliberate attempts to counter such concentration.

In an important sense, however, the game has changed. Within an enlarged Europe, the core countries no longer have all the advantages. Who would have thought, for example, that Britain's motor industry, dying on its feet in the early 1980s, would have enjoyed such a revival, largely thanks to inward investment from outside Europe, in the 1990s? Today, Britain and Spain are the most cost-efficient motor manufacturers in Europe. Greater specialisation will be a powerful force within Europe, increasing the region's overall competitiveness, and it will occur in two ways. First, there will be the 'Savile Row' effect – clusters of particular industries in areas where the proximity of other firms operating in the same business creates a pool of skilled labour and associated expertise. Thus, rather than each European country having its own motor industry, again using this as an example, many will rely on imports, but specialise in other areas. Within such a framework, and this is why restructuring is already in train, no country will be able to afford being inefficient in everything. Second, there will be more Europe-wide takeovers and mergers, to create a smaller number of big international players in each industry. According to Commission figures, the number of annual mergers and acquisitions in industry increased from 720 in 1986 to 2,296 in 1995, and in services from 783 to 2,602. Most, around 70%, of these were within countries, suggesting that the great wave of cross-border mergers in Europe is still to come.

■ *Muddling through in the Single Market*

The most optimistic scenario for economic growth and intra-European trade is one in which there is speedy completion of the Single Market, and the economy of the EU becomes a seamless and efficient whole. Such a picture also challenges reality, however. The history of European integration is often one of painfully slow progress, particularly where national interests are threatened. Thus, while it was possible for the EEC's founder members to create a customs union by 1968, 18 months ahead of schedule, the Common Market (free movement of goods, services, people and capital) which should also have been completed by December 1969 has taken much longer. The Single Market (essentially the Common Market renamed) notionally came into being on December 31, 1992 but, as described in Chapter 2, remains far from complete. Lord Cockfield, who as Commissioner with responsibility for the Internal Market in the mid-1980s was the architect of the Single Market, blames the slow progress towards its completion on 'undue haste' in launching Emu. He also makes the point that those who say the single currency is necessary for the Single Market are presupposing that the latter is functioning as effectively as it can be:

> You cannot have a single currency unless you have a single market on which to build it. You cannot have effective policies to deal with other economic problems, not least in the field of employment and welfare, unless the Single Market generates the wealth to support these policies. . . . This is not a plea, still less an excuse, to slow progress on the single currency or on enlargement. It is a call to recognise that in these and other areas, success demands, and is dependent on, success in the Single Market. (*Is the Single Market Working?*, Philip Morris Institute, November 1996, p. 12)

After 40 years of integration, Europe has a Single Market in name, but it also has a framework that is wrapped in red tape, with more than 400 separate Single Market directives, continued problems of technical harmonisation and the free movement of labour (apart from language, recognition of other countries' qualifications is a particular difficulty). Some of the most communitaire of governments are among the slowest to implement Single Market directives, creating a damaging unevenness. Protectionism, disguised or blatant, is still rife. State monopolies, as the Philip Morris Institute report points out, are a continuing difficulty:

> Among the last bastions to hold out against the Single Market have been the state monopolies in the utilities sector. Some governments have been reluctant to relinquish control over what they consider key sectors of the economy. Five years of laborious efforts have just resulted in an agreement on a directive enabling consumers in one country to buy their electricity from a supplier located in another. But the agreement is a limited one: Initially only large users, representing only 23% of the market, will be able to shop around for a supplier. The Commission is now preparing equivalent draft legislation in the gas sector. (*Is the Single Market Working?*, p. 77)

This, however, was always the way. Europe will never again get the same growth benefits as it did in the 1960s, when the removal of intra-European trade barriers coincided with a liberalisation of world trade under the auspices of the Gatt (General Agreement on Tariffs and Trade). It may take another 40 years before there is a true single market, and even then there could be problems over later entrants. That means the benefits, such as economies of scale and exploiting the gains of comparative advantage, will come through slowly. But they will come through. The Single Market is imperfect but, as the vast majority of businesses would testify, it is worth having. Europe will muddle through towards a genuinely free market, as it always has done.

And muddling through on the single currency

Lord Cockfield's warning on the single currency deserves bearing in mind. On the Maastricht programme, monetary union will be fully operational before Europe has a true single market. That programme has, however, already slipped once – the first target date for the start of the final stage of monetary union, January 1, 1997, having passed. The assumption of this book is that the second of the two Maastricht target dates is more or less met, with a core of countries – France, Germany, Austria, the Netherlands, Belgium and Luxembourg and, possibly Ireland, moving forward on or within months of January 1, 1999. It is already clear, from the pressure Germany exerted during Ecofin (European Council of Finance Ministers) negotiations on the stability pact, that the aim will be a 'hard' euro, uncontaminated by countries whose fiscal and inflation record is questionable. This, as we shall see in a later chapter, could lead to major tensions within the EU. For this scenario, it is assumed that these are held in check, but that Emu grows only slowly beyond the initial core. Thus, Italy, Spain and Portugal will join, possibly before the introduction of the euro notes and coins in 2002, but probably later, around 2005. Others, such as Greece and, because of its distinctive political position even under a Labour government, Britain, could remain in the waiting room for much longer. Sweden may not want to join if Denmark and, obviously, Norway, retain floating currencies. Finland's position may also reflect such considerations.

The key point is that enlargement will interact with Emu in such a way that there are always non-Emu member states. Potential new entrants will, of course, face the same entry conditions as those already inside the single currency, the main difference being that they will be seeking to join an already functioning system. The strength of the euro in international markets will be a factor determining the optimum enlargement path for Emu, as will the state of the European economy. It will be noted that those likely to be in the euro waiting room for longest have the most to gain in terms of interest-rate convergence with the traditional low-inflation economies of Europe. Thus, the process through which Europe's average interest rate is reduced will, like the gains from the Single Market, be more drawn-out than in the 'renaissance' scenario. Such gains will still occur, but they will not happen overnight.

No need for a growth miracle

All of the above suggests that neither the Single Market nor the single currency will bring early and substantial growth gains for Europe. This does not mean, however, that it is necessary to be pessimistic about economic prospects. Europe has suffered, over nearly three decades, from a series of externally and internally generated shocks. The two Opec oil shocks, German unification and the struggle to meet the Maastricht criteria have all taken their toll on growth, which slowed from an annual average of 3.2% in the 1970s, to 2.25% in the 1980s and just 1.7%, so far, in the 1990s. On the face of it, Europe is suffering from a growth crisis. It is hard to believe, however, that Europe's trend growth rate has halved in the space of two decades. The mere absence of internally generated shocks, and the assumed absence of big external shocks such as oil crises, will make a big difference to European growth. A trend rate of expansion of 2.5% is a conservative assumption for the early years of the 21st century, rising to 2.75% as Single Market and single currency benefits gradually come through.

This does not assume any growth miracle, which may not be achievable, on a sustained basis, for mature industrial economies. What it does assume is the removal of constraints, some self-inflicted, on growth. The first thing to say about growth projections of this magnitude is that, while they appear low in relation to much faster rates of expansion in the newly industrialised countries, they are sustainable, unlike current rates of Asian growth, and they start from a much higher base. The second key aspect is that they offer a genuine prospect of a significant fall in unemployment from current EU rates, typically 11.5% of the workforce. The phenomenon of European unemployment being significantly above American rates is, as already noted, a relatively recent one. Not until 1984 did EU unemployment rise above the rate in the US, where it has remained. Currently, US unemployment, at around 5.5%, is half the European rate.

Constraint-free European growth will be one factor pulling Europe's jobless total down. Demography will, in addition, play a useful part. The annual growth rate of the working-age (15–64) population was 1% in the 1979–83 period, and 0.9% for 1983–93. But it slowed to 0.2% in 1994 and 0.3% in 1995, and such slower rates are likely to be the norm for the foreseeable future, reflecting slower-growth (and in some cases declining) populations. The read-across from working-age population growth to unemployment is not a direct one – changes in participation rates complicate the picture. But it makes the task of generating sufficient jobs, and therefore of reducing unemployment, that much easier. The analysis of this chapter is consistent with a drop in EU unemployment to 5–6% by about 2010 – not a miracle but far better than recent experience. The fact that it will occur gradually suggests that it can do so without putting significant upward pressure on wage costs, and therefore inflation. The persistence of high and rising unemployment alongside tight budget constraints is not a sustainable vision for Europe.

Business regains its edge

European business, weighed down for the most part with high social costs and slow growing domestic markets will, in this scenario, find its feet again in the 21st century. The gradual completion of the Single Market and adoption of the single currency will increase the pressure for restructuring and, unlike in the high-growth renaissance scenario, some of this will be painful in its employment consequences. Gradually, however, the exploitation of comparative advantage, the opening up and welcoming into the EU fold of new member states and the realisation that the east Asian economies are not going to claim all Europe's markets, home or overseas, will provide a better environment for business. And, while it will be tempting to regard Europe as one large market, the fact that the Single Market will not be completed overnight, and in one sense will never be completed because all new entrants will require transitional periods – often lengthy – following membership, national diversity will continue to be important for business. As Christopher Gentle points out:

> The diversity of Europe is its Achilles heel: it is also its most valuable future asset. The challenge of the next century is not about how to achieve economies of scale: that was very much a twentieth century problem. The future of business competitiveness will lie in the ability to combine economies of scale together with local tastes and service: this is true for firms and economies alike. Indeed, it is a mistake to view the diversity of Europe as a disadvantage or a handicap on the region's global competitiveness. The direction of economic activity over the coming decade will mean that those economies which can be flexible, produce high quality goods and export to the international economy, will be successful. (*After Liberalisation*, pp. 131–2)

■ *Edging to closer union*

What kind of political structures will emerge in a Europe of gradual economic change? Will the 1996–7 inter-governmental conference result in a huge transfer of powers to the centre? Will the European Parliament, the Cinderella of the EU, quickly come to replace national parliaments at the hub of the decision-making process? And will the twin forces of the Commission and the European Central Bank evolve to represent the most concentrated forces of unelected authority in the age of democracy? Any or all of these things could happen but they are highly unlikely, particularly in a scenario where the further benefits of economic integration make themselves felt only slowly. European political union was formally rejected once, in the early 1950s, a time when belief in the traditional nation-state might have been expected to be far weaker than it is now. The Maastricht process was, as Jacques Delors has admitted, too ambitious. Economic and monetary union was a big enough step on its own. The decision to force the pace on political union in parallel, while explicable in the mood of Euro-optimism of the late 1980s, was badly flawed. As Timothy Bainbridge and Anthony Teasdale point out:

> However well-intentioned, a treaty covering so many heterogeneous issues, some very sensitive, negotiated largely in secret, and for the most part unintelligible to the general public, could hardly be expected to win friends. The period during which it was ratified coincided with a low point in the Community's fortunes: impotence in Yugoslavia, monetary instability, and rows over the Uruguay round of the General Agreement on Tariffs and Trade all contributed to a general impression of a Community that had lost its way. Against this background, the treaty's grander aspirations seemed absurd, and the detailed provisions trivial. At the same time, in spite of assurances on subsidiarity, by moving into areas such as citizenship, police co-operation and a common currency the treaty seemed to portend the much-feared 'European superstate'.
> (*The Penguin Guide to the European Union*, pp. 317–18)

So it has proved. While Emu has remained, more or less, on track, political union has barely moved beyond first base. This aspect of Maastricht, and the subsequent IGC of 1996–7, seems, in fact, to be in direct contravention of Jean Monnet's guiding principle – that European integration should proceed according to practical realities (*réalisations concrètes*) with demonstrable benefits, and not grand visions. Dr Klaus-Dieter Borchardt, in the Commission's own publication, *European Integration, the Origins and Growth of the European Union*, admits as much. 'One thing should not be forgotten', he writes.

> The process of European integration and the progress already achieved can only be brought to fruition if they enjoy the support of the people of Europe and are sustained by a sense of European identity. The sheer complexity of decisions at Community level and the intricacies of the Community's workings make it hard for people to grasp the full implications and tend to hamper the emergence of the necessary sense of solidarity and common interests. European integration must remain credible. That this is something to which people are very sensitive is clearly reflected in opinion poll findings and in the poor turnout for elections to the European Parliament (last held in June 1994). It shows that

people are not prepared to accept the inconsistency between grand declarations of intent and the failure to give substance to them in many areas of daily life. (p. 79)

Not only this but the idea of European government, and all-powerful supranational authorities sits uneasily alongside the rise of nationalism in most countries in Europe. Indeed, acceptance of a single currency – in those countries where it is accepted – appears to go hand in hand with an insistence on guarantees that autonomy is preserved in other areas. What this means is that Europe will continue to occupy some kind of middle-ground between a full federation and a collection of independent nation states. As Michael Welsh puts it:

> The federal idea of a United States of Europe is dead and buried, but few Europeans outside the United Kingdom contemplate a return to a Europe of nation states, pursuing the national interest while attempting to maintain some shaky balance of power. As the pace of change accelerates, frontiers look increasingly old fashioned, the process of integration has been driven forward by the needs of industry and commerce as much as by politicians, and there is no reason to suppose that they will wish to return to a system of discrete national markets. . . . Ever Closer Union implies a constant coming together, but there is no necessary end to the process, merely a constant balancing and rebalancing of our need to live together with a respect for the national traditions and culture which made us what we are in the first place. (*Europe United?*, p. 178)

Europe will muddle through in gradually strengthening its political institutions, as it will on the Single Market and the single currency. In 30 years time people will still be expressing concern about the democratic deficit and members of the European Parliament will still be complaining that they do not have sufficient power and influence. The Council of Ministers, in an enlarged EU, will at times appear fractious and unmanageable, the tensions between the European interest and different national interests often spilling over into outright hostility. But this, for better or worse, is the way it has always been. There is no appetite for significant change, and little likelihood, under the economic scenario sketched out here, of it.

In this scenario, perhaps the thing that changes least will be

European politics. Governments will continue to be torn between national interests and those of Europe as a whole. When such interests coincide, Europe will press on, and the integration process will gain in tempo. When they do not, familiar delaying tactics will be present. This is not a future, however, in which Europe is riven by divisions, or in which nationalism becomes the main political force. Mainstream politics, in all existing member countries and the new entrants, will continue to be based on the central premise that continued co-operation with the rest of Europe is both necessary and desirable. Grand visions may be in short supply but political pragmatism will guarantee that, in this *plus ça change* world, Europe holds together.

▪ *Bicycles can be ridden slowly*

The main argument in favour of the '*plus ça change*' scenario is that it simply projects recent EU experience forward. If it has happened before, why should it not continue in the future? The chief argument against is the 'bicycle theory' – which features in most discussions of international economic diplomacy. This is that, just like riding a bicycle, if you do not keep moving forward at a certain speed you are in danger of falling off. Thus, Europe has to keep setting itself ambitious targets for further integration, and make a fair attempt at achieving them, or else momentum is lost. The Maastricht treaty was given an extra political shove by German unification, because without a new European project, Germany could easily have been diverted into the task of integrating its two parts into a single country. It has already been observed that, even in the case of an exercise with considerable will behind it, the Single Market, many countries proceed only very slowly. The moment that Europe declared itself ready to consolidate could also be the moment in which some member countries decided to 'backslide' into nationalism.

It is, however, a question of degree. *Plus ça change* implies that the integration drive will continue but that, in the context of an enlarged Europe, progress will necessarily be gradual. Somewhat faster economic growth and falling unemployment will, in turn, increase popular support for the EU. There is less danger of further detaching Europe's political leaders, and their vision of Europe, from the public in the context of gradual integration.

Perhaps the most important element of realism involved in this scenario is the recognition that not all member states will proceed towards integration at the same pace but that this (unlike in the next scenario) can be managed without creating undue tensions. Again, this is a continuation of what has gone before. From the six original signatories of the Treaty of Rome, through membership of the exchange-rate mechanism of the European Monetary System, the Schengen agreement and, now, economic and monetary union, Europe has been a multi-speed entity. There is a spectrum of enthusiasm for integration, ranging among the present membership from the Benelux countries at one end, to Britain and Denmark at the other, which could mean that the process has to adopt a lowest-common denominator approach, and gets nowhere, or allows member states to join in when they are ready. The latter offers the best sustainable route to gradually greater integration.

■ *Europe in the world*

Europe's prospects, in terms of share of world trade and economic growth, have been discussed above. The essential message is that a 'normal' growth and trade performance offers an encouraging outlook for Europe. But how powerful an entity would a *'plus ça change'* Europe be in the world, given that there would not be an overarching authority speaking for the continent? As a trading bloc, Europe would clearly be an increasingly important force. The bigger the Single Market, the more influence the Commission has in trade negotiations under the auspices of the World Trade Organisation (WTO). Just as in the Uruguay Gatt round, where the role of Sir Leon Brittan as trade commissioner was a key one, so this role can be expected to gain in importance. Indeed future trade negotiations will essentially be between the EU, Nafta and a representative body for Asia, probably Asean (the Association of South East Asian Nations).

As an economic force, Europe will have considerable clout. The president of the European Central Bank will be at least as important an international player as the chairman of the Federal Reserve Board. Europe, as discussed in the previous scenario, begins from a position of strength in terms of its share of world output – 36.6% for the present EU members. Any losses that Europe incurs on the swings of slower output growth than Asia, it will gain on the roundabouts of enlargement. Michael Emerson, senior research fellow at the Centre for Economic Performance at the London School of Economics, describes the possibility of 'Europe' spreading its effective sphere of influence to cover more than 800m people, taking in the existing EU 15 plus the five front-runners for accession in central Europe (the Czech Republic, Hungary, Poland, Slovakia and Slovenia) – making 450m people – plus Russia (150m), and other European countries, including Turkey, other applicants and the Balkan countries (215m). The key player in this could be Russia. According to Emerson:

> A strategy [for Russia] that secured WTO membership first, and then aimed at free trade with the EU, would have highly interesting properties: it would be analogous to the Nafta which joins the US, Mexico and Canada, all of whom are WTO members. The Russia-EU free trade area would further stimulate a multilateralisation of free trade between all European countries not in or joining the EU, and render the CIS (Commonwealth of Independent States) customs union superfluous. It would be especially positive politically if Russia and the Ukraine together shared multilateral free trade with the rest of Europe. This would be a strong recipe for all-European integration, something sufficiently clear politically and economically to register on the public awareness of the Russian political class, which is less likely to be the case for the language of 'binding of most-favoured nation tariffs' and 'non-discriminatory safeguard measures' of the WTO.
> It would also come close to paralleling the ambitions of the Asia-Pacific Economic Co-operation (Apec), which brings together China, the US, Japan and whole of the rest of the Asian-Pacific (except Russia and Latin America). Apec resolved in 1994 to go for free trade by 2010 among the industrialised countries and by 2020 with the developing countries of the region. . . . The most advanced European integrationist agenda on the economic side would consist of Russia joining ultimately the European Economic Area (EEA), i.e. implying a deep harmonisation of market regulations with the EU's single market laws. (*Re-drawing the Map of Europe*, November 1996, p. 37)

Such a prospect may appear overly optimistic, even fanciful, viewed from the perspective of the mid-1990s. Few people in the early to mid-1980s could, however, have envisaged the changes that occurred in Russia, the other CIS states and eastern Europe in the space of a decade. The logical development of those changes is far closer integration with western Europe, in trade and cross-border investment and, if not for some time, the free movement of people. The kind of timetable envisaged for Apec, free trade by 2010, may be too challenging for Russia and the EU. The target is, however, also probably too challenging for Apec itself. By 2020 the kind of relationship envisaged by Emerson for Europe is perfectly possible.

▌ *The Asian question*

If Europe's sphere of influence is set to grow, we come back to the question of Asia. Tensions between China and Japan could, as set out in the previous scenario, develop into something very serious. Even if this is too gloomy a prospect, it remains difficult to envisage China as a super-tiger economy, the king of the Asian jungle. More likely, the conflicts between the freedoms required for a successful capitalist economy and modern China's instinctive distrust and active prevention of political freedom will result in something rather different. The Royal Institute of International Affairs, in the 1996 report of the Chatham House Forum, *Unsettled Times*, provided a highly plausible vision:

> Here is a credible model for an independently evolving Asia. The current crop of tigers find themselves enmeshed as the external agents of an inward-looking, brittle China. Each serves as a mechanism by which China deals with the external world, as conduits for the commercial aspects of its power. The government of each former tiger will be highly aware of the role that it is to play and the tight rein which leads to Chinese hands. The Chinese remain primarily focused on their internal issues, which may involve the brutal use of power and the enforcement of 'modernisations'. There are alleged to be 50m people in some form of detention, all of them working as forced labour for the Chinese state. Exports based on what is in effect slave labour could well trigger a sharp reaction from, in particular, rejectionist populations in the industrialised world. (*Unsettled Times, Three Stony Paths to 2015*, Royal Institute of International Affairs, 1996, pp. 91–2)

America's role will, of course, be pivotal. The increased US emphasis on the Pacific Basin, including through Apec, and a perceived turning away from Europe has been one of the features of US foreign and commercial policy in the 1980s and 1990s. It has also, in the case of US relations with Japan, been an important source of tension. America has relied upon Japanese investors to fund the federal budget deficit but has grown increasingly frustrated by the lop-sided nature of trade with Japan. Just as this problem is easing, another rather larger one – US trade relations with China – has come along. In this context, and in the context of a larger Europe, committed to the gradual introduction of free trade, America would be expected to tilt back towards the EU.

Sailing along

This is a benign, fairly comfortable scenario for Europe. It embodies the gradual approach to integration that has characterised the region's post-war history. It does not require miracles, either on growth or efficiency, merely a reassertion of Europe's traditional strengths. There will be winners and losers, both among nations and corporations, but the overall perspective is an optimistic one. It is a vision of Europe sailing serenely on, not to disaster, but to gradually improving prosperity and influence. Its message is: 'Don't panic, but don't be complacent either.' Above all, it credits Europe with strengths the continent has exhibited in the past – stamina, creativity, and an ability to rise from adversity.

The idea of a common European culture, even if it were desirable, does not look achievable, even over a century. Barriers of language and taste – the German sense of humour, French pop music – will remain, although increasing freedom of movement will mean a greater interchange of cultures between different countries. This is already happening. Look, for example, at the spread of the 'traditional' Irish pub, Guinness, fiddle music and all, or the culinary revolution that has occurred in Britain, partly as a result of EU membership. Such cultural exchanges and others are not, however, likely to be driven by ambitious European Commission programmes, but by osmosis. They will happen, but they cannot be forced.

■ Fifty years on

Fifty years from now, on this scenario, Europe is still an economic force to be reckoned with in the world, having benefited from, rather than been a victim of, the growth of world trade. There will be those warning, just as now, that the continent is about to be eclipsed. Such warnings will be no more valid than they are now. The second 50 years of European integration will disappoint those who expect to see a European superstate early in the 21st century. The Europe of the middle of the 21st century is both wider and deeper but it remains a grouping of nation states, not a new, borderless, Europa. Mid 21st-century Europe will celebrate the birth of Jean Monnet's vision – and 100 years of peace for the continent – and reflect on the fact that when it came to the choice between practical measures and grand federalist visions, the former won out.

SCENARIO 3

Les Etrangers

Summary

Emu proves to be the defining moment in the history of Europe, and of European integration. A small number of core countries move ahead to Emu – built around five of the Six – France, Germany and the Benelux countries. This does not, however, pave the way for an an extended Emu, taking in other existing EU states, as well as new entrants. Instead, Emu becomes an exclusive club for the core countries, who are able to attract inward investment on the basis of their economic and political stability. After failing to enter in the first wave, other countries suffer significant economic divergence, and are unable to negotiate the hurdles for subsequent entry. In Italy, frustrated by exclusion, pressure for a split between the north and south of the country intensifies. Britain, permanently confined to the EU's fringe, could leave the Union. Emu, rather than uniting Europe, splits it irrevocably.

Scenario 3: Les Etrangers

■ *The Six are special*

It is hard to delve into any aspect of Europe without coming across a reference to the special position of 'the Six'. The original members of the European Coal and Steel Community, Euratom and the European Economic Community are viewed with a mixture of envy and resentment by the others. British Europhiles lament the fact that Britain dithered over EEC entry in the 1950s, allowing the Six to design the Community in a way that was best suited to them and, by implication, only truly suitable for latecomers by happy accident, or not at all. The original six secured for themselves all the plum prizes when it came to the location of the Community's institutions – the Commission in Brussels but with certain departments in Luxembourg; the Council of Ministers, again, with its 'seat' in Brussels but meeting four times a year in Luxembourg; the Parliament's seat is in Strasbourg, but its committees meet in Brussels, an arrangement that has been described as a wasteful travelling circus; Luxembourg has the European Court of Justice, the Court of Auditors and the European Investment Bank. Nor is this confined to the older institutions. London, boasting its position as Europe's most important financial centre, made a strong pitch for the European Monetary Institute (and thus the European Central Bank) but was never in with a serious chance and lost out to Frankfurt. The December 1992 Edinburgh summit committed the EU to give preference to countries other than France, Belgium and Luxembourg in siting new institutions. Denmark thus plays host to the European Environment Agency and London to the European Medicines Evaluation Agency. Welcome though these may be, they are second-rank institutions. European power is centred firmly within the geographical boundaries of the Six or, to be more accurate, within France, Germany and the Benelux countries.

As Keith Middlemas points out in *Orchestrating Europe*: 'It was by no means preordained that six countries would become irrevocably associated with each other in a series of supranational communities, nor that those six would be France, Germany, Italy, the Netherlands, Belgium and Luxembourg.' The process began with the Belgium–Luxembourg Economic Union in 1921, through to the creation of the Benelux customs union in 1948 and the embryonic but unsuccessful Franco-Italian-Benelux (Fritalux) payments union in 1949. In the end, as we have seen, the creation of the Coal and Steel Community provided the spur for the Six to move ahead. Even this, however, could have been merely a Franco-German arrangement but, writes Middlemas, 'the Benelux countries, and to a lesser extent Italy, were pulled into the arrangements because they could not afford to remain aloof from a powerful producer bloc being created on their borders'.

Could there have been a larger grouping than the original six? Certainly. Britain and Ireland could have been in that first wave of integration, if it had not been for the former's dismissive attitude. So too could have been Denmark which, like Britain and Ireland, formally applied for EEC membership only four years after the Treaty of Rome was signed. One or more other of the Scandinavian countries might also, in slightly different circumstances, have been persuaded of the merits of integration in the 1950s as they were by the virtues of joining the European Free Trade Association (Efta). Spain, Greece and to a lesser extent Portugal, all to join later, were not suitable for political reasons. Even without them, however, the Six could quite easily have been, at the outset, the Nine or the Ten.

It was not to be, and the fact that a core group of countries were there at the EU's birth, and for nearly two decades (more if you mark the start of the EU from the ECSC in 1951) had it to themselves, inevitably shaped its development, and will continue to do so in the 21st century. Later large-country entrants, Britain and Spain, have never achieved the influence enjoyed by France, Germany, and to a lesser extent, Italy, although Margaret Thatcher, for Britain, came close in the 1980s but mainly, integrationists would argue, in a negative sense. Smaller entrants, meanwhile, can only look enviously at the central and privileged position occupied by the Benelux countries. This does not mean that later small-country entrants have not benefited from membership, the examples of Ireland and Portugal being a case in point, but they have failed, so far, to join the inner circle. Relative to the size of its population, Luxembourg has 30 times the number of Commission employees, and Belgium 10 times the number, as Portugal. Only Austria, economically if not politically, has enjoyed a fast-track to the EU's core.

As we develop the scenario of *Les Etrangers*, we shall keep coming back to the special status of the Six. It is not the only possible source of a fissure between Europe's insiders and outsiders, however. In the case of European economic and monetary union (Emu), the divisions will play along northern European–hard currency versus southern European–soft currency lines. The position of the eastern Europeans, often regarded by western Europeans as the great unwashed, right on their doorstep, creates its own opportunities for divisions and tensions. Recent experience suggests that the EU will find it difficult enough to satisfy the competing interests of existing members, let alone prevent the development of outsiders among new ones.

▪ Tower of Babel

The bigger that Europe becomes, the more difficult an entity it becomes to manage. This is partly because enlargement brings in countries at different stages of economic development but it is also because the EU's institutional arrangements, while perhaps appropriate when there were just six or nine member states, have become unwieldy and unmanageable in a much larger, and prospectively yet larger, grouping. To give a simple example, it was posited by the original six that French and German be the official languages of the Community, but representatives of Belgium's Flemish population insisted on Dutch as well. Thus, a situation developed where each new entrant would bring their language as an additional official tongue for EU business. There are currently 11 official languages, which means that 33 separate interpreters are required for each Council of Ministers meeting of the present 15 member states, a number that is certain to rise when there is enlargement to the east. Not for nothing is Brussels sometimes described as a modern Tower of Babel.

Part of the EU's current problem, indeed, is that its original designers set out to be scrupulously fair to the smaller member states and probably overdid it. Thus each member state, large or small, takes its turn to hold the six-month rotating presidency of the EU. Belgium and the Netherlands, with a combined population of 25m, less than a third of that of Germany, enjoy a combined vote in the Council of Ministers equal to Germany's. Small countries, when they combine, can use their votes to prevent larger countries from steamrolling decisions through. The combined Council votes of Belgium, Denmark, Greece, Ireland, Luxembourg, the Netherlands and Finland are enough for a 'blocking' minority, even though these countries only account for 14% of the EU's population.

On the face of it, therefore, it is the EU's larger members – France, Germany, Italy, Britain and Spain – who have the most cause for complaint, their only apparent membership 'perk' being that they have twice the numbers of Commissioners (two each) as the smaller member states. In practice, as we shall see, things are a little more complex than that, and it is inevitable that EU power will, even more so than now, become concentrated in the hands of dominant 'insider' nations. The 1996–7 Inter-Governmental Conference (IGC) on EU reform considered a number of proposals to make the institutional structure more manageable, and it had not completed its deliberations as this book went to press. In any event, it may require another such conference before the EU evolves a workable model. One proposal, put forward by the Gaullist RPR (Rassemblement pour la République) party in France, which counts Jacques Chirac as its most influential current member, is that only the big five countries would hold the rotating presidency – and for 2½ years at a time – while the smaller countries would hold the position of rotating vice-president. Every six months there would be two such vice-presidents, one from each of two countries. Unsurprisingly, the proposal has so far been opposed by smaller member states. Another idea is that the Council of Ministers would be slimmed down by putting into practice the idea of regional representation. Thus, apart from the big five, there could be a single (rotating) representative from the other Mediterranean countries, from the Scandinavian countries, and so on. According to Beniamino Andreatta, a former Italian foreign minister:

> During a recent visit to Finland I raised the issue, with the local authorities, of the Council of Ministers possibly becoming excessively large in the future. They replied by reminding me of their history of relative exclusion from European political processes and the intricacies of Community policy. In this, I sensed their fear of becoming a small, remote German province. It is in this sort of context that a membership structure could

develop whereby a given country might say: 'I am one of the Nordic countries, or I am part of the Baltic region, and, on the basis of common historical and geographical interests, my representatives take part in decision-making processes on an equal footing with the great countries of the continental plains'. (*In a Larger EU, Can All Member States be Equal?*, Philip Morris Institute, April 1996, p. 22)

Another proposal, double majority voting, intended to preserve the balance between the dominance of the large member states and smaller countries holding the rest to ransom, stands the best chance of success. Under this scheme, proposals would be approved by the Council of the Ministers on the basis of a two-thirds vote, based on qualified majority voting, supplemented by the requirement that such a vote should also represent two-thirds of the EU's population. On the face of it, such reforms could weaken the influence of three of the original six members, Belgium, the Netherlands and Luxembourg. In practice, their position is so entrenched that it is newer smaller members who will suffer.

■ *Schengenland*

In 1985, Germany, France and the Benelux countries signed the Schengen agreement, committing themselves to the removal of border controls between their countries, including both short-term measures for the easing of frontier delays, closer co-operation between police forces and the abolition of automatic checks, and long-term measures such as the harmonisation of indirect taxes and the strengthening of external borders, i.e. the borders bounding the region. The Schengen agreement was significant in a number of respects. It showed that Europe's core countries (five of the original six) were prepared to co-operate more closely together than, at that stage, were later entrants. And it showed that the core was prepared to take on the process of integration and not submit to foot-dragging by other member states – the Schengen agreement pre-dated the Single European Act. Perhaps most importantly of all, it demonstrated that the multi-speed approach to integration, the core leading the rest, is very much a reality within the EU, and will continue to be so in the future. Indeed, advocates of speeding the pace of integration, such as Germany's Christian Democrat Union/Christian Social Union (CDU/CSU) argue that the only route to avoid the lowest-common denominator problem (if integration has to proceed at the pace of the slowest member it will probably not proceed at all) is for a core of like-minded countries to force the pace. According to Karl Lamers, the CDU/CSU's foreign affairs spokesman, a co-author of a plan for core-driven unification:

> The core of the idea of a core Europe is our firmly held belief – a belief borne out by the entire course of European unification – that if a smaller group of countries presses ahead with particularly intensive and far-reaching economic and political integration, this group or core has a centripetal or magnetic effect on the other countries. As I have said, this is the mechanism underlying the entire process of European unification. (*The European*, November 18, 1994)

In the case of Schengen, a core from the original six forced the pace but this did not preclude others from joining in. Thus, 10 years after the original agreement, the accord had been signed and implemented by Spain and Portugal, as well as by France, Germany and the Benelux countries. Italy, Greece and Austria, meanwhile, had signed but not fully implemented the accord, while Denmark, Sweden and Finland had been granted observer status. Britain and Ireland, however, had declared their intention of not participating in the Schengen arrangements. Thus, one aspect of integration had produced four different gradations within the 15 member states, from the most enthusiastic at one extreme to the non-participants at the other. This is the way of the future.

■ Core monetary union

The Schengen model of integration will provide the framework for the start of monetary union in Europe. No other version, indeed, is available. The idea of Greece entering Emu at the same time as Germany, indeed at all, is as far-fetched as it is possible to be. This does not, as we shall see, make it any easier to manage politically. According to Mica Panic:

> Although a two-tier approach represents the only way to create a lasting European monetary union, it is bound to be resented strongly for political reasons – particularly by the countries whose economies are not strong enough to cope with the pace of change and the discipline of policy synchronisation demanded of those in the top tier. Considerations of national prestige and the pressure from commercial interests confident that they would do well within a complete union, combined with the hope of poorer regions that they would receive a larger slice of foreign aid if their country joined the top tier – all add up to a powerful combination that many governments might find difficult to resist. Nevertheless, given the limited volume of resource transfers that the Community can realistically be expected to mobilise, their long-term chances of remaining in the complete union are likely to be even smaller than those of the countries that found the much less demanding arrangements under the classical gold standard too costly. (*European Monetary Union, Lessons from the Classical Gold Standard*, p. 158)

Panic's analysis is mainly concerned with the position of the economies of eastern Europe, and the mode of their integration into the EU. There is, however, a fundamental question concerning the participation in Emu of existing member states. It is best summarised with reference to the relative positions of Italy and Germany. From Rome's perspective, as one of the original six, participation in the first wave of Emu is almost a matter of right. Italy, by joining Emu, will be able to piggy-back on German credibility, thus gaining in terms of lower interest rates – crucially important for a country whose debt-servicing costs are so large that even a primary budget surplus (i.e. a surplus measured on the basis of current government revenues and expenditure) is not enough, when debt interest is taken into account, to prevent a large overall budget deficit. Viewed from Bonn and Berlin, and perhaps more particularly from Frankfurt, however, the idea of joining a monetary union with Italy is seen as the surest way of sacrificing Germany's hard-won price stability, adherence to which is almost a matter of religious observance. Far from spreading German credibility to fellow member states, that credibility would quickly evaporate. Emu involving France is a risky enough proposition from the German perspective. The further south into Europe it spreads, the greater the risks. Looked at dispassionately, indeed, many would question French participation. Thus, Christopher Taylor:

> There is a core group of structurally compatible and integrated economies in the Community which could probably move safely to a monetary union without delay. Germany and the Netherlands have already gone a long way towards doing so and they could probably be joined by others without much risk – Luxembourg, Belgium, Denmark (if willing) and Austria – to make an Emu of six countries closely integrated with Germany and similar in terms of economic objectives. There are some grounds for thinking that they could be joined by others, notably France and possibly Ireland, but other evidence casts doubts on this. Both economies appear set to meet the Treaty's (nominal) convergence criteria but real factors are less reassuring. In particular both have high, and seemingly increasing, structural unemployment, suggesting the existence of labour market rigidities which could create difficulties under Emu. (*EMU 2000?*, p. 131)

A hard core of countries, a minority of member states, will embark on monetary union. What is less certain about the Schengen model, when applied in this area, is the extent to which, in Emu, others will be able to join later. Monetary union, far from providing the spur to ever closer union, itself a moving target, could create the most serious, and damaging, insider–outsider schism in the history of European integration. Before examining this, let us consider the key EU relationship, the Franco-German axis.

■ *The Franco-German axis*

The drive towards European monetary union has always been a Franco-German project. The goal of Emu was revived in the 1970s by Valéry Giscard d'Estaing of France and Helmut Schmidt of Germany, after prompting by Roy Jenkins, the then Commission president. The Delors report on monetary union, published before the dismantling of the Berlin Wall in 1989, could easily have been swept aside by that event, and the subsequent unification of Germany. In fact, the desire on the part of France to see the unified and more powerful German state contained within an Emu framework meant that the drive towards monetary union was given extra impetus by German unification. In the immediate aftermath of Europe's autumn 1992 currency crisis, proposals were floated which would have brought about an immediate Franco-German monetary union, with the fixing of the franc–Deutschmark exchange rate, followed by the adoption of a common monetary policy between the two countries. The idea, which was framed in the spirit of preventing speculators from unhinging the exchange-rate mechanism's key cross-rate, and thus bringing down the entire system, was taken seriously. A resolution around that time by the Bundestag, which said that Germany should only proceed towards Emu if the conditions of the Maastricht treaty were completed satisfied, can be seen as a successful move to head off such a rush to a limited Franco-German monetary union.

Nevertheless, Emu remains essentially a Franco-German project, deriving directly from the French government's decision in the mid-1980s to adopt the *franc fort* policy, and sustained by the fact that, the more that sacrifices have been made in the maintenance of that policy, the more it is worth persisting with it to its logical conclusion of monetary union. Alain Juppé, the French prime minister, went so far as to say, in 1996, that if there was no monetary union involving France, there would be no monetary union at all. *Franc fort* led to the Delors report, which led to the Maastricht treaty. The motivations of France, in seeking to constrain a too-powerful Germany, and to imitate German economic success, are plain enough, and have been an ever-present feature of European integration, but Germany's apparent desire to be constrained, and to allow others into the secrets of its post-war economic success – price stability and a strong currency – is rather more puzzling. What, in particular, does Germany have to gain from Emu, and are the German people right to be suspicious of the dilution of the Deutschmark within the single currency?

German behaviour throughout the period of post-war European integration has been conditioned by the fact that a pooling of power has offered, not constraints on German behaviour, but greater freedom. Memories of the period after the First World War, when the victorious powers sought to pin down Germany with reparations and economic restrictions, were key. The European Coal and Steel Community unlocked German production, without which a defeated power might have been subject to more rigorous controls. The EEC, similarly, provided a speedy route to economic re-entry. The Emu context is different but reflects similar thinking. According to David McKay:

> A slightly more formal way of putting this argument is that monetary union would, for the first-time in the post-war era, allow the Germans to play a major foreign policy role. Trade-offs across issue areas could be organised to please everybody. The Italians, French and others would benefit from integration with the low inflation German monetary regime, and the Germans, in return, could, via political integration in the EU, play a role in world affairs commensurate with their economic and political status. Such considerations had, of course, long been prominent in the minds of post-war generations of German politicians, but were they sufficiently strong to convince the Germans that the much cherished independence of their central bank could be sacrificed in the name of European union? It seems unlikely that all the advantages of German fiscal rectitude would be given up in return for some vague, longer-term ambition to avoid the emergence of anti-German alliances. A more convincing explanation of German motives is that they believed that Emu *on their terms* would involve little or no economic sacrifice but reap all the political advantages of European union. German terms would, of course, be an insistence that only countries that met their standards of macroeconomic discipline would join the single currency area. As it turned out this is precisely what the Germans insisted on in the negotiations over the Maastricht convergence criteria. (*Rush to Union*, p. 92)

■ *Emu divides the Union*

Emu is thus a Franco-German project, albeit one designed on a German model. At the Dublin European Council (summit) in December 1996, the details of the 'Stability and Growth Pact' for Emu were settled. The terms of the pact, which were variously interpreted as a victory for France, and hence a route to a softer euro, or as a triumph for Germany, provide for penalties for countries which fail to observe the Maastricht budgetary criteria *once in* Emu. Thus, countries whose budget deficits exceed 3% of GDP will normally face financial penalties if they have not acted immediately to correct the position. The pact will work as follows:

- When a country's budget deficit exceeds 3% of GDP it will, unless it has proposed corrective measures considered acceptable by the finance ministers of other Emu states – who will sit on a so-called Stability Council – be required to lodge a deposit equivalent to 0.2% of GDP with the Commission. For every percentage point that the deficit increases above 3%, a further 0.1% of GDP will be required to be deposited, up to a maximum of 0.5% of GDP.
- These deposits, which will be non-interest bearing, will be returned if, within two years, action has been taken to reduce the country's budget deficit to within the 3% limit. If not it will become a fine, and will represent a permanent transfer to the EU.
- Countries will be exempt from these penalties in 'exceptional and temporary' circumstances. The pact, on German insistence, put numbers on these circumstances. If a country's economy is growing, or declining by 0.75% (on an annual basis) or less, the deposits and fines will normally apply. If its economy is declining by 2% of GDP or more, the terms of the pact will not apply. A GDP decline of between 0.75% and 2% will be regarded as a grey area, where the Stability Council will decide whether sanctions should be imposed.

'The stability and growth pact represents an important landmark in fiscal policy within Europe', concluded Goldman Sachs in December 1996. 'Although there are uncertainties about how rigorously the pact will be implemented it is likely to change the focus and stance of fiscal policies in EU countries which join Emu. If the pact provides the right incentives for countries to change their fiscal policies and reduce deficits, government debt ratios will decline significantly.'

The key thing about the stability and growth pact is that it will only operate for those countries which participate in Emu. Unless, therefore, the pact is ineffective, and makes no difference to countries' behaviour, whether in or out of Emu, which is highly unlikely, its introduction sets up the possibility of significant differences in policy convergence between Emu and non-Emu countries. Emu participants, in other words, will have to abide by the deficit criteria, or face sanctions which would be both costly and humiliating. Non-Emu countries *should* abide by the criteria, and will need to do so to qualify for participation, but it will be up to them to decide how urgently to do so. This difference between compulsion and non-compulsion will lead to important differences in patterns of policy behaviour

■ *The Italian question*

Monetary union is likely to divide Europe in several important respects, probably, as with Schengen, with several gradations along the way. Thus, it is highly likely that there will be a smallish group of core Emu member countries comprising France, Germany, the Benelux countries and Austria, next to which there will be a 'waiting room' of states who will probably become eligible after a period, such as Finland, Sweden, Ireland, Denmark and Britain, if the latter two wish to take part (if not, they do not even enter the waiting room). The important dynamic of the insider–outsider scenario is that, beyond these countries, others will find it difficult indefinitely to take part, will not be encouraged by the core countries to do so and, rather than converging towards Emu participation, will diverge from it.

The most obvious example of this is Italy. For the Italian political classes, the country's participation in the first wave of Emu is, as noted, almost a matter of right and is not seriously questioned as a central aim of government policy. Being one of the Six carries, as noted earlier, additional weight within Europe. Excluding Italy from the project would not only underline its essential Franco-German nature, but would provoke a considerable backlash. When France used 'creative accounting', in the shape of a payment by France Telecom to the French government of an amount equivalent to 0.5% of GDP to take on its pension liabilities, a payment which ensured that the government could present a realistic projection of a sub-3% of GDP budget deficit for 1997, Romano Prodi, Italy's prime minister, promised to come up with a few accounting tricks of his own. Italy, with government debt equivalent to around 125% of GDP, is nowhere near meeting the other key budgetary condition (debt of 60% of GDP or below). But then neither is Belgium, with debt of 130% of GDP. Belgium will be waved through into Emu, so why not Italy? In a preparatory move for first-wave status, the lira was re-entered into the

ERM late in 1996, although not until after a hard fought battle over the entry rate.

The German Emu bargain, however, as described above, only works if like-minded countries join the single currency, and are subject to strict conditions once inside it. It does not work, certainly for the German people, if it means admitting a traditionally high-inflation, large-deficit country such as Italy. And for Italy, the question of convergence within Emu, versus huge divergence outside it, is a pressing one. Italy's budgetary problem is essentially a debt-servicing problem. Measures to improve the underlying budget position have worked so well that Italy has a primary budget surplus. Were it not, in other words, for the interest on past debt there would be no budget deficit at all. Thus, Italy has much to be gained from participating in Emu. By doing so she would lock in to the much lower government debt yields, say 6–6.5%, prevailing in the core countries. Outside Emu, however, the sky would be the limit for Italian bond yields. According to one piece of bond market analysis at the beginning of 1997, Italian bond yields 12–18 months into the future could be 7%, or they could be 15%, depending on whether Italy was likely to be in Emu's first wave. In the case of the latter, the effect on Italy's debt-servicing costs would be enormous.

Suppose then, that the situation arises where the markets are open-minded about the prospect of Italian participation right up until the spring 1998 decision date for first-wave eligibility. The lira, and Italian financial markets, will have continued to benefit from the 'convergence play' posited upon Italy's participation. A failure then of Italy to be admitted would result in a sharp fall for both the lira and Italian bond markets, pushing up yields to very high levels. The former would, by increasing Italian inflation, move Italy away from convergence with the Emu countries, while the latter would have an even more detrimental effect on its ability to meet the deficit criteria. Once rejected, Italy would diverge from the others, from which it might take years, or even decades, to be in a position to be accepted for membership.

■ Core success

It has been shown how the drive towards monetary union could lead to serious disunion within Europe, even divisions among the original six. For this to create sustained insider–outsider effects lasting well into the 21st century, as opposed to teething problems in the creation of Emu, two things need to happen. The first is that monetary union delivers economic success for the core, first-wave participants. The second is that the core countries, once they have established an exclusive club, are able to keep 'undesirables' out.

On the face of it, the prospect of significant Emu gains for already-converged core economies is limited. There is no Italian-style gain from lower bond yields, or in the form of lower short-term interest rates, because this has already occurred, either naturally or in anticipation of Emu. Lower transaction costs will provide some benefit, but a limited one. The economic benefits to the core could come about, however, in more subtle ways. According to *Outsiders' Responses to European Integration* (Copenhagen Studies in Economics and Management), edited by Seev Hirsch and Tamar Almor, one of the significant effects of the 1992 programme was a substantial increase in foreign direct investment in the EU, from countries both large and small, for fear of the subsequent exclusion of imports by 'Fortress Europe' barriers. In the same way, one of the effects of a core Emu could be shifts in the pattern of investment in Europe to participating single currency economies because, on the argument that these economies would represent the true single market – through the removal of the 'final' barrier to trade, the exchange rate – such investment would capture all the advantages of a European production base. Hiroshi Okuda, the president of Toyota, said in February 1997 that future investment expansion for his company in Europe was likely to be in those countries taking part in Emu. An analysis by Ray Barrell and Nigel Pain in the spring 1997 edition of *New Economy* came to a similar conclusion.

■ *Building a fortress*

The Fortress Europe analogy, indeed, is not entirely fanciful. Suppose that, with the core having embarked on Emu, a non-participating member state, say Britain, adopted a 'free rider' policy of competitive devaluation against the euro. Such action could be construed as being against the spirit of the Single Market and, in certain circumstances, lead to the erection of temporary barriers to trade against Britain.

Article 109i of the Rome Treaty, as amended at Maastricht, for example, allows any member state to introduce protective measures when faced with sudden balance of payments difficulties. Article 36 provides for restriction on imports where they can be 'justified on grounds of public morality, public policy and public security'. Whether either of these would permit protectionist measures against a country taking advantage of floating exchange rates is open to serious question. But where there is a will, there is often a way.

Suppose, in the extreme, the core Emu economies succeed in developing a low-inflation, strong-currency euro zone but face continual pressure from other, weak-currency EU members, including the new eastern European entrants. The kind of pressure seen from French industrialists after sterling and the lira dropped out of the ERM in 1992 would be multiplied several times, and over a more sustained period. The insiders could erect barriers, parading as temporary measures, against the outsiders. In terms of the integration process, deepening for a relatively small number would have been achieved at the expense of widening.

Could the core countries prevent new entrants into Emu? One of the agreed conditions, insisted upon by likely non-qualifiers for the first wave, is that entry requirements will not be subsequently hardened. In theory, therefore, any country which pursues appropriate convergence policies will, eventually, qualify for Emu. In practice, however, apart from the fact that the dynamics might mitigate against initial non-qualifiers subsequently meeting the criteria, as discussed above, the political momentum geared towards ensuring that a number of countries enter the final stage on January 1, 1999 (including an element of 'fudge' in the achievement of the criteria) would fade once that date had passed and Emu had begun. Not only that, but the participants could plead that, with monetary union bedding in, further time was needed before new entrants could be considered.

■ North versus south – in Europe and in Italy

The prospect is thus of a long-term Emu of a relatively small number of like-minded states, dominated by the Franco-German axis. This also has clear implications for political integration. According to David McKay: 'As of the mid-1990s all the evidence points to the creation of a smaller, more cohesive union based on a core of states dominated by the German economy – Austria, Belgium, Luxembourg and the Netherlands. This group may include France but is extremely unlikely to include the high-inflation peripheral states such as Britain, Italy and Spain' (*Rush to Union*, p. 177).

Unlike McKay, I would see French participation as a certainty in such a situation. The question arises, however: Would the excluded countries accept their exclusion without a fight? In the case of Italy, which has its own internal north versus south dimension, exclusion would strengthen the hand of the Northern League, led by Umberto Bossi, which campaigns for the separation of the prosperous north of the country, which would have no difficulty in qualifying to be part of Europe's core, from the poor south. Emu, which will lead to significant divisions within Europe, could therefore precipitate the break-up of individual countries within it. Northern Italy, with its strong industrial tradition, would fit naturally into the core. All European countries are alliances, Italy's a more fragile one than most.

For other excluded southern states, the choice will be no less stark. Either accept crumbs from the table of the richer northern countries of the core, or try to block their progress. The arithmetic of EU voting patterns was touched upon above. The qualified majority voting weights – ten votes each for France, Germany, Italy and Britain, eight for Spain, five each for Belgium, Greece, the Netherlands and Portugal, four for both Austria and Sweden, three each for Denmark, Finland and Ireland, and two for Luxembourg – provide the southern states with significant blocking powers. An alliance of Italy, Spain, Portugal and Greece, 28 votes in all, would be sufficient to stop progress towards further integration. It could even prevent the core countries from moving to the final stage of Emu. In fact, defining the core as only France, Germany, the Benelux countries and Austria, the outsiders could put together more votes than those on the inside.

The resentment at exclusion that the southern outsiders would feel cannot be overstated. During 1996, a series of tough budgets in Lisbon, Madrid and Rome were framed with the explicit intention of ensuring Emu participation, if not in the first wave, then at least one or two years after the intended 1999 start date for the final stage. Were they to be presented with a *fait accompli* of permanent non-participation in the core, there is no doubt that the southern states would kick up rough. In practice, however, important though blocking votes could be, the core countries are unlikely to be so clumsy as to allow a situation to develop where those excluded would wish to use them.

Thus, the core will move to the start of the final stage of Emu alone, but holding out the promise of early entry to the southern European countries, after they have had a couple more years to converge their economies. By playing on the Euro-enthusiasm of the 'Club Med' countries, and by ensuring that the carrot of full participation both in Emu and closer political integration is continually held out, the core will enjoy relatively unimpeded progress. The Franco-German axis will steamroller on. For the southern Europeans, the world on the fringes of the EU will be a colder one than they have known or were hoping for. But it would be even colder outside the Union altogether. They have nowhere else to go.

West versus east

Enlargement of the EU to the east, on the face of it, merely increases the number of relatively disadvantaged, non-converged Club Med type states in the EU who, like the southern Europeans, would remain outside the elite core in this scenario. In terms of economic philosophy, however, some of the eastern entrants will have more in common with the northern core economies. According to the Philip Morris Institute:

> Until now, geography and economics have separated EU members very broadly into two groups: the northern countries, who are generally richer and more tuned towards free trade and liberalism than their southern partners, and the member states to the south. They are sometimes referred to as the North Sea group and the Club Med. Enlargement will bring in newcomers from central and eastern Europe, representing a third group of countries with broadly similar situations and aspirations. On many economic issues, they can be expected to be on the same side as the Club Med group. Poor as they are, these countries will certainly vie with the southern EU members for support from the Structural Funds. However some may aspire to the northern brand of free market liberalism, although they have a long way to go. Already a number are members of the World Trade Organisation (WTO), while the Czech Republic recently became the first former Soviet bloc country to join the OECD. (*In a Larger Eu, Can All Member States be Equal?*, April 1996, p. 51)

From the point of view of the core countries, subject as they will be to relatively tight domestic fiscal constraints under the terms of the

Emu stability and growth pact, the idea of the new entrants as the equivalent of long-term welfare claimants, reliant on a permanent basis on handouts from the EU budget, is singularly unattractive. The eastern entrants will be required to make their own way, albeit after a period of adjustment. Already there are rumblings about the difficulties of accommodating Poland's agricultural sector within the Common Agricultural Policy. The greater the number of relatively disadvantaged member states, the smaller the amount of cohesion assistance each will receive. It will be a colder world outside the core than it has been for fringe EU members in the past.

Could the embracing of market economics by the former centrally planned economies give them a faster track to Emu than that in prospect for some of the southern European states, and certainly a faster track than new southern entrants such as Cyprus and Malta? It could, but it probably will not. In practice, these economies face problems of economic adjustment that are likely to last for decades. The OECD, for example, while describing Poland as 'one of the most successful transition countries' in its 1997 report on the economy, also noted that 'high inflation persists in Poland, 6½ years after the initial stabilisation measures . . . it was still running at an annual rate of around 20% in the summer of 1996', and that there have been difficulties pushing through necessary structural reforms. Many of the former centrally planned economies suffer from a combination of double-digit inflation and double-digit unemployment. Living standards, as discussed earlier in this book, are far lower than for existing member states. Not only will the adjustment process be long and painful, including the development of modern banking systems, but the core countries will hardly welcome them with open arms. If one effect of the development of a core Emu is the attraction of foreign direct investment to what will become Europe's hub, a move which encouraged the diversion of such investment flows to the lower cost eastern economies would be against the core's interests.

■ *British schizophrenia*

The discussion so far has been concerned with the position of reluctant outsiders – those countries which would want to be part of the core, including Emu and the development of a political union, but are prevented from doing so. For others, notably Britain, but also

Denmark and possibly the other Scandinavian states, the position is rather different. With no wish to be part of a federal, single-currency Europe dominated by the Franco-German axis, but no wish either to be isolated in this position, the prospect of a core of like-minded economies moving forward at a pace which suits them, leaving a sizeable number – a significant majority in an enlarged Europe – frozen at a much earlier state of integration, would seem to satisfy the requirements of the 'willing outsiders'. In fact it would do no such thing. The former British Conservative government, having apparently embraced the idea of a multi-speed Europe, took fright at its implications. The idea of Britain being in the EU's second tier, among the Club Med economies and the eastern European entrants, would not only offend national pride. It was also seen as threatening the trick Britain had successfully played – attracting foreign investment by being part of the Single Market and enhancing its appeal as a location for such investment by being 'semi-detached' from certain aspects of Europe such as the Maastricht social protocol (a distinction that has disappeared anyway following Labour's May 1997 election victory). The scepticism of Britain, and Denmark, has been relatively costless, and may have brought advantages. Under the insider–outsider scenario, the stakes would be far higher. One of Britain's lasting conceits has been that, were it to show willing, the rest of Europe would welcome it into the fold. The evidence has, however, been to the contrary. As we have seen, British membership of the EEC was twice rejected. In the 1990s, Britain has been regarded with impatient bemusement by other member states, who fail to understand its stance of being 'in but not really of' the EU. A British conversion from sceptical fringe-player to enthusiastic member of the core is more likely with Labour in power but it could be resisted by the core countries, not least on the grounds of economic eligibility.

The question that would then arise, with some countries moving towards full monetary and political union, is whether Britain would remain part of the EU at all. Departure from the EU is unlikely under Labour but possible, at some future stage, if a nationalist Conservative government were to be elected. In the eyes of many British Eurosceptics, certainly, this would be enough to precipitate withdrawal. Martin Holmes, in *The Eurosceptical Reader*, sets out the argument:

> The intergovernmental conferences ... provide a golden opportunity, an heroic pretext, the Conservative party to look afresh at

the whole relationship with the European Union. The Conservatives should renegotiate a free-trade deal with the European Community to safeguard Britain's economic interests and to ensure that we have a full and functioning single market with the EU countries. But they also need to remove any possibility of political union, a single currency and the moves towards integration that are the very essence of the Community, as pursued by the federalist troika of the Commission, the French and the Germans. If they can renegotiate a deal to this effect so will be solved the 30-year old problem of the Conservative party and EEC membership. But if such a deal is not forthcoming a Conservative prime minister should cast aside the failures of those 30 years by leading his party and his country out of the federal superstate which the Continentals are determined to create. Britain should withdraw from the EU rather than acquiesce in a federal state which few in the Conservative party welcome and which the vast majority fears. (pp. 123–4)

For the Conservatives, such considerations will have to wait for some future negotiations, but the prospect of a yet more Eurosceptical and nationalist Conservative party in the early years of the 21st century, faced with the choice of being permanently lodged on the fringes of the EU, an EU essentially run by the core countries, is a very real one under this scenario. The traditional argument of pro-Europeans in Britain's Foreign Office, that the country can 'punch above her weight' internationally by being in the EU, would be rendered obsolete. So too would the argument that, by being part of Europe, Britain attracts more than its fair share of foreign direct investment. Withdrawal, which any British government committed to could persuade the electorate of the virtues of, would be seen as preferable to inferior 'outsider' status within the EU. It remains to be seen whether Labour can render Euroscepticism obsolete.

■ Insiders and outsiders – in 30 years time

Europe will, on this scenario, develop in a multi-tiered way, with one group of countries almost fully integrated economically and politically, but with others at different stages of that process, and some stuck at those stages. Toughest to predict, but clearly a strong possibility in this setting, is the break-up of Italy into its northern and southern parts, with the former part of the core, the latter among the outsiders. Thus, we have, in 30 years time, the following broad split of core insiders consisting of France, Germany, Belgium, the Netherlands, Luxembourg, Austria, and, possibly, Northern Italy, Sweden and Finland.

Looking in from the outside, reluctantly and resentfully, would be a collection of reluctant outsiders, consisting of Spain, Portugal, Greece, Southern Italy, Cyprus, Malta and, as an 'honorary' Club Med country, Ireland, together with the newer eastern entrants, the Czech Republic, Hungary, Slovakia, Poland, Slovenia, Estonia, Latvia, Lithuania, Romania and Bulgaria. Denmark could either be a willing outsider or join Norway as a complete outsider, leaving the EU. Britain, in certain circumstances, would no longer be an EU member.

Culturally, Europe according to this scenario would be more diverse than ever. For the outsiders, not only would freedom of movement be restricted, but resentment of the core, and its success, would give rise to a greater emphasis on national identity and culture. The idea of a cultural common market for the whole of Europe, like that of the Single Market itself, would have been proved to be unachievable. Within the core, things would be different, although greater cultural integration within a relatively small number of countries will not offer a serious challenge to American dominance.

The situation would be reminiscent, albeit with a larger number of countries involved and far closer integration of the core countries, to that in Europe in the late 1950s and 1960s, when the EEC was up and running, with Efta as a second-best solution for non-members. Deepening and widening the EU at the same time would have been shown to have been conflicting ambitions, with the former winning out but only for a limited number of states. Europe would have travelled full circle, turning itself into a more dangerously divided and unequal continent in the process. The power and influence of the core countries, effectively developing, as the Eurosceptics fear, into a superstate, would be enormous, both within Europe and in the outside world. The core would represent Europe in international councils, and use its huge economic and political weight to steamroller through advantageous arrangements both in respect of the European outsiders and with the wider world. The old democratic arrangements, embodied in qualified majority voting, would be gradually eroded, removing the power of veto from smaller, outsider countries. Thanks to its economic weight, the core would become the seat of European military power, as it already is the seat. The former centrally planned economies would have exchanged one dominant power, the Soviet Union, for another, the new western European superstate. Their ability to influence the latter would be no greater than for the former.

■ An explosive political cocktail

A divided Europe will be a potentially dangerous place. Outside the core, the loss of economic advantage and the prospect of permanently high unemployment will give rise to nationalism, reflected in mistrust and resentment of foreigners and a tendency towards protectionism. The far right, in particular, will present exclusion from the core as an indication of the bankruptcy of the European project, and a powerful argument for strengthening national borders. Those politicians, and parties, which have given greatest emphasis to European integration could find themselves unpopular and increasingly marginalised. Even in the core, the drive towards federalism and a loss of national sovereignty will also give succour to nationalist movements, even during a period of relative economic success. The biggest dangers will come among the outsiders, however. For nearly a half a century after the Second World War the behaviour of European countries was conditioned, either by the cold war division of the continent – and the combination of fear and discipline this exerted – or by the promise of the economic and political benefits arising from European integration. Without either of these forces any longer affecting the majority, European politics will become fractious, bitter and ultimately dangerous.

■ And an uncertain business environment

For business, operating within an insider–outsider Europe will be at best unsatisfactory, at worst impossible. The benefits of the core economies – an integrated market, a single currency and high living standards – will be obvious. Business, however, will be torn between the access advantages of directing investment towards the core economies and the lower costs of other European locations. This will, above all, be a Europe of great uncertainty – uncertainty about trade liberalisation, with the ever-present threat that the core economies will establish their own fortress Europe; uncertainty about the extent to which eastern Europe, for example, can maintain its reform process without the carrot of a realistic prospect of EU entry; and uncertainty about the sustainability of a Europe divided into haves and have-nots. The spur for restructuring, for improving competitiveness, will remain powerful, driven by competition from outside Europe but, combined as it will be with persistent mass unemployment in the outsider economies, business will find itself facing a popular backlash. In this insider–outsider Europe, the prospect of new pan-European alliances, of exploitation of a true single market and of the opening-up of eastern Europe will all be but pale echoes of the two previous scenarios, if they are there at all.

■ Dangerous inequality

Is a Europe along these lines sustainable 30 years into the future, let alone 50 or 70 years hence? For the core, economically enriched and politically powerful, the danger would be of resentment spilling over into violent instability on its borders. Fortress Europe would become a reality in more ways than one. It could maintain the carrot of occasional entry into the inner circle for suitable applicants from the outside, although at a slow enough pace to not damage its vested interests. The outsiders, making up a diverse set, could be played off against one another by the offering of economic aid and preferential trading arrangements. Britain might be assumed to be content ploughing its furrow elsewhere, across the Atlantic and in Asia.

Ultimately, however, the insider–outsider scenario raises only disturbing possibilities, of pronounced economic inequalities between European countries, of outsider regions of persistently high unemployment and permanent depression, and of unrest and armed conflict within Europe. The basic goal of integration, of avoiding a repetition of the damaging conflicts of the 20th century, would risk abject failure, brought on by the ambition of a relatively small number of countries to take that integration to its logical conclusion. Europe, on this scenario, becomes an uncomfortable place.

■ Fifty years on

For some of the economies that participated in those early moves towards European integration in the immediate post-war years, what in 50 years will be the approaching centenary of their efforts will be a cause for modest celebration. Germany will not have gone to war again with France, and the Benelux countries will have enjoyed nearly 100 years of peace and privilege. Modest, however, will be the operative word. Like some rich, walled community, they will know that outside their gates lies a sullen underclass and, from time to time, an angry mob. For the small number for whom integration has deepened, there are far more who are effectively excluded from the process. The Karl Lamers idea of the core leading the rest along on the integration process will have been proved fundamentally misconceived. Instead, the 21st century record of integration will have been one of lamentable failure, sparked off by the decision to push for Emu at the wrong time, and in the misguided belief that it was a force for integration when, for most of Europe, it was precisely the opposite. Europe, divided into 'haves and have-nots' will have been shown to be a region of accelerated economic decline – the relative success of the core countries insufficient to compensate for economic failure and political instability outside that core.

SCENARIO 4

The dark ages

Summary

Europe's slow growth of the 1990s is not a consequence of temporary factors – it is the new reality. Emu reinforces Europe's sclerotic tendencies, before other forces condemning the continent to a grim future – mainly the burden of ageing populations – come into play. Emu, in these circumstances, does not last, but there is no economic liberation for Europe – it is too late. As average unemployment in Europe climbs towards 30%, EU countries adopt protectionist measures to try and protect their remaining industries, only exacerbating the problem in doing so. Far from becoming a cohesive, united force, the EU does not even survive as a free trade area.

Scenario 4: The dark ages

■ *Faded glories*

Empires rise and fall. Unions form and then, when they lose their way, they disintegrate. Europe's 50-year journey towards union is but a brief interlude in the grand sweep of history. The bigger picture is more accurately painted by longer-run trends. Europe has seen its colonial interests, and its 19th-century world hegemony, dismantled and consigned to the history books. Like Miss Havisham in Charles Dickens's *Great Expectations*, what was once a hugely influential economic powerhouse has become a monument to past glories, with, to quote Dickens, 'everything within my view which ought to be white, had been white long ago, and had lost its lustre, and was faded and yellow'.

The basis of this scenario is that in the 21st century Europe suffers, not merely old age, but relative, and in some respects absolute, decline. The efforts to deepen integration in the 1980s and 1990s are seen to have taken European countries down a blind alley. When all energies should have been directed to improving Europe's competitiveness and restructuring welfare provision to make it affordable, European leaders chose instead to concern themselves with grand and irrelevant projects. The expectations of its citizens, to maintain the Dickensian theme, remain great, but the capacity of their economies to deliver the wealth necessary to fulfil them does not. This is the era when Asia, having lived in Europe's shadows for so long, gets its own back. It is also the era when America reinforces its dominance of global culture and, in its own interests, switches its economic emphasis decisively from the Atlantic to the Pacific.

For Europeans, the new dark ages become associated with declining living standards and, their sclerotic economies long having lost the art of job creation, permanently high unemployment, averaging 20% or more of the workforce. This will bring with it social decay, the emergence of a growing underclass, rising crime and random violence. There will, as always in periods of high unemployment, be rising racial tension. The most dynamic, skilful and entrepreneurial will seek their fortune on the other side of the world, leaving the continent denuded of its best talent and so caught in a vicious circle of decline. European markets, once the lure of multinational corporations and their inward investment, will become a slow-growing backwater.

The disturbing thing about the scenario sketched out above is that it is not reliant on new external shocks for Europe. The ingredients of slow growth, uncompetitiveness and welfare burdens stretching well out into the 21st century are already in place. So is the shifting of the world economic axis to the east. This is, in many ways, only a slightly gloomier version of my second scenario, 'Plus ça change', except that this one assumes that recent trends in Europe, and in particular slow growth, reflect fundamental forces and are not simply a consequence of relatively high post-unification interest rates in Germany and the struggle by member countries to achieve the Maastricht criteria for monetary union. It also assumes that pending changes do nothing to put Europe on a different path from these recent gloomy trends and, instead, may serve to reinforce them, a process beginning with economic and monetary union.

■ *Emu stultifies Europe*

In early 1997, the European Monetary Institute released a paper, 'The Single Monetary Policy in Stage Three'. Although much of the paper was concerned with as yet unanswered questions, such as whether the European Central Bank (ECB), which will succeed the EMI, will operate a system of inflation targets or, like the Bundesbank, target the money supply, one thing was abundantly clear. The ECB, said EMI president Alexandre Lamfalussy, would aim to ensure that the single currency, the euro, would be at least as strong as the Deutschmark. In practice, although he did not spell it out, this, in turn, would entail two things. In the early years of monetary union, and possibly for a decade or more after its inception, the ECB would have to operate a tougher monetary policy and hence higher interest rates than those prevailing in Germany at the time monetary union starts. The reasons for this are straightforward enough. This credibility-building exercise would start from a position where, even with a narrow Emu, all entrants would not, could not, be Germany, nor regarded as synonymous with Germany by the financial markets. In order to establish Emu as a low-inflation, hard-currency zone, the one thing the central bank would want to avoid most would be providing traditional higher-inflation economies with a monetary boost in terms of significantly lower interest rates. The wider Emu is, the greater the difficulty. In the extreme, interest rate policy would have to be set according to the rate prevailing, at the time of the start of the final stage, in the highest inflation country, which could be two or three percentage points above German levels. Even if the central bank does not go as far as this, it will need to set interest rates at a level which makes things extremely tough for the low-inflation economies, while avoiding an inflationary boost for the others. The Maastricht criteria, it should be noted, provide little help in this regard. Although there is an inflation condition for Emu entry – an inflation rate no more than 1.5 percentage points above the average of the three member states with the lowest inflation – the treaty says nothing about the level of short-term interest rates needed to achieve that goal.

The countries that qualify for Emu will thus have faced a long and difficult journey, involving tough, and in some cases draconian budget measures, to make it through the gateway to the promised land. But, if they were expecting relief, in the form of easier monetary policy, once they got there, they will be sorely disappointed. In most cases interest rates will be no lower, in some cases higher, than those prevailing prior to the start of the final stage of Emu. This will reinforce the reality of Europe under Emu, whether the single currency zone is narrow, wide, or somewhere in between, as a slow growth region, the more so because faced with a tough monetary policy, these countries will also be required to pursue tight budgetary policies in order to avoid fines under the stability pact discussed in the previous chapter.

The credibility-building period, as noted above, could be long, indeed is likely to be. After it, however, surely Europe will enter the sunny uplands of non-inflationary growth, with low interest rates the norm because the markets believe in the euro as much as they used to believe in the Deutschmark? Even in the longer term, unfortunately, history would not be erased. Different countries would be affected differently by the monetary policy decisions of the ECB. Julian Callow gives an example:

The sort of problem that could occur under Emu would be the following. Suppose there were a new Russian revolution soon after Emu began. The natural response of the Bundesbank under such situations historically has been to fight any currency pressure through higher interest rates. Let us suppose that the ECB decided to behave like the Bundesbank would do, and hike rates in order to prevent the euro from depreciating (and thereby endangering the ECB's nascent credibility). The German, French, Austrian and Dutch economies could withstand a sharp tightening in short rates since little of their private sector debt is financed at the short end. But the impact on household and corporate sector cash flow for economies more susceptible to short term rates, such as Italy, Spain and the UK, would be much more dramatic. (*Life After Emu*, pp. 11–12)

Even if monetary systems converge sufficiently to remove such problems, which itself would be a very lengthy process, this would leave a second difficulty, that arising from the declared ECB aim of making the euro at least as strong as the Deutschmark. Part of the reason why the Emu credibility-building exercise is likely to be a long one is that the financial markets have tended to assume a softer euro, in other words one reflecting the traditional strength of some of its hard currency constituents, such as the Deutschmark and Dutch guilder, but also the influence of some of its component currencies with a weaker history, including the French franc. But central bankers are a particular breed. National interests and characteristics will always take second place to their determination to pursue a prudent and responsible monetary policy. Indeed, the hardest line on the ECB council could come, not from Germany, but from the central bankers of traditional soft currency countries. Consider what this might mean. In the 30 years leading up to Emu, the franc has lost nearly two-thirds of its value against the Deutschmark. Other currencies have lost more, sterling, for example, 75%. In Emu, not only does that depreciation process of individual European currencies which take part have to come to an end, but the new currency will be expected to hold its own with the best in the world, including the currencies of the rapidly growing, highly competitive, Asian economies. Exchange rate policy in Emu, in fact, could be highly confusing. As in national economies, finance ministers rather than the central bank will have responsibility for framing the policy. If European finance ministers, aware of the strains on their economies, tried to pursue a weak euro policy, however, they would soon find themselves in dispute with the ECB, which would be minded to raise interest rates in response.

Emu, far from providing a liberating growth boost to Europe, will reinforce deflationary tendencies in the region. As Rudiger Dornbusch has put it: 'The struggle to achieve monetary union under the Maastricht formula may be remembered as one of the most useless battles in European history. The costs of getting there are large, the economic benefits minimal, and the prospects for disappointment major.' Any small benefit in terms of lower transaction costs will be wiped out by the insistence by the ECB on tough monetary policy. At the very time Europe needs a growth boost, Emu will condemn the continent to slow growth, a start to the 21st century from which the region will never recover.

European labour markets don't work

The poor performance of European labour markets since the early 1970s has been frequently commented upon. Thus, the OECD in its 1994 'Jobs Study', said of Europe's record:

> Weak employment growth, most of it until the mid-1980s in the public sector, has been accompanied by strong productivity growth, achieved mostly through labour-shedding in traditional sectors rather than through shifts of production in high-technology and skill-intensive activities. Unemployment has ratcheted up over successive cycles, resulting in rising long-term unemployment. Inflows into unemployment have been relatively low but outflows even lower – suggesting poorly functioning labour markets. (p. 25)

The disturbing thing about Europe's jobs record, of course, is that it has progressively deteriorated, at a time when the challenges of running successful labour markets have become greater. Europe, it appears, has been faced with that challenge – and flunked it. At the beginning of the 1950s, North America and Europe both had 5% unemployment rates. For the remainder of that decade and in the 1960s, Europe's record, with unemployment rates typically 2–4%, was better than that of North America, where unemployment rates averaged 4–6%. Even in the 1970s, when unemployment worldwide rose, there was little to choose. European unemployment rose more gradually than in North America in response to the first global oil price shock, although in both regions the jobless total at the end of the decade was around 7% of the workforce. In the 1980s and 1990s, however, the combination of slower economic growth and what the OECD defines as an inability to adapt to change has seen the European record deteriorate decisively. EU unemployment in 1997, at 11.5% of the workforce, was running at more than double the rate in the United States, with 5.5%. And, while unemployment in North America is cyclical in both directions – falling during upturns and rising during downturns – the pattern in Europe has been that economic upturns produce a pause in the rising jobless trend but fail to take the total significantly lower. With each successive cyclical unemployment peak two to three percentage points above the previous one, this points to 15% EU unemployment in the early years of the 21st century, rising to 20% between 2010 and 2020, 25% between 2020 and 2030 and 30% or more before the middle of the century. For Europe's unemployed, these will indeed be the dark ages.

Europe's rigid labour markets are bad in themselves. In the context of monetary union, they are positively dangerous. In May 1996 Lawrence Lindsey, a governor of the Federal Reserve Board, gave evidence to the House of Commons Treasury and Civil Sevice Committee on the flexibility of labour markets in another large monetary union, the United States. A sixth of Americans move home each year, mainly for employment reasons, and a third of those aged 20–30 do so. As for inter-state moves, 3% of Americans do this each year. Lindsey gave the example of the contraction of the Californian defence industry over the 1990–4 period, with 1.2m people leaving the state, many finding jobs in neighbouring states: for example Utah saw a gain of 200,000 jobs and Colorado 300,000. The north-eastern recession of the same period produced a fall in the state populations of Rhode Island and Connecticut, at a time when the overall US population was growing.

Europe, in contrast, suffers from low levels of geographical mobility within countries, let alone between them. Norman Tebbit, a British government minister, famously recommended in the early 1980s that the unemployed 'get on their bikes' to seek work elsewhere. Few heeded his advice, the interaction of Britain's housing market and the conservatism of British workers leading most to stay put. Between European countries, the constraints on mobility, not least differences in language, culture and recognition of qualifications and experience, are multiplied. In 1994 regional unemployment rates in Europe ranged from 3.4% in Luxembourg to 33.3% in Sur in Spain. The free movement of people under the Single Market is a fine ambition, but the reality is that cross-border movements of people in search of jobs are limited. According to the Commission's own assessment: 'A large market without borders is not enough. It is even more essential that the citizens of the European Union feel at home everywhere within the Union's territory. This feeling will be the flesh to the bone of the great economic area' ('Freedom of Movement', p. 3).

In a study published by UBS, 'Labour Markets and Emu', George Magnus and Paul Donovan found that labour mobility within Europe had declined in the two decades from the mid-1970s at a time when, in preparation for Emu, it should have been increasing. In the case of France and Germany, mobility in respect of other EU countries had roughly halved. A survey by the Commission in 1995 found that two-thirds of EU citizens did not wish to seek employment elsewhere for the simple reason that they preferred to stay at home. For the two economies at the heart of Europe, France and Germany, the proportion was highest, at over 80%. In Germany, despite good language skills among the people, more than 70% cited language differences as a reason for not seeking jobs elsewhere in the EU.

Magnus and Donovan cited four principal reasons for declining labour mobility in Europe:

- Linguistic and cultural barriers. Even in the United States, there are problems of mobility for population groups where language is perceived as a barrier, for example Hispanics in California. In Europe, with so many different languages, the constraints are that much bigger.
- A lack of cross-border job information. Although there is some limited information, for example for jobs with the EU institutions themselves, or within multinational companies operating across Europe, the emphasis, particularly for government-sponsored employment services, remains strongly national in character.
- The problem of diverse state benefit systems. High social costs in the EU have been identified as a cause of competitive problems for the region as a whole. For individual employees, variations

in benefit and tax systems also form a significant barrier to mobility.
- A perceived lack of opportunity elsewhere. Although there are substantial variations in unemployment rates between countries and regions, the fact that unemployment is generally high throughout Europe severely limits the incentive to move to other countries in search of work. Those hardest hit by rising unemployment, the unskilled, will tend to find that opportunities are as limited in other countries as at home.

The combination of an immobile workforce and an Emu which reinforces Europe's low-growth tendencies is a dangerous one. While Europe's average unemployment rate rises inexorably there will be regions, as there are now, where unemployment rises significantly above the average. Within the context of an EU average unemployment rate of 11–12% there are regions with more than 30% of the workforce out of work. EU unemployment of over 20% would conceal a diversity in which some areas would have rates of more than 60%.

Geographical immobility of labour is, of course, only one symptom of European labour market inflexibility. The working time directive, imposed on a reluctant British government by the European Court of Justice in November 1996, institutionalises restrictions on working hours, one of the areas in which, according to John Llewellyn, writing in the *Oxford Review of Economic Policy* (Autumn 1996), Europe badly needs to improve its flexibility. According to Llewellyn:

> The European socioeconomic system has for several decades been underperforming relative to the aspirations of many of its citizens, particularly in respect of the capacity to create jobs. This is increasingly ascribed to a lack of competitiveness, by which is meant not insufficient cost or price competitiveness, but rather a lack of the full array of factors that lead to good economic performance. Much of this lack of European competitiveness in all probability derives from poor structural policies. . . . It is very difficult to be sure which structural policies matter the most in Europe at present, but five are suggested as being of particular importance: greater flexibility, both of real wages and of working time; better policies to top-up low wage incomes; a fundamentally revised social attitude towards entrepreneurship; markedly

enhanced education and training of the workforce, particularly in later working life; and better educated markets. (p. 96)

Although some of this is motherhood and apple pie, there is scant evidence that this broad message is getting across. Continental Europeans refer disparagingly to the 'Anglo-Saxon' labour market model. Establishing the famous level playing field across the Single Market too often means ensuring a common level of inflexibility. Nor will rising unemployment trigger a change in such attitudes. Rather, it will harden the attitude of those in work to retaining the job protection they enjoy.

No escape from slow growth's grip

Emu and European labour market inflexibility, together, presage a grim future for Europe of slow growth and permanent mass unemployment. Surely, however, this is only a future for those who take this road. Will not non-Emu countries bless their escape from the system's yoke and prosper outside the single currency?

Let us assume, as in the previous scenario, that only a core of countries move to the final stage of Emu and that slow growth adds to the difficulties of the initial non-qualifiers in achieving the Maastricht criteria. The experience of the post-ERM period would suggest that, freed from system constraints, countries can achieve faster rates of growth. In Britain, and to a lesser extent Italy, such freedom resulted in export-led growth which would not easily have been available within the ERM. It is precisely because this occurred, however, that it would be unwise to apply such experience to predict significant differences in the economic outlook for Emu and non-Emu countries when the single currency is a reality. The relationship between the 'ins' and the 'outs' was a topic of much discussion between European finance ministers in the final formulation of Emu. With the exceptions of Britain and Denmark, who can apply their monetary union opt-outs, non-Emu countries will be regarded as in the waiting-room for entry. Thus, their currencies will be required to stay within a set range against the euro in a new exchange-rate mechanism, and their economies will be expected to abide by the Maastricht convergence criteria. New entrants to the EU will be expected to enter the single currency waiting-room. Indeed, it is likely to be a condition of entry. Liberation from the dead hand of Emu will not be an option.

Slow growth will also be reinforced by the fact that, even if it were possible for non-Emu economies to pursue independent exchange-rate, monetary and fiscal policies, the prospect of a sclerotic, high-unemployment European core would, in any case, be enough to snuff out any glimmerings of strong revival elsewhere in Europe. Britain and Italy, despite gaining a strong competitive advantage in the wake of the departure of their currencies from the ERM, were held back by weak growth in other European markets. So it would be for Emu.

It may be thought that this is an excessively gloomy view. Emu's ability to reinforce the continent's slow growth tendencies could, it will be argued, be put down to teething troubles, albeit lengthy ones. Apart from the fact that Emu could, as is argued here, entail a permanent growth sacrifice, there is another factor looming into view that will help ensure a grim 21st century for Europe.

■ *The burden of ageing populations*

Europe's economies, in common with those of other developed countries, face the problems of ageing populations. Greater longevity means that the number of elderly people is rising, while numbers in employment, relative to the elderly dependent population, are declining. The majority of public pension systems are 'pay as you go' schemes. In other words, current pensions are funded by transfers – taxation – from the incomes of the present workforce. For most European countries, the problem of a growing elderly dependent population is made worse by the fact that, so poor has been the record in generating employment that early retirement has been encouraged. In Germany, according to OECD figures, only 45% of men aged 55–64 are in employment, in the Netherlands 40.7%, France 39.1%, Finland 34.3%, Luxembourg 33.4%, Belgium 33% and Italy just 30.7%. Britain, Portugal and Sweden are unusual in the EU in having employment-to-population ratios for men aged 55–64 above 60%.

The consequences of ageing populations for Europe's economies, with only a few exceptions, are alarming. Projections by Giorgio

Radaelli and Ryan Shea of Lehman Brothers, in an April 1996 paper, 'Public Pension Systems: The Challenge Ahead', suggest that elderly dependency ratios – defined as retired people as a percentage of those in work – will rise in Germany from 34% in 1990 to 52% by 2050, in Italy from 38% to 61%, in France from 35% to 54%, in Belgium from 39% to 55% and in the Netherlands from 30% to 49%. To take Germany, France and the Netherlands as representative of Europe's core economies, change is in prospect which will mean that a current situation in which each retired person is supported by about three people in work is transformed into one in which there is one dependent retiree for every two, or slightly under two, workers. The dependency ratio rises everywhere, although, to take an example of a country where the problem is less severe, the increase in Britain is from 33% in 1990 to 43% in 2050.

European countries have taken decisions which, while convenient in the short-term, pose huge problems for the long-term. According to Radaelli and Shea: 'A factor behind ballooning pension provisions is that in some instances disability and early retirement pensions are granted as a hidden subsidy to older workers in difficulty, either because of underemployment or long-term unemployment. In Italy, for instance, generous public pensions have occasionally been justified as ways to buttress personal incomes in the *Mezzogiorno*' (p. 11). The OECD, in its June 1996 'Economic Outlook', cited the effect of measures to reduce the workforce and thus limit the rise in unemployment:

> It will be important to reform labour market policies which reduce labour supply, such as mandatory reductions in working hours, early retirement schemes or excessively generous invalidity schemes. Such schemes may have only a limited downward effect on unemployment but, by reducing the available workforce, they reduce aggregate output and reinforce the fiscal pressures which arise from population ageing. While employment rates for men aged 55–64 have been on a declining trend in virtually all OECD countries, Japan being the outstanding exception, the decline has been more pronounced in European countries since the late 1970s which, at least partly, is likely to reflect early retirement legislation. (p. 26)

The difficulty of reversing such measures, in order to address the consequences of ageing populations, is that in the case of Europe it will be in the context of slow growth and a continuation of the recent appalling record of job creation. Politically, the pressure will remain intense to retain measures which restrict the available working population, despite the fiscal penalties of doing so.

The disturbing thing about such projections is that much of what underlies them is already in place. So too, therefore, barring early and fundamental reform of public pension systems, are the economic and financial consequences. Figures compiled by Professor David Miles of Imperial College London, largely based on OECD work on the consequences of ageing populations, show that *as a percentage of GDP* spending on public pension schemes in Europe will rise by between 2% (for Britain) and 12% (Austria and the Netherlands). For France the projected rise is 7%, Germany 8% and Italy 9%. Belgium is 7.2%, Denmark 6.7%, Finland 8.5%, Greece 4.7%, Ireland 2.1%, Norway 4.1%, Portugal 4%, Spain 4.9%, and Sweden 4.9%. Britain's low rise, and hence its more sustainable state pension system, is largely due to an early decision by the Thatcher government to link public pensions to prices rather than faster-growing earnings, together with the encouragement of private personal pensions in preference to the state earnings-related scheme.

The first thing to note about these figures is that the countries with the biggest projected increases already have a high level of public spending as a percentage of GDP. As Miles points out:

> In the absence of a change in spending patterns the share of government in total output might significantly exceed 60% in several countries. Only in the UK, Ireland, Spain and Portugal would government spending be under 50% of GDP if the projected rise in pensions spending were to be added to the current level of spending. At the other extreme come Sweden and Denmark where rising pensions expenditure could take the government's share of GDP to close to 70%. ('The Future of Savings and Wealth Accumulation', p. 12)

The figures, in rising order of government spending to GDP in 2030, are: Ireland 43.6%, Britain 44.9%, Portugal 47.1%, Spain 48.3%, Greece 50.2%, Norway 50.3%, Germany 57.8%, Italy 60.3%, France 61.2%, Belgium 61.7%, the Netherlands 62.5%, Austria 64.5%, Finland 64.5%, Denmark 69.6%, Sweden 71.5%. Europe's starting point is one where government spending accounts for a significantly higher proportion of GDP than the United States (33%), Japan (36%) and the emerging economies of Asia. Research by economists at the International Monetary Fund in Washington has found a clear relationship between the state's share of GDP and long-term growth potential, for fairly obvious reasons – a large public sector crowds out private sector activity, not least by imposing a rising tax burden on private sector employers and employees.

In the case of Europe, this will be reinforced, damagingly, by the interaction of rising state pension burdens for the elderly and the need to run low budget deficits and keep a lid on the public debt burden under the terms of the Maastricht convergence criteria, as they evolve into the more rigorous Emu stability pact. It is a crunch recipe for a sharply rising tax burden in most European countries including, crucially, those at Europe's core. It is also a recipe for grindingly slow economic growth. The only alternative is radical surgery on Europe's unaffordable state pension systems and, while some action is being taken, for example the proposed pension reforms in Germany, it is mainly too piecemeal and too modest to substantially alter the picture.

Emu irrelevance

In the circumstances set out above, or indeed those described earlier in this scenario, it can be argued that monetary union would be unlikely to survive, or at least not in a form that condemns its members to a permanent condition of slow growth and mass unemployment. The more countries that enter Emu at its inception, when their economies are not sufficiently converged to enable them properly to do so, the greater the risk that Europe's 21st century will be characterised by the new dark ages. In this situation, it is quite likely that Emu will start to disintegrate, beginning with the exit of non-core members. This would not, however, change the broad parameters of this scenario. The constraints of tight monetary policy initially would, in any event, give way to the fiscal policy problems created by the impact of ageing populations on already excessive state sectors in Europe. Underlying it all is Europe's competitivity problem. Emu is a significant aggravating factor, particularly in the early stages. Even in its absence, however, these problems are unavoidable.

■ *American century*

As the 20th century draws to a close, which of the 'older' industrial regions is displaying the dynamism and innovation which will carry it forward in the 21st century? It is not, sadly, Europe. Any hope of a European economic miracle is based on shaky, perhaps non-existent, foundations. Dynamism is not, either, to be found in Japan. The 1960s, 1970s and 1980s were remarkable decades for the Japanese economy as it emerged, from virtually nowhere, to become the second largest global economic power. The 1990s have not, however, been kind to Japan. Slow growth has exposed structural weaknesses in its economy at the same time as competition within its own home region has intensified. Japanese dynamism has faded and the Japanese model, like that of Germany, has come to be called increasingly into question.

The prize, instead, goes to America. The US economy has exhibited a dynamism and an ability to generate jobs that is the envy of the rest of the industrialised world. Within the past two decades America has been prey to deep industrial gloom and the loss of its domestic markets, to Japan in particular. Now, however, the USA has rediscovered its self-confidence. According to Alfredo Valladão:

> The 21st century will be American for the simple reason that America alone possesses the three pillars of power: military, economic and cultural. As a result of the final collapse of the Soviet Union, the United States has become the co-ordinator of planetary security. The US must now decide where and when an international 'police operation' is needed; and Washington alone has the privilege of being able to intervene anywhere in the world. America also comprises the world's largest, wealthiest homogeneous market; the combination of advanced technology with control of the great flows of petroleum, finance and audio-visual images produces economic hegemony. American culture is not shy about its universal vocation. It is proud of its capacity to integrate all other cultures, and has diffused across

the entire planet to be incorporated into all other societies. (*The 21st Century Will Be American*, p. xi)

Valladão's compelling thesis is that those who postulate the decline of the American 'empire' are at least four or five centuries premature. The best historical analogy, he argues, is with Ancient Rome which, after its triumph over Carthage in the 1st century BC, had a period of internal division and strife before mutating into a universal empire. There was 'declinist' talk in Rome then, as there is in America now, but it was no more appropriate. At the start of the 20th century, the key industries in which to gain a winning lead were in manufacturing – steel, shipbuilding and the emerging automobile industry. At the start of the 21st century they will be in information technology, communications and related industries. From personal computers, through mainframes, system architecture (Apple, Microsoft, Intel) to supercomputers, American dominance is formidable. Others can, and do, copy, but they cannot displace America at the technological frontier. Nor, it appears, can Europe take full advantage of existing technological developments. Thus Tim Berners-Lee, now of the Massachusetts Institute of Technology, writing of the World Wide Web (which he designed while working at CERN in Geneva):

> The Web has rushed through the US in a way that it cannot through Europe. The heat of excitement about the content already on the Web fuels the pouring of greater and greater resources into providing more content, more facilities, better organisation and cataloguing. The more interesting content there is on the Web, the more incentive for readers to get connected; similarly, the more people browsing, the more incentive there is for people to put public content onto the Web. In the US this happens very quickly, as each morsel of information is available to anyone throughout that largely common-language, common-currency bloc that is (in oversimplification) the US. There is an incredible economy of scale. Europe, however, has firebreaks between its cultures: disparate languages, history, institutions, even long-nurtured antagonisms. The explosion of servers and readers exists, but it has moved more slowly. . . . Add to this the historical facts that the Internet was invented in the US and that in European states telecommunications monopolies have manacled the development of communications, and it is not

surprising that Europe seems to be a few years behind the US. (*Time*, Golden Anniversary issue, Winter 1996, p. 140)

■ *No United States of Europe*

The expression 'United States of Europe' usually enters the European debate in the context of the degree of federalism that the continent might move to over the medium to long term. In this scenario, as will be discussed below, even retaining Europe's existing economic relationships will prove difficult. The United States of Europe analogy is relevant, however, in another context. That America has a single currency and a common, if not universal, language is an enormous advantage in terms of the coherence of the US as a single market and a single economy. The single currency has been in place, with one obvious break, since shortly after independence – the dollar was defined in law in 1792 – more than two centuries ago. Although composed of peoples of a huge range of different languages and cultures, including all the European languages, English came to dominate.

The contrast with Europe is striking. America had a single currency prior to economic maturity. Europe is trying to create one, and at best it will only apply to part of the continent, after economic maturity has been achieved and, on this scenario, relative decline has set in. America has a system of huge federal transfers, effectively shifting resources from rich to poor states, which is barely in prospect for Europe, and certainly will not be in place when, on the current timetable, the single currency begins.

More than this, Europe is a continent divided by language. There is no prospect of a European common language – national languages and culture are jealously guarded, ferociously so in the case of the Académie Française. All of this is understandable, but then so are the consequences. America's common language provides it with the unified home market essential for the kind of global domination described above. In the case of popular culture, global success is not attainable unless a particular movie or rock group plays well in the US market. This, in turn, provides the springboard for Hollywood's domination of global popular culture and the pivotal world role of the US television industry. There is no comparable market for popular culture in Europe, and never will be. And this does not apply to culture alone. From Coca Cola downwards, American brands dominate the planet in a way that few European brands can pretend to. A long-established single currency and a common language have provided the basis for American success in a way that Europe cannot hope to emulate. In the case of the latter, an English author hesitates to suggest that Europe's best course would be to adopt the world language of English. In any event, it will never happen.

Little fortresses

The consequences of slow growth in Europe will be that, even if monetary union survives – and this is surely a heroic assumption – free trade within Europe, and between Europe and other areas, will not. The classic response of countries experiencing extreme economic strains, and in particular high and rising unemployment, is to seek to protect their own markets. So it was with the 'beggar-my-neighbour' tariff protection of the 1930s, and so it will be for Europe, in this scenario, in the 21st century. Trade liberalisation and the preservation of free markets occur in an environment of economic growth and rising prosperity; they do not when both are under threat.

There is already evidence, indeed, that slow growth has delayed, possibly permanently, the completion of the Single Market. In the case of financial services, national markets have remained largely protected at a time when they were due to have been liberalised:

> Four years have come and gone since the magic date when the single European market in financial services was supposed to have come into being. But for ordinary consumers, the dream of a free choice of cheaper products and services in banking and insurance has not materialised. Most people don't yet have the option of choosing a cheque account with a French bank, a mortgage-loan from a German bank and motor insurance with a British company. Despite the much discussed 'single passport' for banks in the EU, the difficulties of competing with established national institutions and of overcoming remaining regulatory barriers have prevented banks and insurance companies from

making much headway in neighbouring markets. (*The European*, 16–22 January 1997, p. 19)

What has happened in financial services is an indication of the shape of things to come in a slow-growth era. Not only that, but where freedoms have been established, they will be gradually eroded. Europe already suffers from low geographical mobility of labour, as discussed above. In the new higher unemployment era, this will be reinforced, with different national qualification standards emphasised and available jobs, in effect, reserved for the citizens of the country concerned. More generally, Europe has a collection of national bureaucracies which are adept at throwing up informal barriers to trade when conditions require it. In the extreme, as discussed in the previous scenario, such barriers could become formal, initially to prevent short-term balance of payments difficulties, but retained in the name of longer-term problems. Europe is not, instinctively, a collection of free-trading nations. The different economic philosophies that compete for supremacy within Europe contain a heavily protectionist bias, emphasised in the approach of France and Italy, but present, where national interests are at stake, in many of the others. Brian Hindley, writing of Europe's approach to world trade liberalisation, described it thus:

> The primary characteristic of EEC trade policy is sulky obstinacy. The EEC is the world's largest trading entity, but it cannot seem to find positive uses for the influence that its mass can bring. It uses its bulk in stubborn defence of its own narrowly-defined interests, without apparent thought for the effects on the world trading system. . . . Those who are urging a federal future for the EEC often do so on the basis that a federal EEC will have more influence on the world at large. That might be true. But those who support the federalist position seem to assume as a matter of course that greater EEC influence will make the world a better place. The performance of the EEC in trade policy, which the Treaty of Rome places in the hands of the EEC institutions, does not bear out that assumption. That performance suggests the possibility that a federal EEC would create an immobile and introverted lump in world affairs, whose primary effect would be to neuter the better instincts of individual member states and

to give them more power to pursue their worst instincts. (*The Eurosceptical Reader*, pp. 129, 146–7)

Even without a federal Europe, the continent's natural response to economic adversity will be to erect barriers to trade with the outside world – the evolution of the much-feared 'fortress Europe'. Within this there will be a series of little fortresses, as member countries seek to protect their markets from the predations of other European countries. History tells us this is a road to nowhere. It does not mean, however, that it will not happen.

■ *Extra-European links*

For some European countries, the response to the continent's profound 21st-century difficulties will be to seek solace elsewhere. Two possibilities, in particular, stand out. One is Britain, which has always emphasised that it has a foot in at least three camps – the EU, the 'special relationship' with America and the historical links with the countries of the former empire, the Commonwealth. A slow-growing, sclerotic Europe is exactly what British Eurosceptics have predicted, in urging the rebuilding of such links and a turning away from the EU. Britain's success in attracting inward investment from the Far East, it is further argued, shows that a special relationship is being built with the current most dynamic economic region in the world. Thus, according to one vision of its future, Britain should become a signatory to the North American Free Trade Agreement (Nafta) and thus piggyback on to America's development of free trade links with the Asia-Pacific region. In 1963, rejecting British membership of the EEC, de Gaulle had said: 'Britain is in fact, insular and maritime, linked by her trade, her markets, and her supply routes to very varied and often very remote countries. She is entirely industrial and commercial: hardly agricultural at all. . . . How can Britain, being what she is, come into our system?' In more than three decades some things have changed. Britain's trade links with Europe have expanded to the point where more than 50% of visible trade, in either direction, is with other EU members, although this is not true for either invisible trade or investment flows. Britain's commitment to Europe, and to the European ideal has often been, however, as half-hearted as de Gaulle suspected. Britain could be the first country to leave a slow-growing, increasingly protectionist EU. The adjustment, however, would not be easy. Substituting trade elsewhere in the world for that with the other EU countries would also condemn Britain to a period of economic pain and slow growth, albeit with a light at the end of the tunnel.

The other central possibility concerns Germany which, with only economic stagnation to the west, would reach out increasingly to the east, forging a new *Rapallo* (after the Treaty of Rapallo signed by Germany and Russia in 1922, in which the two countries agreed not to pursue compensation claims – for the Soviet seizure of German assets and war losses respectively – but also agreed to develop new economic relations 'with mutual feelings of goodwill'). Germany's sensitivity to developments in central and eastern Europe is both logical and long-established. Europe's ideological divide between communism and capitalism physically divided Germany uniquely. When the Berlin Wall came down and the old regimes collapsed, in a reverse domino effect, throughout eastern Europe, Germany's position within Europe became even more pivotal than before. Germany was the bridge between east and west, the nation best placed to co-ordinate, and benefit from, central and eastern Europe's emergence from its dark ages. Political tensions in Russia, and risks to the process of westernisation, reverberate in the financial markets to the detriment of the Deutschmark. According to Hans-Georg Ehrhart, of the Institute for Peace Research and Security Policy, Hamburg University:

> The new Germany has experienced rapid, seismic internal change in a world which is itself undergoing dramatic reorganisation. The variety of challenges and expectations, both internal and external, have created a kind of double-bind in which she must negotiate between contradictory expectations and impulses while attempting not to harm anybody. The result seems, unsurprisingly, to be a state of some confusion. Nevertheless the challenges are real and have to be faced. Germany will do this in her traditional way, following the, until now, successful policy of deeper European integration, while at the same time attempting to juggle her various interests in eastern and central Europe (CEEC), Nato and the EU. As to the first of these, she must at all costs forestall the threat of once again being Nato's front line. She is determined to prevent its borders with the CEEC from

becoming a social-economic and, in the long-term, a military frontier. This would have serious consequences for Germany's political and economic stability. The preferred scenario is, of course, that the CEEC becomes its, and Western Europe's new frontier, an extremely attractive 'big idea' which would stimulate economic growth, stabilise European security, and strengthen Europe's standing in world politics. (Parliamentary Brief, March 1996, p. 11)

What happens, however, if the process of deeper integration is stalled, and reversed, by the EU's grim economic state? What happens if, instead of opening itself up to central and eastern Europe, the EU develops a series of little fortresses, and is encouraged by French influence to itself become a rather larger fortress against the outside world, including its neighbours to the east? The consequences for Germany in this scenario are potentially very serious. The former Comecon countries, excluded by the very capitalist countries they had hoped to emulate, would become dangerously bitter and resentful, and risk reverting to something like the old regimes, only more unstable than before because of weaker central control from Moscow. Germany's strategy in these circumstances will be to redefine its *Ostpolitik* in terms of new relationships between Berlin and Moscow, and between Berlin and the capitals of central and eastern Europe. Germany, in its own national interest – economic as well as security – would turn away from the sclerotic, protectionist EU, and towards the east. Again, this would not provide a comprehensive insurance policy against western Europe's woes, but it would help.

■ *Nationalism rules*

In the previous scenario I described how European politics might develop under an insider–outsider future for Europe, with politics in the outsider countries becoming increasingly nationalist and isolationist. In this scenario, those same forces of nationalism and isolationism would apply, but they will cover all countries. The tendency of countries to want to cut themselves off from their neighbours, in the mistaken view that this is the route to national salvation, will have the same effect as in the famous tariff wars of the 1930s – merely exacerbating an already difficult situation. In the new dark ages, the idea of European integration will be seen as a historical relic. The new politics of Europe will emphasise national self-interest and suspicion of neighbours. Anti-immigration rules will become draconian, effectively making refugees of 'guest' workers. A new generation of political leaders, with no direct memories of the Second World War, will take over. As the economic gloom deepens, even these are unlikely to be able to satisfy the nationalist cravings of their peoples. The political mainstream will come under threat, from both right and left.

■ Business suffers

For European business, the dark ages will mean what it suggests – a prolonged period of struggle and retrenchment. All those hopes of a dynamic, integrated European economy will have been dashed, replaced by a series of separate, stagnant markets. The burden of high social costs, far from diminishing, will be exacerbated by the effects of even higher unemployment and ageing populations. Businesses will, of course, look outside Europe for the best opportunities – and shift production to lower-cost regions, thus adding to Europe's difficulties. The problem of this west-to-east shift is that it will bring European business into direct competition against the best of Asian and American companies, which will have the additional advantage of buoyant domestic markets as well as lower costs. High European tax levels will mean that, for many international businesses, even maintaining headquarters in Europe will prove prohibitively expensive. In this declining Europe, business survival may mean emigration.

■ A living museum

What kind of Europe would result from a shift in the world economic axis away from Europe and the transatlantic trading relationship, and towards Asia and the Pacific rim? What kind of future would be faced by an uncompetitive region, burdened by high costs and high taxation, its industry dazzled by the reality of better, cheaper producers in other parts of the world? The answer is that a once-dominant civilisation, like other once-dominant civilisations before it, would become a museum piece, a kind of modern-day Ruritania, of interest to the newly wealthy for its crumbling symbols of a glorious past, French chateaux, English castles and Italian opera houses. Like Egypt or Ancient Greece, Europe would be of interest to visitors for the contrast it offered with their modern, dynamic world, and for what they had read about in their history books. 'Once', the Chinese visitor would say to his children, 'this was a formidable power. Until they were dragged down by their decadence and greed, most of these countries had colonial interests stretching across the world. Now they cannot afford to keep their old people in a comfortable state. We must never let this happen to us.'

Perhaps such a judgement would be too harsh. Europe, after all, did not do that badly. Its world dominance began in the Middle Ages and relative decline did not set in until the 20th century. Inevitably, though, this relative decline has continued, and is likely to be accompanied by absolute decline, in the 21st. Thus, according to one of Europe's most formidable intellects:

> Europe now has, compared with its main competitors, the lowest birthrate (with the exception of Japan), the highest unemployment rate, the oldest population, the highest social expenditures, the lowest industrial-growth rate, the weakest industrial research in key areas of information technology, the fewest new patents. Even its renowned financial markets are heading towards fragility. And though its share of worldwide GNP remains large, this too will drop rapidly in the future. Thus, everything is shaping up for a 21st century Europe to become little more than a 'Venetian Continent', visited by millions of Asians and Americans, inhabited by tourist guides, museum caretakers and hotelkeepers. In the big global bazaar, the place occupied by European companies, products, ideas, literature, music and cinema will soon be taken over by objects, services, sounds, noises, words and images from elsewhere. . . . Faced with a rapidly growing membership, the Union will no longer be able to remain a decision-making centre with a coherent economic and security policy, or a credible defence. Lacking a strong common will, moreover, most of the European Union countries will be

unable to reduce their tax burdens. They will cease to be competitive because of high labour costs, which will move various activities toward Africa and Asia and thereby increase European unemployment. According to this scenario, only Germany will be able to get by, if it manages to maintain its social consensus, its banking resources and its lead in certain key sectors. Even then, Germany will be held back by the recessionary climate surrounding it. At the same time, all European countries will raise military spending because of a double threat. To the east, there will be a Russia in turmoil, financially drained and gradually fragmented into more or less autonomous provinces, several of which have nuclear armies run by one or more local generals. To the south there will be a Maghreb tested by a radical Islam, where millions of desperate inhabitants will be tempted to cross the Mediterranean, thus multiplying the risks of all kinds of destabilisation. (Jacques Attali, *For a New Political Order*, *Time* Golden Anniversary issue, Winter 1996, pp. 142–3)

Attali's 'dark ages' scenario is intended as a warning, a plea for Europe's political leaders to wake up to the uncomfortable realities that could be facing their nations in the 21st century. His wake-up call, however, consists of urgent recommendations that in the present climate look unattainable. He urges the creation of powerful political institutions, alongside the single currency, notably a European treasury, supreme court and senate. Turkey and Russia must be speedily integrated into the EU, he says, the former to send a signal to Islam that Europe is no longer a 'Christian club', and that modernisation is rewarded, the latter to tap into Russia's vast natural resources. Finally, Attali says Europe should use the model of Nafta to create a common market with the countries of North Africa and Central Asia, and thus prevent destabilising flows of population from these regions to Europe.

The nature of Attali's action plan underlines how difficult consensus would be to achieve on any of these points. While some would agree with his recommendations, many would argue that they, and in particular his idea of powerful centralised institutions, are precisely the opposite of what is required to lift Europe out of the doldrums. This may mean that ultimately, there is no escape.

■ Fifty years on

When people warned at the end of the 20th century that Europe had forgotten the techniques of economic growth and job creation, the optimists laughed such warnings off. The first half of the 21st century is proof, however, that all such fears were justified. The idea of Europe as one of the richest regions of the globe has become a distant memory, and so too has the integrationist drive that characterised the second half of the 20th century. The EU has ceased to function as an effective alliance, consigned to history as much as the Austro-Hungarian empire is to late 20th-century students. Mass unemployment is rife, those lucky to have a job are a rarity in some regions. The old are increasingly also the poor – in these new dark ages the old promises about pensions and security in old age count for nothing. Europe is a failing, moribund region.

SCENARIO 5

The apocalypse

Summary

Europe, beset with tribal and nationalist tensions, becomes a dangerous place, with conflict, small wars and the danger of a big war. The rest of the world not only achieves economic dominance over Europe but the rise of Islam and an aggressive China forces European countries to increase defence spending when they can ill afford to do so. Emu fails catastrophically, either when it has imposed chronically high unemployment on member states, or forced a splitting of the Franco-German axis. This Europe is dirty, with widespread, choking pollution as the costs of clean industry become unaffordable, and acutely vulnerable to nuclear disaster. The apocalypse can come in many ways.

Scenario 5: The apocalypse

■ *War and peace*

In February 1996, in a celebrated speech at the University of Leuven in Belgium, Chancellor Kohl set out his explanation of why the goal of completing the process of European integration was so important to him. 'There is', he said, 'no reasonable alternative to ever closer integration among European peoples; we all need a united Europe.' The most prominent reason on Kohl's list of explanatory factors was also the most stark. 'The policy of European integration is in reality a question of war and peace in the 21st century', he said, echoing the view of his old ally, François Mitterrand, that 'nationalism is war'. Kohl continued: 'We have no desire to return to the nation state of old. It cannot solve the great problems of the 21st century. Nationalism has brought great suffering to our continent – just think of the first 50 years of this century.' From a German chancellor, this is perhaps bolder than it would be coming from a Belgian, Dutchman or Frenchman, but it reflects a consensus view. 'The Schuman plan for the creation of the ECSC (the coal and steel community) saw Franco-German reconciliation as the keystone of a new European order and explicitly sought to create conditions that would make any future war not only improbable, but impossible', writes Dr Klaus-Dieter Borchardt in the Commission publication 'European Integration'. 'The Community and the Union have succeeded in making that ideal a reality. Military conflict between the member states is quite unthinkable today.' Or consider this from Donald Sassoon, in an Institute for Public Policy Research paper, 'Social Democracy at the Heart of Europe': 'German political stability is now one of our best guarantees for lasting peace. She is now united. The German question has been finally resolved. This is the great European and international diplomatic masterpiece of the second half of the 20th century' (p. 47). Not everyone was so sanguine about the idea of a unified Germany. Margaret Thatcher, coming to the end of her period as British prime minister when the two parts of Germany were united, attempted to resist it, referring to 'bitter memories of the past', and adding: 'You cannot just ignore the history of this century as if it did not happen.' Briefly, she appeared to have persuaded Mitterrand of the need for similar caution – playing on the old adage that France liked Germany so much she was glad there were two of them – but this was always an unlikely alliance, and the more powerful pull of the Franco-German axis exerted itself.

Kohl's central point was that it is not enough for Europe to rest on its laurels. To keep the forces of nationalism at bay, including those in his own country, the integration process must go on. It is not enough for Europe to be a relatively tightly knit trading bloc, or to co-operate in a whole series of other arrangements. The status quo is not enough. The bicycle theory applies, and Europe must press ahead with ever closer union or risk falling off. There are new countries to integrate, and nationalism remains, indeed has increased. Kohl's 'nation states of old' have not been eliminated.

European tribalism

In September 1991, after months of rumbling tension, Serb forces launched a full-scale offensive against the breakaway Yugoslav republic of Croatia. This was not the comparatively bloodless displacement of old regimes and structures that had characterised the former communist countries of eastern Europe. It was the beginning of an old-style military conflict which was to last five years and which had its bloodiest incarnation in Bosnia-Herzegovina. Yugoslavia, an unhappy alliance of six republics which concealed, largely due to the repressive nature of Tito's long regime, deep tribal rivalries and hatred, broke up in perhaps the worst way imaginable. The war in Yugoslavia was a deep blow to Europe's self-confidence. Yugoslavia's Adriatic resorts were places where western Europeans holidayed, not embattled enclaves subject to savage aerial bombardment. Wartime atrocities – concentration camps, brutal rapes, the torching of villages and the summary execution of their inhabitants – still happened in the world, but many thousands of miles away from Europe. Their return in modern-day Europe was the most powerful and horrific indication that the birthplace of modern civilisation had not expunged from its collective character the ability to inflict the cruellest and most inhuman treatment on its own citizens. In all, about 200,000 people died in the conflict in former Yugoslavia. In Bosnia alone, according to the United Nations High Commissioner for Refugees (UNHCR), 2.4 million people were displaced by the conflict. Of these, 600,000 sought refuge outside the boundaries of the former Yugoslavia, with more than half (320,000) obtaining asylum in Germany, 80,000 in Austria, 57,000 in Sweden, 24,000 in Switzerland and 13,000 in Britain. Apart from the sheer horror of the conflict itself, and Europe's seeming inability to respond effectively, without the eventual leadership of the United States, the fear that the conflict would spread well beyond the boundaries of the former Yugoslavia was a real one. According to Lord Owen, the unsuccessful European negotiator in the conflict from 1992 to 1995:

> The main strategic concern associated with the wars in former Yugoslavia was the fuse line which runs from Sarajevo to the Sandzak Muslims to the Albanians in Kosovo (both within Serbia), to the Albanians in Macedonia, to Albania itself, and then to Greece and to Turkey. This powder keg could have ignited in 1991 and then again in 1992 after the appalling rapidity with which the Serb ethnic cleansing campaign developed in Bosnia-Herzegovina in the spring and summer of that year. Greek–Macedonian disagreements only added to the tension. There was a real risk of Turkey and Greece being on opposite sides in any Balkan war, particularly one which brings the Serbs and Albanians into confrontation. Such a vital war would have affected the vital interests of the EU as well as Nato and the US. (*Balkan Odyssey*, p. 11)

About the only comforting aspect of the war in the former Yugoslavia was that it did not spread in this way. There were, however, three important lessons for the rest of Europe. The first was the weakness of the EU's foreign policy response, the second the continuing potential for devastating tribal conflicts within Europe, and the third the fact that the likelihood of such conflicts is heightened when different peoples are absorbed into artificial unions, as was the case with Yugoslavia.

■ *Dangerous nationalism*

The question of whether tribalism and nationalism is heightened within a more integrated Europe has been widely debated. Peter Lynch, in his *Minority Nationalism and European Integration*, puts forward three different models in which European integration and minority nationalism are, respectively, compatible, incompatible and a third variation, in which European integration and a pooling of defence interests in Nato, supports the continued existence of even very small nation states. Some nationalist movements, as Lynch points out, see their interests enhanced within an integrated Europe which would devolve power to smaller units than some of the existing nation states. The Scottish National Party, for example, supports this view. Others see a concentration of power at the centre as reducing national identities and the power and influence of nation states. Two things are clear. The first, as Keith Middlemas points out, is that the forces of nationalism have increased:

> The Community is at present confronted by several sorts of nationalism in wider Europe, each as likely to prejudice integration as their predecessors were in the 1920s: among political groups, usually on the extreme right, in certain regions, and in an inchoate form among whole publics confused by a search for national identity more unsettling than any which has been experienced in the memory of people younger than ninety. This is the EU's current ideological burden, not class divisions or conflict between rival capitalisms. . . . If there is to be a European common culture, the EU's institutions have to contain these nationalisms in forms which allow them to develop fruitfully but without the sort of conflicts which have erupted in three great waves since the 1890s. (*Orchestrating Europe*, pp. 696–7)

Nationalism has increased alongside the process of deepening European integration. The two are clearly related. Integration, particularly post-Maastricht integration, has aggravated tensions within Europe and increased popular support for the forces of nationalism. Emu is seen, by many, as an integration too far, the sacrifices necessary to achieve it unnecessary.

The second effect is economic. During times of economic adversity and high unemployment, people return to their tribal roots, becoming increasingly resentful of others, particularly immigrants, and increasingly convinced that their ills are inflicted upon them by others. This is how it will be in the 21st century. According to Felipe Fernández-Armesto:

> Europe today is being ground between two vast, slow and apparently contradictory changes: an integrative process, which tends to extend the limits of Europe and the reach of European institutions; and a fissiparous process, which threatens empires and federations with break-up and other states with erosion by devolution. Under the shell of integration and homogenisation, the old historic communities – out of which the familiar Europe of nation-states and modern empires was formed – are being re-fertilised. Some have attained devolution or autonomy; others are calling or fighting for it. The re-fashionings of the Soviet Union and the Yugoslav federation are only the most conspicuous and violent examples of a Europe-wide phenomenon of self-discovery by resurgent peoples. Seen from a distance – or even from the height of some seats of European government – the nation-state is still the cultural unit of which Europe is composed. Yet even after generations of attempts to 'purify' some states by deporting or exterminating minorities in their millions, most so-called 'national' frontiers enclose a variety of highly self-aware historic communities. In some ways, Europe's complexion resembles South Africa's in the last days of apartheid: a well-stirred tribal mixture, imperfectly divisible into maddeningly complex Bantustans. Future constitutional problems in European states could be as daunting as those of South Africa. . . . In eastern Europe, ethnicities are so dangerously mixed that concessions can provoke civil wars. (*The Times Illustrated History of Europe*, pp. 201–2)

Europe's failure to deliver jobs and prosperity for its citizens will fuel nationalist and tribal tensions, while Europe's leaders, pursuing a lofty vision of ever closer union, will be seen as remote and irrelevant. Such tensions will increase to dangerous levels.

■ Emu – damned either way

The role of monetary union will be crucial in this. Future historians are likely to regard Europe's decision to persist with the single currency goal, inflicting a tough fiscal and monetary policy regime on European economies at a time of slow growth and high and rising unemployment (and thus exacerbating these factors) as the riskiest phase of integration. It could work, but there is a good chance it will not. There are two pessimistic models for the future of Emu, both of which would contribute to the apocalyptic scenario for Europe. The first is the model in which monetary union, by removing the ability of countries to ease their way out of economic difficulty by varying the external value of their currency, renders entire regions of Europe uncompetitive. The second is that Emu is exposed as an unrealistic folly, incapable of being sustained even among Europe's core economies, and results in a huge political and economic fissure at the very heart of Europe. Both are sub-sets of this scenario. Let me take them in turn.

■ A euro nightmare

This is how it might be: Emu starts more or less on time and, by 2005, has 14 of the 15 current member states within it. Italy overcomes German objections and is a first-wave member. Spain and Portugal make it within three years, as does Britain, fearful of being left out of another European arrangement at its inception. Sweden and Finland see more advantages to being in than out, particularly when the initial effects of not joining in the first wave are rising bond yields and currency turbulence. Denmark, like Britain, reluctantly abandons its opt-out. Only Greece, as expected, is on the outside, but expressing the confident hope of membership within 10 years. Initially, everything goes well. Having achieved membership with 'one more heave' to meet the convergence criteria, traditional high-inflation economies experience a growth boost with the lower interest rates that Emu participation brings which, in a benign world inflation environment, does little immediate damage to their inflation rates. The follow-through of pre-Emu fiscal policy measures and the re-emergence of growth, at trend rates, within Europe means there is no early pressure on budget deficits in a way that would require the penalty provisions of the stability pact to be invoked. Unemployment is high, 12% for the EU as a whole, but it has stopped rising.

This honeymoon period appears to confound the fears of the Emu sceptics. Then, however, the European economy enters its first post-Emu cyclical downturn, at the same time as the traditional high-inflation members of the currency bloc are running up against growing competitive pressures because, for the first time in the modern era, they are effectively required to keep pace with the Deutschmark, in its new incarnation as the euro. Unemployment rises to 15% on an EU-wide basis, but this disguises huge variations, with rates of 30–40% in parts of Spain, southern Italy and Germany's eastern *Länder*. There are moves to ease such pressure – European finance ministers clash with the European Central Bank over the former's majority wish to make the euro a weaker currency on world markets. But this does not overcome the central problem of larger areas being fundamentally, and increasingly, uncompetitive *within* Europe. And so it goes on. Each cyclical upturn appears to moderate the problem but, crucially, does not significantly reduce unemployment. And in each downturn unemployment ratchets inexorably higher. Emu is seen as irreversible – no country dares risk the turbulence and the inability to service its debt on international markets that dropping out of the system and trying to re-establish a national currency would entail. By the middle of the century some parts of Europe are effectively non-employment regions, with unemployment rates of 50–60% and most of the jobs that remain in place being in the public sector. Migration could, in theory, ease some of these pressures, and may do so. But in a Europe where unemployment is generally high the incentives to move in search of work are limited. And, as Peter Jay has pointed out, this would represent a deeply unsatisfactory prospect for Europe:

> However much money and power the Commission have, it is improbable that they will be able to have any significant impact on the competitiveness imbalance problem which a single currency will pose. This will leave the problem to nature's remedy – the migration of population. It seems hard to believe that the political, economic and social success of Europe, whether one approves or disapproves the objective, will be promoted by

establishing at the heart of its economic functioning a mechanism which depends for equilibrium on the enforced migration, on pain of destitution, of its population in the tens of millions:

- Away from the places to which they are tied by natural affection, by family relationships, by social capital and by individual will.
- Across frontiers of language, culture, historical experience and law.
- To places of which they know little, which they like less and where they are so far from welcome that they are likely on arrival to be violently assaulted.
- If this is the character of monetary union, conceived by politicians who saw it as little more than a trite gesture of nationhood, to go with a blue flag and a jolly anthem, then we can say that it is not in the long-term interests of Europe and very far from being a sensible economic sacrifice even for the sake of a large political goal. Indeed, one may wonder that anyone who professes to hope for the success of political union in Europe could wish to implant in its foundations such an engine of mass destruction. (The Darlington Economics Lecture, November 17, 1995)

■ *Shock treatment*

If this seems like an excessively gloomy view of Europe under Emu, it could, in economic terms, be a lot worse. The above analysis merely assumes a gradual emergence of competitive problems which, over a number of economic cycles, and after a period of half a century or more, results in regions of chronically high unemployment – within a Europe where overall unemployment is high. The crunch could, however, come much sooner than this. The problem of underlying competitive differences, and the emergence of large areas of Europe as economic 'no-go zones', is but one potential Emu danger. The other concerns the different, or asymmetric, response of European economies to external developments, or shocks. The usual example of this is North Sea oil, and the beneficial impact on UK public finances and the balance of payments resulting from a rise in world oil prices, in contrast to the negative impact this would have on other European economies. This is only one of many possible asymmetric shocks, some more damaging and far-reaching, as Stephen King has pointed out:

> Some argue that most of the 'major' asymmetric shocks for Europe have already happened – the collapse of Communism, German unification. But this view is surely naive. There are plenty of potential upsets with important economic – and, particularly, fiscal ramifications. Civil war in Russia would raise the risk of a massive influx of refugees into Germany. A rise in Islamic fundamentalism in North Africa could lead to a surge of refugees into France, Spain and Italy. France or the UK might be forced to defend territories outside Europe, implying a one-off surge in military spending. Italy or Belgium could split in two. Parts of the Netherlands could be destroyed via a tidal wave from the North Sea. A nuclear reactor accident could, potentially, wipe out thousands of square miles of one particular country. A sharp rise in oil prices would have a significant differential effect on the UK. An exchange rate shift would not necessarily be the most appropriate response in all of these circumstances. However, the possibility of asymmetric shocks does suggest that exchange rate shifts can still serve a useful purpose. In their absence, other mechanisms will be required. And here, serious problems arise.
> (*Emu, Four Endings and a Funeral*, p. 50)

We come back to a familiar problem, that of the likely need for massive resource transfers within Europe once Emu is in operation, and the near impossibility, under present arrangements, of providing them. Thus, Europe's uncompetitive regions, of which there will be many, will fester and decline, forced to accept the loss of their best talent to other areas, unable to attract investment and dependent upon tiny handouts from Community regional and cohesion funds. If some countries were notably successful within Emu, of course, some of this could change. In those circumstances there might be spare resources to direct to the permanently depressed parts of Europe. This is not, however, the expectation under this scenario. Even the more successful Emu countries, such as Germany and the Netherlands, will by past standards achieve only weak growth and high unemployment. If there is little amelioration in the form of resource transfers, anger and resentment at the perceived injustices of a system that condemns large parts of Europe to economic misery will come out in other ways – against the central bank in Frankfurt, against the politicians, and against other countries, and people within their own countries. As Bernard Connolly, a former Commission official, in a bloodcurdling footnote in his *The Rotten Heart of Europe*, put it:

> The analogy between present circumstances in Europe and those in 1940 should not be overplayed. Kohl, Mitterrand, Delors and their supporters and successors do not *intend* the abominable, pagan barbarism of Nazism; they are not threatening recalcitrant countries with military annihilation; they do not intend to unleash racial pogroms or establish death camps. But their ambitions, if realised, would create the conditions of economic decline, political illegitimacy and resentment among 'regions' in Europe in which xenophobic, as opposed to liberal, nationalism would flourish, and military superpower status would, as in Wilhelmine Germany, produce a temptation to engage in 'adventurism' on the world stage as a distraction from intractable domestic problems. Three years ago, who would have dreamt that the world would again be confronted with pictures from Europe of emaciated, broken men staring numbly out from behind the barbed wire of a concentration camp? Bosnia should be a dreadful warning to all those who want to destroy the political structures in Western Europe that have kept its countries in peace, friendship and prosperity for half a century. (p. 395)

Permanent mass unemployment will be a powerful and dangerous cocktail, a 21st-century parallel to the 1920s and 1930s. The analogy with the rise of Hitler is, however, less appropriate than that of the rise of angry nationalism and powerful regionalism across a range of countries. Nationalism has become a powerful force in the Emu 'phoney war' of the 1990s. When the real conflict begins, it will have increasingly violent expression. In the latter part of the 20th century, western Europe watched, fascinated, as unpopular regimes in eastern Europe, in thrall to a greater external power, were overthrown by their people. Under this scenario, this will be the fate of some western European governments in the 21st century.

▪ Splitting the axis

If one apocalyptic Emu scenario has its roots in the attempt, which ultimately proves misguided, to apply a single monetary regime to economically divergent economies, another would, if anything, be more dramatic in its effects. It is not that long since analysts seriously questioned whether France would be in the first wave of monetary union, seeing the pioneering members as a small, tightly knit, German bloc, of perhaps Germany itself, the Benelux countries and Austria. Latterly, of course, this has come to be seen as impossible. In the EU all members are equal but some are more equal than others. Thus, while it is regarded as feasible for Emu to go ahead without Italy (although Italy would disagree), or for that matter Spain or Britain (the two other largest population member states), a single currency without France would be a non-starter. There has even, as discussed in an earlier chapter, been some discussion about France and Germany alone forming a monetary union.

So determined has France been to participate – without the *franc fort* policy it is highly unlikely that there would have been a serious drive towards Emu at the time it occurred – that the question of the sustainability of the French economy's position within the single currency has been a secondary one. It is, however, a legitimate question. The *franc fort* policy has been in place for little more than 10 years, if one dates it to the January 1987 ERM realignment, and wobbled alarmingly, to the point of crumbling completely, in the 1992–3 ERM crisis. The economic convergence between France and Germany that has occurred in recent years has, with the exception of inflation, been largely the result of a deterioration in German performance, rather than an improvement in that of France. Thus, German unemployment has risen to approach already high French levels. The French budget deficit has been on a downward trajectory in the approach to Emu, partly due to artificial measures such as the one-off payment to the government from the France Telecom pension fund. Prior to unification, German per capita GDP, on a purchasing power parity basis, was around 20% higher than in France, with a similar gap in economy-wide productivity. Unification has been a great leveller for Germany, dragging down the country's economic performance so that it is far closer to that of France. This may, however, only be a temporary phenomenon. Fundamentally, Germany is a lower-inflation, stronger-currency economy than France, historically, has been. The French franc left the snake, the ERM's predecessor, in January 1974, rejoined in July 1975 and then left again permanently in March 1976. In the first eight years of the ERM's existence, from March 1979 to January 1987, the franc was effectively devalued six times against the Deutschmark. The adoption of wide, 15% ERM bands in August 1993 provided for a temporary devaluation of the franc, although its central rate remained unchanged. As a platform upon which to build a permanent absence of exchange-rate adjustment with respect to Germany, this is a very shaky one.

Indeed, for France one disturbing aspect of the present situation is how widespread is the view in the financial markets that there will be crisis, possibly soon after the start of Emu, which puts France's continued participation in it under extreme strain. The ingredients are well-known – monetary union locks the French economy into slow growth and high unemployment, while at the same time requiring deep budget cuts to escape from fines under the stability pact. The full force of the power of organised labour in France is brought to bear against Emu, forcing the government into a corner from which the choice is to stay with the single currency, negotiate 'softer' arrangements for the policing of monetary union, or drop out altogether. Part of the reason for scepticism arises from a study of the history, but there was powerful supporting evidence in the attempt by the French government to politicise, and therefore soften, the arrangements for policing Emu in the run-up to the Dublin European Council in December 1996. So what might happen?

■ *The crash*

David Lascelles, of the Centre for the Study of Financial Innovation, graphically and entertainingly sets out such a scenario in his paper 'The Crash of 2003 – An Emu Fairy Tale', which, despite its title, raises possibilities that should be taken extremely seriously. In this, Emu starts conventionally enough, with Germany, France, Austria, the Benelux countries and Ireland as the first-wave countries moving forward on January 1, 1999. Italy and Spain join a year later, but only after speculative attacks on the lira and peseta have dragged down their entry levels into Emu. Just two years after the start date, however, the problems, and the signs of economic divergence between France and Germany, particularly on fiscal policy, begin to mount. With France's difficulties exacerbated by the exchange-rate advantages of Italian and Spanish industry, unemployment rises to 15% and, according to Lascelles, sketching out an imaginary contemporaneous report:

> The combination of rising joblessness and ECB (European Central Bank)-mandated austerity led to a sharp tightening of political tension in France. Two years after the launch of Emu, Alain Madelin (who had replaced Juppé after the 1998 elections) was forced to admit that fiscal adjustment to the single currency would be 'a long and hard road'. In an ill-judged TV interview in September 2000, he raised the possibility of an income tax increase to square the budget. This unleashed the first of a string of violent demonstrations by students, the unions and the unemployed, fomented by the increasingly powerful voice of Jean-Marie Le Pen, whose *Front National* was making strong gains in the opinion polls. By late 2000, Madelin had himself become as much of a political liability as Juppé had been, and Chirac was forced to dismiss him. In his place, and with evident reluctance, he appointed the populist Philippe Séguin. Notwithstanding his avowal of the Gaullist party line on Emu, everyone in France remembered that Séguin had been an open Eurosceptic in the mid-1990s. There was, therefore, intense speculation in Paris that he might reverse policy on what was seen as ECB-imposed austerity. (p. 17)

It gets worse. Séguin attempts to seek approval to issue dollar-denominated French government bonds to ease the economy out of the Emu straitjacket but the plan is vetoed by other members of the European Council. Chirac, in a desperate attempt to seek re-election in 2002, calls for a formal end to the stability pact, a rewriting of the ECB's mandate to emphasise its duty to promote growth and an emergency EU import tariff of 10%, the proceeds to be used to finance job creation schemes. Edmund Stoiber, successor to Helmut Kohl as German chancellor, initially appears sympathetic to the French scheme, but eventually roundly rejects it. France faces its first fines under the stability pact. With tensions between France and Germany out in the open and the markets sensing the imminent collapse of Emu, the European Commission proposes the creation of a European Treasury to take over the existing debt of member states, issue new debt on behalf of member states and manage revenues for the purposes of funding the debt. The new Treasury would be given the power to set European-wide taxes. The Commission's proposal comes up for discussion at a crisis summit in January 2003. Lascelles takes up the story:

> As expected, Stoiber demurred. In a clear statement of Germany's opposition to the plan, he said he was unable – politically, constitutionally and as a freedom-loving German – to support what amounted to a surrender of economic control. The Treasury, he said, would be a device which, 'far from strengthening the European Union, would surely destroy it'. Although he attacked the plan on the grounds that it would infringe sovereignty, distort the EU economy, and encourage fiscal irresponsibility, the true basis of his opposition was glaringly obvious: it would turn the German taxpayer into the underwriter of other Emu countries' debts. Stoiber's powerful outburst, untempered by any conciliatory reference to the need for unity, left the meeting stunned. After several minutes silence, President Chirac quietly gathered up his papers and walked out of the room, followed by his retinue. He returned directly to Paris where he and Séguin summoned an emergency meeting of the Cabinet. Here the decision was taken to leave Emu and to resume the issuance of a national French franc. The necessary legislation was prepared overnight and presented to the National Assembly the following morning, where it passed without opposition. Within 48 hours, a proclamation was issued on the terms for exchanging euros back into francs. Bank balances would be automatically converted into francs at midnight on December 31, 2003. (pp. 23–4)

Is it possible, or just a fairy tale? It is certainly possible, not necessarily in the way that Lascelles sets out, although his scenario is eerily plausible, and not necessarily on his timetable, although if such a crisis is to occur, the further into Emu it happens the more difficulties it would create, not least in re-establishing one or more national currencies. The combination of slow growth, rising unemployment and the need for fiscal retrenchment is, however, one which would expose dangerous tensions even within Europe's core in which, for a variety of reasons, France would be the first to reach breaking-point. It might happen within Emu's first five years. It might take 10 or 20. But in these circumstances there is a very good chance that it would happen.

■ Divided and unstable

What would be the consequences for Europe of a Franco-German split of this type, of France being effectively expelled from the core? It would be preceded, and followed, by violent protest in France, much of it directed towards Germany. It would reawaken fears in France about German domination. It would kill the Single Market, as France imposed import controls in an attempt to provide protection for its battered industry, and reimposed border controls. It would represent the severest blow to the Franco-German bargain that has been the basis for European integration since the early 1950s, much more serious than de Gaulle's 'empty chair' policy or the snake and ERM episodes, and could mark the effective end of the EU as a functioning body. Rival armies probably would not cross the Rhine but, at the very least, the diplomatic war between France and Germany would be a long one. Ultimately, such a fissure would very likely herald the splitting of Europe along north–south lines, with, on one side, a group of hard-currency, predominantly industrial countries and, on the other, the southern, more agricultural, mainly Mediterranean states, envious of the greater prosperity of their former partners to the north, putting into practice their natural inclination towards protectionism and a breeding-ground for violent nationalist and regionalist groups.

France, effectively kicked out of Emu, would storm off in a huff. But what of Germany, the other half of the partnership? Kohl, in his Leuven speech, had in mind the role of European integration, over a 50-year period, as an agent for peace in Europe. Who, however, has been the main 20th-century aggressor in Europe? Germany's EU policy brings to mind an image of a man with a past full of serious wrongdoing begging to be shackled for the good of himself and others. Freed from such constraints, and easily the dominant nation within Europe, both in terms of population and economic strength, could Germany become dangerous again? Under the present political leadership, certainly not. But think of the reaction of the German people when they learn that they were forced to give up the Deutschmark in the cause of a failed European venture. Consider the return of racism and aggressive nationalism in the post-unification period. And combine that with high unemployment and struggling German export industries as the protectionist shutters go up again all over Europe. Late 20th-century German tolerance would be tested to the extreme in the 21st century. And it could easily fail.

■ Rough neighbours

If the outlook within Europe is for economic failure, political division and, at the very least, localised uprisings and small wars, it might be thought that things could not get any worse. In the preceding chapters various economic scenarios for the world outside Europe have been discussed, some of which plainly have political consequences, but mainly in terms of Europe's influence on the world stage. What happens, however, if alongside a shift of economic power away from Europe, there is a related tilting of the geopolitical axis in a way that becomes, not merely economically painful for Europe, but threatening in other ways?

The notion that the world economy is run by the Group of Seven, four of whose members (Germany, France, Britain and Italy) are European, the other three being the United States, Canada and Japan, will become increasingly outdated as the world moves through the 21st century. In place of this workable late 20th century co-operation will come a dangerous rivalry of conflicting interests. Stability will be replaced by global instability, emanating from Russia, a Chinese-dominated Far East, and the re-emergence of Islam as a global economic force. The 1996 report of the Chatham House Forum, operating under the auspices of the Royal Institute of International Affairs, developed such a global scenario, and named it 'Rough Neighbours'. Thus, within 20 years:

> Unemployment drifts towards an average of 15% of the workforce across the industrialised world. As many as four successive generations in some families may never have worked. Those most affected are the groups who have the weakest skills and the lowest level of linkage into anything beyond everyday

life. Their interests may be dissected by age, ethnicity, gender and culture. Their ability to generate a coherent response is, therefore, low. Political intentions are not always constructive, however, and the situation continues to worsen. Failing industries call for protection. Populist politicians seek measures which are as dramatic as they are unlikely to solve the fundamental issues. The other regions of the world are not standing still, although their absolute growth is somewhat slower than has been the case in recent history. They are, however, converging faster on the industrialised world than ever before. The Asian seaboard integrates around a Chinese centre of weight. This grouping becomes increasingly dominated by Chinese power. The export-oriented members of it act as China's agencies in the outside world. The rejectionist states see the apparently chronic decline of the West as the confirmation of their deepest intuitions. They seek integration and collaboration among themselves, each in their own way. Predatory nations take advantage of the security vacuum and the poor nations, in particular, are confronted with a difficult choice between weak growth and dependency on hard task-masters. (The 1996 Chatham House Forum Report, pp. 127–8)

As set out by the Chatham House Forum, the whole of the industrialised world is confronted, and weakened, by the emergence of these rough neighbours. There is reason to believe, however, that Europe would be more seriously affected than North America. Japan would have the choice between remaining part of the 'Western' industrialised world, or seeking an accommodation with the Chinese-led power bloc in its own region. For Europe there would be no such choice. One consequence of the emergence of new, and potentially unstable, power blocs in other regions, some of them on Europe's doorstep, would be the need for higher levels of defence spending. Added to the other public expenditure pressures facing most European countries, many of them emanating from the consequences of ageing populations, the effect would be to raise already high and rising levels of taxation to an economically destructive level. The United States, beginning from a position of lower taxation and already-high defence spending, would be less exposed.

Capitalist reversal

The striking feature of this 21st-century view of a struggling European economy, of new and aggressive players on the world stage, and of fiercely competing religions and cultures, will be that it is diametrically opposed to the 'end of history', triumph of capitalism view of global development, so popular after the collapse of Communism in the eastern bloc. The new powers in the world economy may borrow from western capitalism, they may be dependent upon it, at least initially, for know-how and capital and joint ventures. Ultimately, however, their vision will be different. When Mao led China, the people were bombarded with images and accounts of western decline, of the poverty and decadence of capitalist societies. In eastern Europe for many years, governments successfully persuaded their populations that their lifestyle was superior to that enjoyed in the west, while simultaneously conveying to the west the impression that, behind the iron curtain, strong, competitive economies were thriving.

In the 21st century, such deceptions may be unnecessary. When Europe is racked by mass unemployment and internal conflict, Japan has become a poor Asian relation to China and America is working desperately to turn the new, eastern-dominated world economic environment to its advantage, the western capitalist model will begin to look like a spent force. According to Professor Samuel Huntington of Harvard:

> The west is and will remain for years to come the most powerful civilisation. Yet its power relative to other civilisations is declining. As the west attempts to assert its values and to protect its interests, non-western societies face a choice. Some attempt to emulate the west, others – especially Confucian and Islamic societies – attempt to expand their own economic and military power to resist and to 'balance' the west. A central axis of post cold war politics is the interaction of western power and culture with the power and culture of non-western civilisations. ('The West and the Rest', *Prospect*, February 1997, p. 37)

With the exception of Hong Kong, the successful East Asian economies have emphasised that their development has been due, not to blind adherence to the western capitalist model but to the characteristics and strengths of their own culture. Their modernisation has occurred in tandem with a preservation of Asian values, of a non-western way of doing things. Mahathir Mohamad, the Malaysian prime minister, told European heads of government in 1996: 'European values are European values; Asian values are universal values.' So it will be for China and India.

For Europe too, the model of economic liberalism and free trade which has come, sometimes reluctantly, to be adopted as the standard for 20th-century economic prosperity will come to be increasingly questioned in an era where it is seen to be manifestly failing to deliver that progress. As Lester Thurow puts it:

> The danger is not that capitalism will implode as communism did. Without a viable competitor to which people can rush if they are disappointed with how capitalism is treating them, capitalism cannot self-destruct. Pharaonic, Roman, medieval, and mandarin economies also had no competitors and they simply stagnated for centuries before they finally disappeared. Stagnation, not collapse, is the danger. (*The Future of Capitalism*, p. 325)

Despite describing himself as 'the last Euro-optimist on the globe', Thurow sees Europe as highly vulnerable unless there is fundamental change in the continent's ability to foster entrepreneurship, particularly dynamic medium-sized firms, in regulatory intrusion, and in increasingly burdensome welfare commitments. In short, the 'Rhine model' needs to be scrapped. But the conditions in which Europe could so liberate itself will not be present in this scenario. Instead, Europe will be caught in a vicious circle, where rising unemployment and deep-seated social discontent prevent governments from pushing through necessary reforms, and this, in turn, exacerbates these problems. It is the road to nowhere.

If the perceived failure of capitalism will not, as Thurow says, necessarily mean a revival of communism, in eastern Europe, where its grip is more recent, that may occur. It does mean, however, a probable attempt to define and develop a kind of European version of Asian values, with greater emphasis on national, rather than European culture, a questioning and a reversal of the ethos of free trade, both within Europe and between Europe and other regions, and a backlash against big multinational corporations. Europe, confused and uncertain, will turn in on itself; the idea of the continent as an outward, expansive free trading bloc will come to be seen as a late 20th-century fantasy, the EU as a victim of its own unrealistic ambition

Dirty Europe

The loss of hegemony for the western capitalist model will have another consequence. The standard model of industrial development is one where countries go through a 'dirty' phase, often lasting for many decades. The description by Friedrich Engels of Victorian Manchester, in *The Condition of the Working Class in England in 1844*, is a classic of its kind:

> The view from this bridge – mercifully concealed from smaller mortals by a parapet as high as a man – is quite characteristic of the entire district. At the bottom the Irk flows, or rather stagnates. It is a narrow, coal-black, stinking river full of filth and garbage which it deposits on the lower-lying bank. In dry weather, an extended series of the most revolting blackish green pools of slime remain standing on this bank, out of whose depths bubbles of miasmatic gases constantly rise and give forth a stench that is unbearable even on the bridge forty or fifty feet above the level of the water. (1973 edition, p. 81)

Concern for the environment can thus be seen as the equivalent of a luxury good, something that consumers demand and expect as prosperity increases. Progress towards this end can be slow, particularly when the worst-affected industrial areas are some distance away from the most prosperous markets. It is, however, a relationship that holds pretty well. It is no accident that the two most recent periods of greatest concern for the environment, 1972–3 and the late 1980s, came during powerful booms for the western economies.

Such progress can, however, be reversed. The economies of eastern Europe initially experienced some 'luxury good' environmentalism but, during nearly half a century of economic failure under communist rule, much of it was reversed. When the centrally planned economies were liberated after the demolition of the Berlin Wall one of the biggest shocks, not least to western firms seeking to take over existing industrial sites, was the degree of environmental degradation that was encountered. In chemicals, steel and a range of other process industries, economic survival had only been achieved – and then often with huge subsidies – at the cost of environmental vandalism. Much of the industry of eastern Europe was associated with outpourings of dangerous pollutants and irreversible land contamination. Nearly a century and a half after Engels wrote, the conditions he described still prevailed across large areas of the European continent.

Nor should eastern Europe be thought of as a special case. For many of the industrialising countries, and notably the emerging giants of China and India, western attempts to insist that they skip the 'dirty phase' of industrial development, and move straight to the emission and other standards of the mature economies, are falling on deaf, and ultimately resentful, ears. Such insistence is seen as an attempt to block their industrial progress. Thus, John Naisbitt, in *Megatrends Asia*:

> No one can turn back the clock, but many wish to slow down the rate of development long enough to examine the impact of growth on people and on the environment. In three years, China's economy expanded 40%. Steel production has helped China maintain that phenomenal growth rate. But sulphur dioxide emissions from the coal-fired blast furnaces have made Beijing one of the world's most polluted cities. Pollution is evident in Hong Kong, Bangkok, Manila and in India's largest cities. In Indonesia, logging for paper and pulp has stripped the nation of its trees with no organised plan for reforestation. Major infrastructure projects like China's Three Gorges Dam will uproot tens of thousands of peasants. Many will drift to urban areas where there is little work for the unskilled and nowhere to live. (p. 139)

In a world where the old industrial countries are dominant and prosperous, it may be possible for them to insist on high environmental standards for the emerging economies. Even then it is a tall order. But what happens when large areas of the old industrialised world, and most notably Europe, are themselves experiencing economic stagnation or decline? The 'luxury good' driving force for improving environmental standards, both within Europe and beyond it, gets replaced by a more naked desire for economic survival, and jobs, even if this means descending back into dirtiness. Environmental standards converge, not around those of the mature industrial countries with their caring consumers of the late 20th century, but rather in terms of convergence towards the lowest common denominator of the emerging industrial economies. As the Chatham House Forum puts it:

> The chief issue of inter-regional pollution is that of agreement across boundaries. If, for example, the emissions in one country affect the health of another, as was abundantly the case during and immediately after the fall of the Soviet Union, then this becomes a matter for negotiated settlement. One key issue is that of embodied pollutants. European refineries are laboriously being converted to meet emission and product standards. This will be hugely costly: between Ecu30 and 50 billion, a sum that has to be recovered from the electorate which ordered this improvement, in the shape of higher prices. Imported refined goods may have to meet product standards but could have been made with the crudest and most pollutive technology imaginable. It can become impossible to recover the costs associated with pollution abatement if the competition does not have to shoulder these costs. ('Unsettled Times', p. 103)

Europe's rivers become dirtier and incapable of supporting living things, as do Europe's seas and beaches. The cities become, once more, choking, inhospitable places, a serious threat to human health. Chest diseases multiply. Life expectancy for city-dwellers declines. Even in the country, environmentally damaging methods of super-intensive agricultural production come to dominate. Europe goes backwards.

Loose nukes

On April 28, 1986, the world's worst nuclear disaster occurred at Chernobyl, 80 km north of Kiev, causing devastation in the surrounding area and spreading nuclear radiation across northern Europe, with effects that continue to this day. The explosion of Chernobyl's Block Four reactor sent, on a conservative estimate, 100 times more radiation into the atmosphere than the atomic bomb dropped by the Americans on Hiroshima in 1945. The fall-out of radioactive caesium-137 and strontium-90 was heaviest on farmland in the Ukraine, Belarus and Russia, but its spread reached across Lithuania, Latvia, Poland, Sweden, Norway and Britain – the hills of Snowdonia in Wales were contaminated by a nuclear explosion which took place in the heart of what was then the Soviet Union. In most cases it will take until well into the 22nd century before the land is clear of contamination. More than 10 years later, in 1997, the wrangling continued over western aid to shut down Chernobyl.

No one knows whether Chernobyl was a one-off, or a reflection of more fundamental problems stretching across the former Soviet Union and the old eastern bloc countries. After all, America had a serious nuclear accident at Three Mile Island in 1979, and Britain has had accidents at Windscale (Sellafield) and Dounreay. Before Chernobyl, there had been serious accidents at Chelyabinsk in Russia and, almost certainly, others kept secret from the west. Perhaps accidents, and the occasional disaster, are in the nature of the industry, wherever it is located.

There are, however, particular worries about the old Soviet bloc. We know that environmental standards there were well below those that had come to be accepted as the norm in the west. It is reasonable to extend this to questions of nuclear safety and to the handling of radioactive material. In the eastern part of unified Germany, near the Czech border, the Zwickauer Mulde valley is known for the mining of silver, cobalt, bismuth and nickel. It is also known for the giant slag heaps that dominate the landscape and overshadow the homes of the miners. The area is also, however, rich in uranium and the slag heaps are highly radioactive, with the high incidence of cancers giving it the name Death Valley in the German press. Despite a massive clean-up programme financed by Bonn, the area remains heavily contaminated. The Zwickauer Mulde valley is perhaps fortunate – unification has produced the beginnings of a solution to its problems. Other parts of the former Soviet bloc are less fortunate. In countries hit by economic adversity safety will be compromised. The prospect of another Chernobyl, perhaps a more serious one, right on Europe's doorstep, is a real one.

The risks of disaster from peaceful-use nuclear technology are but one aspect of the problem. Those arising from nuclear weapons are potentially more serious. In 1995, Russia had 726 inter-continental nuclear missiles, 95 nuclear bombers and 45 nuclear submarines, making it still the world's second nuclear power after America, with a quarter of its budget spent on defence. The west, say Richard Layard and John Parker in *The Coming Russian Boom*, has a vested interest in the success of Russian economic reform because 'the failure of Russian reform would raise the prospect of instability in a nuclear country, with all that implies for Russia's neighbours, near neighbours and the world'. Successful reform is, however, far from guaranteed, still less political stability, as Layard and Parker point out:

> The chief threat of this kind comes at present from Vladimir Zhironovsky, but new threats could arise over the next decade. The most dangerous moment is not necessarily at the depth of recession. As expectations begin to rise, the danger of political unrest often increases. A series of bad experiences in the 'near abroad' could create a very nasty climate in Russia – with refugees fleeing to Russia while at the same time the west condemns Russian aggression. Nationalism and anti-Semitism are never far below the surface, and one can never rule out a period of rule by a fascist populist. (p. 334)

The cold war provided a reasonable degree of security, although it did not always seem so at the time, because the Soviet response was relatively predictable. It is in the unpredictability of the post cold war situation – nuclear weapons in the hands of dangerously unstable warlords – that the risk arises in the 21st century. In November 1995, as Jeremy Hall records in his book *Real Lives, Half Lives*, the Chechen rebel Shamil Basayev told alarmed Russian television viewers that he had placed a 'hot' package in the centre of Moscow. A package of caesium-137 was duly discovered in a park in eastern Moscow. Basayev said that his next target would be a nuclear power station. According to Hall:

> Up to now the world has been lucky to escape the wrath of a nuclear terrorist. Yet it was not only in Russia that Basayev's action unlocked a deep-rooted fear. Having witnessed the Oklahoma bombing and the sarin-gas attacks on the Tokyo subway, nobody can underestimate the hypothetical danger posed by a political activist or religious fanatic or madman obtaining a nuclear device or perhaps highly radioactive material. The rudiments of atom-bomb making have been widely known for decades. Indeed any physics graduate, with the right ingredients and technology, would be able to assemble a crude but lethal

prototype. In the 1960s a book was even published about how to build the bomb. The problem, however, is getting hold of the necessary fissile materials. And for this reason the nuclear industry continues to be the most regulated and security-conscious in the world. Nevertheless, the success or failure of any regulatory system depends upon its safeguards, its checks and balances, being properly maintained. In recent years the nuclear equilibrium has been upset by miscellaneous arms reduction treaties and hectic decommissioning, not to mention economic and political chaos following the break-up of the former Soviet Union. Keeping tabs on fissile material nowadays is proving to be difficult. (pp. 189–90)

The threat of 'loose nukes' or of nuclear accidents is not confined to Europe. Europe, however, was the focus of the cold war and thus has an unusual concentration of nuclear firepower within its borders or in the near vicinity. Many nuclear power plants in Europe – east and west – are old but energy needs, combined with a lack of available finance for building new plants, mean that they cannot be phased out. The one 21st-century certainty is that there will be nuclear accidents affecting Europe. How bad they will be, whether they will be deliberate terrorist acts, or whether they will involve the misuse of nuclear weapons is impossible to say. The combination of deep economic difficulties and the presence of so much dangerous material could, however, be devastating.

▪ *The end of politics*

In this scenario, conventional politics will not survive. The democratic process will be destroyed by the forces first of nationalism and then of tribalism. Local leaders will emerge, backed by violence, and wrest power from national politicians. City states will reappear. The old left–right distinctions will matter less than the power of individual despots and warlords. This may seem fanciful in today's mature western European democracies but it will happen within Europe, starting with the newer democracies and spreading. In this apocalyptic environment, conventional politics will prove to be a luxury that few can afford.

▪ Business apocalypse

Just as conventional politics will gradually cease to exist in the Europe of the apocalypse, so will conventional business. The normal parameters of business, tax, markets, means of payment, convertible currencies, will disappear as Europe splinters. The black market will become the market – think of Russia after the collapse of communism. The more tribalistic Europe becomes, the more vulnerable business will be to asset seizures and other, unpredictable losses. Like the worst Third World countries, much of Europe will become a no-go area for business.

▪ Apocalypse when?

This scenario has sketched out a grim vision of Europe's future, in which economic adversity provides the breeding ground for conflicts, certainly minor, possibly major, within and between European nations. Ugly nationalism will become the dominant force within Europe. It is a future in which Europe's decline leaves it vulnerable to external threats and to the exertion, by other cultures, of their hegemony over a once-dominant region of the world. In some respects, Europe will take on Third World characteristics, with widespread poverty and deprivation, and an obsession with eking out economic growth at any costs taking precedence over the environment and other late 20th-century concerns. At its most apocalyptic, it is the devastation of nuclear accident, or nuclear weapons getting into the wrong hands and being used. Few would have predicted at the end of the 19th century the depths to which Europe would sink in the following 50 years. By various means, such depths could be plumbed again in the 21st century.

▪ Fifty years on

Looking across their continent in the middle of the 21st century, Europeans wonder how things could possibly have gone so badly wrong. Instead of a unified Europe, Europe is characterised by conflicting power factions, including states within states. The grand European alliance of the second half of the 20th century, the Franco-German axis, has become a footnote in history, replaced by the new reality of mutual distrust between two neighbours, the peoples of which dislike and resent the other intensely. Germany is once more attempting to claim back border territory from France. Europe in 2050 is like the scrapyard of an abandoned industrial town, heavily polluted, no longer of any economic relevance and dangerous. Small wars have become a commonplace in Europe, with the fear of 'the big one' ever present. The Swiss, scoffed at for their obsession with nuclear shelters even after the end of the cold war, are seen to have been wise in their foresight. As Europeans look to the second half of the 21st century, they know that anything can happen, most of it bad.

Probabilities

The one certainty about the future is that it will throw up surprises and shocks – good and bad – of the kind that it is impossible to envisage looking forward. In Europe in, say, 1980, few could have envisaged the counter-revolution that was to sweep through eastern Europe before the decade was out. In the cheap oil era of the 1950s and 1960s, the prospect of producer power exerting its influence over world oil prices, to the considerable detriment of the industrialised countries in the 1970s and early 1980s, seemed remote. Change happens with a suddenness that is impossible to predict. Those who predict sudden and dramatic change not only risk being proved entirely wrong but are likely to be accused of scaremongering or excessive optimism. The scenarios set out in this book are thus presented with due humility, in the knowledge that none of them is likely to turn out exactly right. This is not because the broad thrust of one of them will not turn out to be on the right lines – it probably will. The fault of the scenarios is most likely to be that they mainly assume gradual change, whereas real-world change is often much more sudden. With that health warning in place, let us look at some probabilities.

■ *Scenario 1: The renaissance – probability 10%*

The idea of a powerful European economic comeback, built on the coming to fruition of the Single Market, and the removal of the 'final barrier to trade' – transactions costs and exchange rate volatility – with the single currency, is an appealing one and has its adherents, not least in the European Commission. Certainly it is possible to see these effects as beneficial, not least if the start of Emu coincides with a

European cyclical upturn, which eases the pressure for further action to reduce budget deficits. An initial period of strong growth, if it eased the passage of policies designed to improve Europe's structural performance, essential if a faster rate of trend growth is to be maintained in the future, would be highly beneficial, and begin to correct the scourges of modern Europe: persistently high unemployment and a feeble rate of job creation. A Europe with a properly functioning single currency and Single Market would be a positive, outgoing continent, better able to absorb new EU entrants from eastern Europe and, in turn, for the entry of these countries and their economic rehabilitation to bring substantial benefits for both eastern and western Europe. A confident, strong, growing Europe could also, as in the original Renaissance, become associated with cultural revival and technological advance – the way of the future for mature economies.

Standing back a little from these hopes, however, it is necessary to be realistic. The Single Market and single currency (assuming beneficial effects from both) are developments in the degree of, respectively, intra-European free trade and European monetary co-operation. Emu represents more of a sea change than the Single Market but neither are likely to presage a benign revolution for Europe's economies. Mature economic groupings may be able to grow a little faster, over time, under the right circumstances. They are unlikely, sadly, to be able virtually to double their trend growth rate to 3.5–4%. Economies, like people, tend towards steadiness – slower rates of sustainable growth – as they mature. If Europe's mature industrial countries can maintain a steady growth rate they are doing well. The hope has to be that they do not develop another characteristic of human ageing – unsteadiness and a tendency to stumble. Even with everything conspiring in its favour, the chances of a European economic miracle are slim, the probability attached to it correspondingly low.

■ *Scenario 2: Plus ça change – probability 35%*

Notwithstanding world-changing events like the collapse of the Berlin Wall and the beginnings of the economic liberation of eastern Europe, events in western Europe, and in the EU in particular, have tended to move at a slower pace than those who designed the integration process in the post-war years had hoped. Thus, the Single Market, coming together 40 years after the Treaty of Rome was signed by the Six, is more or less what was intended as the original Common Market. Emu was planned, in detail, in the late 1960s, but in the late 1990s is not yet a reality. Europe is not yet a politically mature grouping, and the relationship between national governments and the supranational institutions not a comfortable one. Real-life events happen quickly but integration occurs only slowly. So it has been in the past, and so it is likely to be in the future. Europe will display that sometimes endearing, sometimes infuriating combination of 'muddling through'.

This is one reason why I give this scenario the highest probability of the five. There will be no brave new world of a fully integrated Europe as we move into the next century. In 30 years, the Commission will probably still be issuing pleas for recalcitrant member states to introduce remaining Single Market measures. Such is the way of Europe. The other appealing aspect of this is that it is based on a much more realistic assessment of Europe's economic prospects. There is no reason, in other words, to expect a European growth miracle, but there are good reasons to believe that some of the factors that have held down European growth in recent times, notably tight German monetary policy in the post-unification period and the tough fiscal measures that have been required, in many countries, to meet the Maastricht criteria, will prove to have been temporary, and not a sign of a permanent slowdown in growth. Add in a small, and gradual, growth boost from the Single Market, the single currency (within which the most important factor may be consolidation around a lower average level of European interest rates) and the development of eastern Europe, and the prospect becomes rather encouraging.

The key thing about this scenario, again an important lesson from history, is that Europe is above all resilient. After both world wars the continent could easily have been written off economically but bounced back. The current position is infinitely better than in either of those two periods. Europeans are resourceful and, when it comes to it, adaptable. 'Sleepwalking to disaster' may seem to many to be Europe's current path, but the very fact that there is awareness of the dangers is likely to prevent disaster from happening. *'Plus ça change'* is perhaps not the most exciting prospect and, as a description, it perhaps does Europe something of an injustice – some favourable change is assumed. It is, however, perfectly attainable.

■ *Scenario 3: Les Etrangers – probability 25%*

Running like a thread through Europe's future is a central question. Some European countries are at a more advanced stage of economic convergence, and preparedness to engage in more intense political integration, than others. The idea of a multi-speed approach to integration, with leaders and followers – the Karl Lamers view, emanating from Germany's Christian Democrats, of a core of countries being willing and able to take the process forward – is now well-established. The alternative, that integration should only proceed at the pace dictated by the country which is only willing, or able, to travel at the slowest speed – and perhaps not travel at all – is unacceptable to many European governments. The image is of a car pulling a caravan on a narrow country road, followed by a convoy of faster vehicles growing increasingly impatient at their inability to overtake. A multi-speed approach is therefore well-established, and is already a reality in the Schengen arrangements, and will almost certainly be a reality when Emu begins its final stage. The question is whether this approach can continue without imposing significant disadvantages, and effective exclusion from the benefits of integration, from those not in the fast lane.

One of the paradoxical arguments put forward by the pro-Emu lobby in Britain is that the British government should enter Emu in the first wave because to delay would be to repeat the error of previous episodes of integration – not joining at the outset and being left with the second-best option of participating on disadvantageous terms later. The same people argue, however, that Emu will be flexible in its operation, capable of taking in new entrants when they meet the conditions for membership, and accommodating them into the framework on exactly the same terms, and with exactly the same influence, as the pioneering group which first embarks on monetary union. Both, I would say, cannot be true, and the former is more likely to be a more accurate assessment of reality than the latter. Emu will further increase the distance between the core – France, Germany, the Benelux countries, Austria and any other countries which can make it into Emu's first wave – and the rest within Europe. This is well understood, and it is one reason why countries such as Italy, Spain and Portugal, for whom a more sensible strategy might be a more leisurely progress towards Emu – not least because this would give them an opportunity to see how it works – are so desperate to get in. There is a catch-22 at the very heart of the Emu question, in that those who do not make it initially may find themselves diverging from the rest – in Italy for example because of sharply rising government bond yields – and unable to do anything about it.

The question, then, is one of degree. The core will secure an advantage, as Europe's low-inflation, stable currency zone, and attract inward investment as a result. They will dominate, even more so than the Bundesbank does now, the setting of European monetary policy. But will this lead to the kind of discrimination against those outside the core, discrimination enough to, for example, make northern Italy split from the south in order to be able to make it into the top tier? The answer is that it could, and has to be taken as a serious possibility. This is not wholly dependent, remember, on Emu. The Lamers view of a core of countries moving ahead and pulling the rest along applies to political integration as well. In reality, this has always been the way of European integration. What may be in prospect now is something more divisive than has occurred to date. Whether or not a Europe of insiders and outsiders is sustainable is another matter. The difficulty for the outsiders may be that there will be nowhere else for them to go.

■ Scenario 4: The dark ages – probability 20%

This is, as I have already noted, the malign version of the *'Plus ça change'* scenario, except in this one, the 'no change' carries forward the trends already evident in the 1990s, and adds in a few other emerging difficulties, notably those arising from ageing populations and more intense competition from China and the other Asian economies. There is a deadly logic about this scenario, which has Europe initially struggling to meet the monetary and fiscal requirements of Emu – which will guarantee that there is no sudden post-Emu liberation for the economies of Europe. Then, just as it seems there might be a light at the end of the tunnel, the consequences of ageing populations come into play, simultaneously slowing economic growth and raising tax burdens. Europe is an old continent in more ways than one and, without early action to ameliorate the economic consequences of this, will suffer for it in the 21st century. There is a logic too about the west-to-east shift in the balance of world economic power and, while Europe has theoretically much to gain from the expansion of world trade triggered by the emerging economies, it is questionable how big that gain will be as long Europe struggles with competitiveness.

Europe has had its dark ages in the 20th century, in two world wars and their aftermaths, and recovered from them. The difference, looking into the 21st century, is that the range of genuine competitor countries, capable of taking the economic baton from Europe and running with it, is much wider. At the same time, 50 years of prosperity have made the people of Europe less willing to make the sacrifices necessary to guarantee a sound basis for economic success in the new millenium. There is barely a consensus on the kind of action needed in Europe, to reform labour markets and welfare provision, let alone firm action plans in place. So why, if many of the trends that could consign Europe into a new dark ages are already in place is this not the favoured scenario? The answer, I think, is that Europe's loss of economic influence, and the pauperisation of her citizens will be more likely to be a very gradual, almost imperceptible process than something more sudden. Of course, over 50 or 70 years the effects of even gradual change become cumulatively very important. By the end of the 21st century, Europe is almost certain to be a relatively poorer region than now – the rise of other parts of the world virtually guarantees that. Whether or not she is absolutely poorer, which would be a much gloomier prognosis given even sluggishly improving living standards, and would be needed if the dark ages scenario is to come true, is more doubtful. Even if this does not happen, relative to the 20th century, the 21st may feel like the dark ages for Europeans.

■ *Scenario 5: The apocalypse – probability 10%*

In my first scenario, a European renaissance is made possible because everything that could go right for Europe, in terms of economics, political unity and developments elsewhere in the world, does so. Because such a favourable combination of circumstances, repeating themselves over and over again through the 21st century, is stretching credibility, I argued that it would be unwise to invest too much hope in it. The apocalypse is, in many respects, the mirror image of the renaissance, in that it assumes many things can go wrong, and keep on going wrong, to drag Europe inexorably towards disaster. For Europe to be prey to so many adverse developments, even over a prolonged period, may seem as unlikely as for everything to keep coming up sunny. There is, however, an important difference between the two scenarios – it takes many events to produce a lasting economic, social and cultural rebirth for Europe but it could take only one to give it an apocalypse.

No one, of course, talks lightly of the possibilities of wars in Europe, even small ones. To speculate on nuclear disaster, environmental catastrophe, widespread racism and permanent mass unemployment is perhaps to indulge in scaremongering. Bad things have happened in Europe before, however, and plenty of them. The ability of struggling European industry to perform according to high environmental standards must be open to question, particularly if the environmental rules are being broken elsewhere – or there are no rules. A similar thing could happen, incidentally, in the treatment of labour, if standards elsewhere in the world are low.

Not to allow for the possibility of, for example, serious wars in Europe in the 21st century would be to adopt far too rosy a view. Europe has had half a century free from major wars but that is no reason for complacency. Economic wars are another matter and can be discussed more dispassionately. The combinations of economic circumstances described in this scenario, with either Emu breaking up in an atmosphere of mutual recrimination, after effectively bankrupting the French economy, or imposing rising unemployment and economic austerity on its members indefinitely, are those where something, eventually, is bound to snap. Protectionism and other weapons of economic warfare would be quickly wheeled out, the idea of the EU as a trading bloc dead in the water. Deeply gloomy though this scenario is, it should not be dismissed out of hand.

Part III

The players

The scenarios set out in Part II have very different implications, both for individual countries in Europe, and for those beyond its shores. They also suggest a range of strategies, both for national governments and for business. The difficulty, of course, is that a strategy that is dependent on one outcome may be wholly inappropriate in the context of one or all of the others. It may be that a scenario that is good for Europe will not be beneficial for all its states, and vice versa. In this chapter, some of these strands are drawn out, beginning in Europe itself.

■ Germany

For Germany, the encouraging aspect of the future is that, despite its economic difficulties of the late 20th century, few see it as anything other than pivotal in Europe in the 21st century. Europe's future is, in very important respects, bound up in the course Germany takes, just as was the case in the past. This book sees a future for Germany that is, at the very least, optimistic in relation to most other countries in Europe, except for the final, apocalyptic scenario. Even in the 'dark ages' for Europe, Germany does better than most, although worse than in the second half of the 20th century.

For Germany, the strategic vision of the late 20th century is clear. It begins with Chancellor Kohl's wholehearted commitment to European integration, embodied in a vision in which German unification is followed by genuine European unification, an achievement which would, arguably, give Kohl a more prominent place in history than Adenauer, Erhard or Bismarck. The difficulty is squaring that vision with the practicalities. The immediate source of tension arises over economic and monetary union. Kohl's vision implies a wide Emu, because the exclusion of a significant number of member states, particularly Italy and the other southern states, let alone new entrants, would raise the chances of a divisive, 'insiders and outsiders', future for Europe. On the other hand, a wide Emu would risk the permanent loss of one source of German comparative advantage, a strong currency, low inflation economy. Germany in a 'soft' euro zone would be a different Germany from the one that, for nearly half a century, has set the standards of price stability for the rest of Europe, if not the world, to follow.

It may be that, although the German people do not yet see it, there is method in Kohl's apparently contradictory 'madness'. The argument goes like this: stern anti-inflationary policies and a strong Deutschmark served Germany well in the post-war period. Latterly, however, the game has changed. The world is now a less inflationary place than it was before, so the loss from any pooling of monetary sovereignty is substantially less than it would have been in the 1960s, 1970s or 1980s. Moreover, German industry appears to have run out of room for manoeuvre in terms of its ability to cope with an ever stronger currency and faces a future in which the only possibility is to locate an increasing proportion of production in other countries. Add to this the fact that, in order to put in place policies to make the German economy more flexible and reduce the burden of state pensions and other aspects of the welfare state, the economy requires robust growth – such unpopular policies are difficult to sell to the public in an environment of austerity. Within Emu, Germany's natural competitiveness will exert itself, because other member countries will be unable to use competitive devaluations to ease their difficulties, and the strategy begins to make sense. Finally, the presence of an independent European Central Bank, and an Emu stability pact to prevent fiscal irresponsibility, will mean that, while the euro will not be as hard as the Deutschmark in pre-unification days, it will not be a banana republic currency. A wide Emu strategy for Germany thus has much to commend it.

The other key questions for Germany concern its future global political role, and its position as a pivot between eastern and western Europe. Germany's European strategy has been based, at least in part, on the fact that the world will only accept a particular version of German power – that which is embodied in the power and influence of Europe. It could be that this represents a 20th-century view which will fade as the 21st century progresses. But it remains prevalent and, as long as it does, that European strategy remains valid. As for eastern Europe, the time when Germany could have turned its back on western Europe, in favour of its new allies to the east, has probably gone. This does not mean, however, that Germany has nothing to gain from the economic development of eastern Europe – it has much. The best way for those gains to be realised is in an EU which is enlarged to the east.

The Kohl strategy, which is under pressure from within Germany, thus appears to be the optimal one as we move into the 21st century. Going it alone, monetarily or in other respects, would raise fears that the old, belligerent Germany was reviving itself. In the event of accidents, over Emu, failed enlargement, or in other respects, it remains important that Germany does not shoulder the blame. The revival of nationalism, racism and other minor echoes of Germany's past, are disturbing, but they are no worse than in many other European countries. On most of the scenarios in this book, Germany is well-placed. In some of them, she will do very well in the 21st century. Getting through the next 5-10 years, while maintaining something like the existing European strategy, presents the biggest challenge.

■ France

France, in the context of European integration, has long presented something of a mirror image to Germany. France, with a weaker economy and industrial base, and bitter memories of Germany's political and military past, has sought the means of harnessing both within a more integrated Europe. The Franco-German axis has become the pivotal relationship in Europe. France has succeeded in gaining a greater influence over Europe's institutions, and in steering Europe in the direction that was most advantageous to its national interests, than any other country. Like Germany, however, she has reached the late 20th century under strain, with the economic prizes to be gained by further integration in doubt, and the sacrifices required to maintain the *franc fort* policy into Emu widely questioned by the French electorate. Nationalism has a more powerful political voice, much of it directed against further European integration, in France than in

Germany. The narrow approval the French electorate gave to the Maastricht treaty – only 51% were in favour – was both a shock to the political consensus and an important warning signal.

France, perhaps even more than Germany, requires a wide Emu – even with a new exchange rate mechanism in operation the French economy would be highly vulnerable to the competitive gains that Emu outsiders could achieve as a result of currency shifts. The question remains, however, whether France is yet competitive enough not to lose out in a permanent single currency arrangement with the intrinsically more competitive countries of Europe's northern core – notably Germany, Austria and the Netherlands. It is possible, as we have seen, to construct scenarios in which Emu comes spectacularly unstuck for France, just as previous, looser, currency arrangements have done so in the past.

France, too, cannot expect to exert the same influence over Europe's institutions in the future as she has done in the past. The triumph of French diplomacy has been the exploitation of trade-offs – a wide-ranging Common Agricultural Policy in return for German industrial access to its and other European markets, even, as is now suggested, a French president of the European Central Bank in return for it being located in Frankfurt – and so on. There is widespread recognition that, as Alain Juppé has put it, that without France (and of course Germany) there will be no Emu at all. The Emu stability council is a French plan designed to ensure that, however large is Emu's composition, it will come to dominate economic policy – fiscal as well as monetary – within the EU.

But in a wide Emu, and a wider EU, some French pretensions will be shattered. The idea of the single currency as a stepping-stone to a new world system of more or less fixed exchange rates, as a means of controlling 'Anglo-Saxon' speculators, has long been a French ambition but it sits uneasily alongside free capital movements and the sheer power, which will not be reversed, of the international markets. France, indeed, may yet feel the force of these international markets on the 'one last assault' principle, even before Emu is in place. More fundamentally, the wider the membership of the EU, and the greater the pressure to reduce the democratic deficit, the more that France will have to accept a loss of national sovereignty. This has been a problem for France stretching back to its rejection of a European Defence Community in the 1950s and de Gaulle's 'empty chair' crisis of the 1960s. If French nationalism proves to be an enduring force, as is likely, the conflict between that and the drive towards political union that will follow Emu will be intense.

France's optimal strategy thus differs from that of Germany. Germany's economic weight guarantees a degree of dominance over Europe almost regardless. No such guarantees exist for France. Its national political interest lies in the maintenance of some kind of two-tier structure for Europe in which an inner core, heavily influenced by France, makes the key decisions. But its economic interest lies in the widest possible Emu. The two things may be incompatible. Nor is it clear that France, which requires structural reforms of its economy just as much as Germany, can generate either the economic growth or develop the political will needed to achieve it. Again, the next 5-10 years are crucial. A continuation of recent austerity will mean that France begins the 21st century in poor shape to face the challenges ahead.

Britain

The 1990s have been a decade of fevered UK Euroscepticism. Instinctive suspicion of European integration, given voice by Margaret Thatcher in the 1980s, gave way to outright hostility in many quarters following the country's failed two-year membership of the ERM from 1990 to 1992. With the Eurosceptical genie out of the bottle, many doubt that it can ever be put back. Both main political parties have been required to offer a referendum on British participation in Emu, on which Britain, as well as Denmark, retains the right to opt in at a time of its choosing. Even with a more pro-European Labour government now in power, there seems little doubt that such a referendum would reject membership by a substantial majority, making Britain a highly unlikely first-wave participant in the single currency. A more fundamental debate, over whether Britain should be part of the EU at all, will rumble on in the background and – although the political consensus rejects this as an outlandish option – could in certain circumstances come to the forefront of the political debate, notably with the emergence of an even more nationalist Conservative party.

Britons are nothing if not pragmatic, however. Just as initial doubts over the EEC gave way to belated enthusiasm – after Britain had been instrumental in establishing Efta – so the same thing could happen with a successful Emu, or even an Emu which is seen to confer significant advantages upon its members relative to non-member countries. Thus, if the pre-eminence of the City of London as Europe's leading financial centre was threatened by exclusion from the euro zone – which does not at present look likely – attitudes could quickly shift. Or, more likely, if inward investment into Britain from overseas, or re-investment by multinational companies based in Britain, was seen to be critically dependent upon Emu membership, there would also be a change. Already, Toyota and Unilever have warned that exclusion from Emu could affect their future investment decisions in Britain. A change in attitude driven by business could also emerge if, outside Emu, and outside the new ERM – along with Denmark, Britain is not required to join it – sterling became a highly unstable currency. The shift in favour of ERM entry in Britain in the 1980s came partly as a result of sterling's volatility during the period.

During the 1990s, the Conservative government coined the phrase 'enterprise centre of Europe' to describe Britain's relative success in creating jobs, large-scale privatisation, attracting inward investment and fostering peaceful industrial relations. Although some of this success can be put down to the accident of sterling's post-ERM devaluation, and the competitive advantage it provided for British industry while not triggering significantly higher inflation, there is no doubt that Britain in the 1990s reaped the benefit of the reforms painfully pushed through by the Thatcher government in the 1980s. One significant long-term advantage, for example, arises from the future costs of state pension provision which, thanks to a decision taken early in the Thatcher years to link the basic state pension to prices rather than earnings, together with far higher levels of private provision, does not loom large as a significant 21st century problem for Britain, as it does for other countries in Europe. Industrial relations reforms have limited the ability of unions to engage in disruptive strikes, which again is not the case for most of Europe, while the economy is significantly less regulated than most Continental countries.

To a large extent, therefore, Britain should have much to gain from economic integration in Europe, and in particular the opening up of markets. This, of course, was why Britain was an enthusiastic supporter of the Single Market programme, in which a British commissioner, Lord Cockfield, was in the vanguard. If other countries in Europe have yet to undertake the kind of reforms undertaken by the Thatcher government in the 1980s, with no guarantee that they will succeed in pushing them through and if, in several important respects, the model adopted by Britain becomes one, albeit in adapted form, for the rest of the EU, Britain would have, at the very least, a 20-year start, and could look to further integration with enthusiasm. There remains a significant possibility, however, that particularly in the slow-growth scenarios described earlier in this book, the dirigiste and protectionist instincts of some European countries, notably the southern states, would win through. In such circumstances Britain would have the choice of following this European model – on the grounds that if you cannot change them you might as well join them – or pursuing its own course. The former could be the choice of a Labour government in Britain, having opted in to the Maastricht social protocol, and determined to operate at the 'heart of Europe' much more than the Conservatives. The latter choice, that of pursuing a very different course, more likely in a Conservative-led Britain, would imply that, perhaps at best, Britain remains a 'semi-detached' member of the EU or, in the extreme, that withdrawal becomes a serious option for the political mainstream.

Italy

Italy, in many respects, presents the most fascinating 21st-century possibilities in Europe. As a founder member of the EC, one of the Six, Italy can lay claim to being at the centre of further integration in Europe. In fact, however, when set against the momentum established by the Franco-German axis, the EU's driving force, Italy has always been, to an extent, somewhat off the pace. Thus, in the ERM from 1979 to 1990 the lira was a wide band currency, with fluctuations of 6% either side of its central rate permitted, a recognition of the greater volatility of the Italian currency. Italy, unlike the other five members of the original Six, was not a signatory to the Schengen agreement. This is the context in which Italy approaches the start of Emu and other aspects of European integration. Can it still hope to be part of the inner circle or does it have to bow to the inevitable and accept that, in many ways, the Italian economy is not compatible with the hard-currency nations of northern Europe? France, after all, has had a decade of *franc fort*, has achieved a high degree of economic convergence, particularly on inflation, with Germany and yet legitimate questions are asked about whether the French economy is strong enough to lock itself in to a permanent, no-devaluation, currency arrangement. In the case of Italy, whose currency was so recently the subject of a major devaluation, and which has a record of significantly higher inflation, interest rates and budget deficits than the other core economies, as well as a history of unstable government, the idea appears fanciful.

Yet Italy, perhaps more than any other EU member state, relies on early Emu entry. Early entry would justify the financial markets in their 'convergence play' on Italian financial assets, which has seen government bond yields move significantly closer to those in Germany and France, at a time when the economic fundamentals would suggest a much larger gap. For Italy, this is no small consideration. With a national debt around 140% of GDP, it is debt-servicing costs that create the country's budget deficit. With low government bond yields, there is a virtuous circle, in which the budget deficit is reduced, which requires less bond issuance, and those that are issued are on lower yields. A failure to enter Emu would reverse that convergence play, replacing the virtuous circle with a vicious one, and pushing Italy further and further away from subsequent entry. Not only that, but the 5.5 trillion lire ($3.6 billion) 'Euro tax' for 1997 – introduced as a one-off measure to reduce the budget deficit for qualification purposes – would be seen to have been pain inflicted in vain. Achieving reform of Italy's costly and inefficient welfare state, necessary for the long-term good of the economy, would be difficult, if not impossible, without the spur of Emu – unlike in most other countries there is a powerful domestic constituency in favour of participation.

If Italy fails to enter Emu, missing not only the first wave but subsequent entry windows in the early years, the consequences could be far-reaching. There would be disenchantment with the existing political leadership, with Italy's new ruling elite still trying to find its feet after the corruption scandals which brought down the old order, and there would be a revival of north versus south resentment. Umberto Bossi's Northern League has failed to find favour with the majority of northern Italians, partly because of the personality and tactics of Bossi himself. The idea that the south is holding northern Italy back from its rightful place in Europe's core, and that separation should be given serious consideration is, however, one that would gain ground in an Italy excluded from Emu, and apparently condemned to inhabit the second-class world of Europe's lower tier. The break-up of Italy during the 21st century, under such circumstances, would be a real possibility.

Italy's strategy of pushing in the most determined way for first-wave Emu entry is, therefore, understandable, even if on most economic measures, the country cannot be said to be ready for it. The worrying thing about the strategy, however, is the absence of a 'Plan B' or fallback position. In the end, Italy's hope has to be that a wide Emu is seen to be in the interests of both France and Germany. If not, turbulence looms.

Spain and Portugal

Spain and Portugal entered what was then the EC at the same time, at the beginning of 1986, after gradually emerging from their respective political wildernesses. Both joined the ERM, the peseta (1989) prior to the escudo (1992), and suffered a series of devaluations, but not suspension from the system, in the crisis of 1992–3. Neither country enjoys being lumped together with the other, or with Italy. Spain, as the fifth largest economy in the EU, sees itself as having achieved more genuine economic convergence than Italy, as being more pro-European than Britain, and thus having a genuine claim to being one of Europe's core, big-hitting economies. Portugal has but a quarter of Spain's population – 9.9m against 39m – but also sees itself as having made enormous economic strides towards sustained economic convergence, in terms of both budgetary policy and inflation. In the early 1990s, Spain had 6.5% inflation, Portugal 12.5%. By 1997, both were in the 2.5–3% range.

Although exclusion from Emu's first wave would not present as big a symbolic blow to Spain and Portugal as to Italy, there is no doubt that both countries rely on being part of Europe's core within the relatively near future, and have based their political and economic strategies upon it. In particular, with chronic high unemployment in Spain (with a rate of over 20%, three times that of Portugal), inward investment is vital, competition for that inward investment from the even lower-cost producers of eastern Europe alarming to the Spanish and Portuguese. Thus, they require a long period in which they are part of Emu, but the new entrants from eastern Europe are not. Spain, which has competed with Britain for inward investment, particularly in the motor industry, would regard it as an advantage if Britain is not part of the single currency zone.

Looking beyond the immediate question of Emu entry, both countries have a long way to go before they catch up with per capita GDP levels in the more mature European economies. Spain, in particular, requires extensive labour market reforms. The key question, touched on above, is whether the success they have achieved in Europe from being low-cost producers can translate itself into lasting prosperity as that advantage is reduced by enlargement to the east.

■ *The EU's other economies*

The standard argument for European integration among smaller countries is that, in comparison with a situation in which they are dominated by larger neighbours, any pooling of sovereignty adds to their weight and influence. It is not surprising, therefore, that further integration is at the heart of their economic and political strategies. This applies particularly to monetary union. For countries such as Austria and the Netherlands, whose interest rates have long been effectively set by the Bundesbank Council, meeting fortnightly in Frankfurt, the prospect of a voting seat on the council of the European Central Bank is a step up. The smaller EU economies are not uniform, however, in the attitudes of their people. Danish voters rejected the Maastricht treaty, before being given concessions, an echo of earlier rejections by the people of Norway of EU membership itself.

Austria, economically and geographically at the heart of Europe, has become an instant member of Europe's core, with few doubting that the country will be a first-wave Emu member. Despite the fact that EU membership is recent, and was comfortably approved in a 1994 referendum on accession, nationalism is a rising political force in Austria, with Joerg Haider's Freedom Party winning nearly 30% of the vote in special European Parliament elections in October 1996. Austria's fortunes are tied closely to those of Germany and the outlook is thus relatively optimistic, except in the gloomiest scenarios. The spur for Austrian EU membership was economic – the Single Market programme – the question is whether the enthusiasm of the Austrian people for integration is already evaporating in the light of economic adversity. Long a neutral country (this was a condition of the departure of Soviet troops in 1955), the relative fortunes of Austria and **Switzerland**, which rejected membership of the European Economic Area in a 1992 referendum, will be one of the interesting side issues of Europe's 21st-century development. A successful Emu would prove highly attractive to the Swiss, particularly if one of its effects is a volatile Swiss franc. Switzerland has, however, proved immune to the general argument that smaller countries have a bigger influence if part of larger groupings. The loss of national identity and an influence that is disproportionate to its size (7m people) are larger concerns.

Belgium, unlike Switzerland, is the classic example of a country which has gained significantly, in status and influence, from European integration. By being at Europe's hub – home to the Commission and other institutions and venue for the majority of Council meetings, Belgium is guaranteed a pivotal role. European integration is almost instinctive for Belgium – the creation of the Benelux customs union preceded the start of the EEC by 10 years, while subsequent developments, such as the removal of border controls, came ahead of the wider Schengen arrangements. Belgium is unusual, for a small country, in the degree of regionalisation and federalism which characterises its political system. As in other countries, however, the demands of the regions, and the pressure for Flemish autonomy, can be seen as more likely to be catered for in an integrated Europe. Interesting questions would arise, however, in the event of any rupturing of the Franco-German axis. While Flemish Belgium would stay with the smaller German core, francophone Belgium would probably split away. Belgium's position means that it is difficult to see the country not being in the vanguard of Emu (despite having a debt-to-GDP ratio of roughly double the 60% level specified in the Maastricht treaty).

Denmark, as the longest-serving Scandinavian member of the EU, is also the most Eurosceptical – Finland and Sweden apparently embracing integration more willingly. Norway, of course, is not an EU member at all, because of the desire of its people to remain independent. If the UK is the most likely of the bigger European countries to leave the EU, Denmark holds that position among the smaller member states. The Danish people only supported the second Maastricht referendum on condition that Denmark would not participate in the third stage of Emu – reversing that position would require a further referendum with little likelihood, in present circumstances, of public support for Emu participation being achieved. As in Britain, majority opinion in Denmark favours the free trade aspects of the EU – the original reason for converting Efta membership into EC membership in 1973 – but is highly suspicious of moves towards political union and the EU's strong Catholic influence. The challenge for Denmark, outside Emu and on the fringes of the EU (although again, like Britain, Denmark has been quick to translate European directives into national law), will be not to get squeezed by the potential monetary leviathan on its doorstep. The Norwegian example provides encouragement if Denmark decides to part company with the EU although, unlike Norway, Denmark does not have the cushion of North Sea oil.

Finland applied for membership of the EU after emerging from the long shadow of the former Soviet Union. Linguistically (Finnish is the only non-Indo-European official EU language) and geographically distant from Europe's core, Finland is also economically distinct, being highly dependent on its dominant forestry industry. The economy has recovered from the deep recession that followed the break-up of the Soviet Union – and the loss of a huge amount of trade – but the legacy of that recession is high unemployment, at around 15% of the workforce. The Finnish people appear enthusiastic about EU membership, partly because it represents a clear break with the country's Soviet-dominated past, but are less clear about the virtues of Emu, although the government took the preparatory step of taking the markka into the ERM in 1996. Much will depend on the decisions of Sweden, Finland's main trading partner, but it is difficult to see Finland being a core EU country for the foreseeable future.

Greece is in a class of its own when it comes to the integration process. Even the Commission, in its optimistic assessment of the likely early Emu entrants, was obliged to leave Greece off the list – as the only country which will fail to meet all five of the Maastricht criteria. As recently as 1994, the country's budget deficit was 12% of GDP. It is hard to be optimistic about the prospects for Greece. Although economic development has occurred, this has been hugely dependent on transfers from the EU budget (under, initially, the Integrated Mediterranean Programmes and latterly the Cohesion Fund) but despite this Greece's growth record has been lacklustre. Greek governments have been, at times, unenthusiastic about EU membership, despite the direct benefits it has brought. What it has not done is correct fundamental economic weaknesses, which will be exposed in a wider EU, when there are a greater number of competing demands on EU structural funds and other programmes. Greece's main political contribution during more than 15 years of membership has been to make the admission of Turkey to the EU very difficult, if not impossible.

Ireland has earned the sobriquet 'tiger economy of Europe', to the embarrassment of some of its citizens, thanks to an impressive growth record in the 1990s, with GDP rising by an average of 6% a year over the 1992–6 period. Ireland, like Greece, Spain and Portugal, has been a substantial net beneficiary from the EU budget, both the Common Agricultural Policy and the structural funds. This has been combined, however, with an improving record of job creation, low inflation and fiscal consolidation. Ireland is caught between enthusiasm for European integration and a desire not to be on the wrong side of currency moves affecting the euro and the British pound. The great fear is that Ireland will enter Emu, only for this to be followed by a significant sterling devaluation – trade with Britain has diminished in importance but remains substantial. Competitive devaluation by Britain would pose very serious problems for Irish-based industry. In the end, however, political will is what matters, and there is a strong political will in Ireland to break free from over-reliance on Britain. Emu will be one route to achieving it. The 21st century will continue to see Ireland attempting to align itself with Europe's core.

Luxembourg, tiny (population less than 400,000), economically successful – the only country guaranteed to meet all five Maastricht criteria without any 'fudging' – and accustomed to pooling sovereignty, including monetary sovereignty in terms of a shared currency with Belgium which dates back to 1922, will ally itself to any hard-core, hard-currency bloc, with or without Belgium. Luxembourg's enthusiasm for the EU and Emu is not in doubt. The former provides Luxembourg with more than its share of European institutions, while the latter will arguably give the country a greater influence over monetary policy – in the form of a seat on the council of the European Central Bank – than now.

The Netherlands, as the biggest of the Benelux countries (population 15.6m, compared with 10.2m for Belgium), has been a considerable economic success in recent years, combining low inflation and a hard currency with a notably better record than other continental European countries in creating jobs and reducing unemployment (which, at just over 6%, is half the rate in France and

Germany). Participation in Emu is virtually a foregone conclusion for the Netherlands which, at the end of the ERM crisis of 1992-3, formalised the tight link between the guilder and the Deutschmark. The Netherlands, along with Austria, Germany and Luxembourg, is part of Europe's hard core which, in Emu, will argue against any softening of the anti-inflationary emphasis of monetary policy. Dutch pragmatism has helped steer the EU through crises in the past, and will doubtless do so in the future. For the Netherlands, committed to the cause of European integration since the 1950s, Europe has to work. There is no alternative nor, given its geographical position and intertwined economic links with the other EU countries, can there be.

Sweden came late to the EU, joining with Finland and Austria on January 1, 1995. Until its application for membership in the early 1990s, this famously neutral country did not appear to need economic alliances. The Swedish social and economic model succeeded in maintaining low unemployment even as the rest of Europe was suffering. Levels of social provision were the envy of the world. Successful multinational firms emanated from Sweden and, in their employee relations, exported a version of the Swedish model around the world. The model was, however, of limited use in the new aggressive world of tougher competition in terms of relative wage and tax rates – generous Swedish social provision had its direct consequence in punitive levels of taxation, forcing the reform of some aspects of the model. Like Finland, the end of the cold war had the effect of encouraging Sweden to turn to the EU. There remains a sense, however, as with the other Scandinavian countries, in which Sweden is not yet a whole-hearted member of the EU. The government has no formal opt-out from Emu but remains equivocal about membership. For Sweden, Denmark and Finland, one key question in the 21st century is whether there will be pressure for harmonisation of welfare provision. At present, in spite of some reforms, the Scandinavian countries tax and spend to the equivalent of around 60% of GDP, compared with about 50% for Europe's core economies, and 40% for Britain and Ireland. In a true single market, activity will gravitate towards the lowest tax economies. The Swedish model may require further surgery, in a way that will prove unpopular to the Swedish people, accustomed as they are to their particular approach.

New entrants

For potential new members of the EU, the way Europe develops in the 21st century is the $64,000 question. Existing member states, for the most part, are stuck with the EU, come what may. They can influence Europe's future outcomes by their actions but do not have the luxury of deciding whether, at this stage, they want to be part of the process at all. Those striving to join are different. Will they join an EU which is in terminal economic decline, or one that is about to embark on the most successful period in its history? Will they become second-class members of a bloc dominated by its inner core – in the EU but condemned to inhabit its outer fringes? Or would staying out mean that they will, at some stage, face a fortress Europe which, in response to economic adversity, reaches for the protectionist button?

Of the current applicants, **Cyprus** and **Malta**, who applied for membership in 1990, are at the head of the queue, following a decision by the European Council, meeting in Corfu in June 1994, that they would be given priority in the next round of enlargement. Cyprus and Malta face different challenges. **Cyprus**, with successful tourism and agricultural sectors, as well as some industry, has a per capita GDP level above that of Portugal and Greece and, economically, looks well-placed to prosper in the EU. Its difficulty is political, and the island's split, with the Turkish Republic of Northern Cyprus now having existed for more than 20 years. The Turkish enclave, which is not recognised internationally, would in theory be part of the EU on Cyprus's entry – the Cypriot government applied for membership on behalf of the whole island – but in practice it would remain separate. Greece has already lodged objections over the position of Turkish northern Cyprus, threatening to block enlargement if it is to be admitted as part of Cyprus's entry. Cyprus's entry will also aggravate relations between the EU and Turkey. **Malta**, economically weaker than Cyprus, has an economy which, while also heavily dependent on tourism, is largely made up of small, inefficient firms, heavily dependent on state subsidies. It will require a lengthy transition period before it can face the rigours of the Single Market without these subsidies. The question of voting rights will also loom large. It is difficult to envisage Luxembourg accepting equal status with these island states, which have similarly small populations.

Switzerland, which applied for membership in June 1992, has, as noted above, yet to get beyond the first base of public approval for membership of the European Economic Area. Its chances of eventually making it into the EU are critically dependent on the success, or otherwise, of Emu. For **Turkey**, which applied as long ago as 1987, and was the subject of an unfavourable Commission opinion in 1989, the obstacles to membership remain considerable. Turkey is a large country (population 64m), most of its territory is in Asia and it is considerably poorer on a per capita basis than Greece, currently the EU's poorest member. Turkish entry would trigger huge demands for resource transfers from the EU budget. These economic obstacles, however, are minor compared with continuing objections on the basis of the country's human rights record. Political rehabilitation may be possible – Turkey is, after all, a member of Nato – and several of the existing member states have come in from the political cold. Turkey will continue to press hard for membership, while the calculation for the rest of the EU may come down to the question of demonstrating that it can accommodate a large, substantially Muslim country among its membership.

■ *Eastern applicants*

For the EU, enlargement to the east is the culmination of a process that began with the collapse of the Berlin Wall in 1989 and the unification of Germany a year later. For the former Comecon countries, it would be a sign that, after more than four decades of economic and political repression, they had crossed the Rubicon and become paid-up members of European capitalist society. **Hungary** applied for EU membership in March 1994, **Poland** a month later. They, along with the **Czech Republic,** the **Slovak Republic** and **Slovenia**, are generally seen as the first wave of eastern entrants, followed by **Estonia, Latvia** and **Lithuania**, and then **Bulgaria, Romania** and, possibly, **Croatia.** Two main problems affect the eastern applicants. The first is economic. To avoid the kind of problems West Germany encountered on unification – and the massive resource transfers that were required to bring the East German economy up to even a rudimentary standard – the eastern applicants need many years of economic development. Average living standards are well below those in the EU and economic structures remain weighted towards heavy industry and agriculture.

This suggests a long period in the EU waiting room, during which time frustration will build, as will allegations that existing member states are blocking their progress by delaying entry. The second problem is that, despite the strong wish of most of these countries to join the EU, it may not be best for their economic development. This would be true if the EU becomes a region of chronically low growth and creeping protectionism. But it could also occur in another way. It has already been noted that some of these eastern European countries are likely to pursue a hard-currency, free-market economic model, which would square with aspects of the northern European model, but sit uneasily alongside southern traditions. Vaclav Klaus, prime minister of the Czech Republic, noted this danger at the Davos World Economic Forum in February 1997. Apart from the economic transformation of the countries of central and eastern Europe, about which he was optimistic, the key question for western Europe, he said, was 'how successful will be the dismantling of over-regulated and over-paternalistic welfare states in western Europe'. 'I do not know whether we will succeed in winning the battle with overlegislation and with corporatism and syndicalism in ourselves', he added. 'I am afraid that both tendencies are deeply rooted in the intrinsic fabric of our societies. To extrapolate in 1997, the year 2007 is not a very rosy picture.'

Apart from the curiosity value of the leader of a former communist state telling western Europe how to go about being good capitalists, Klaus's comments showed that eastern Europeans are not viewing the EU through rose-tinted glasses. They know, as people who have lived through the nightmare of unaccountable bureaucracy and stifling regulation, about the EU's tendencies in these areas. They also know that most EU member countries view questions of enlargement in a self-interested way and, in particular, will strive to neuter eastern Europe's low-cost advantages to avoid the loss of jobs to these new entrants.

■ *Europe's institutions*

This is not a book about Europe's institutions. Plenty has been written about the **European Commission,** the **European Parliament** and the **European Council,** and the relationship between them. Plenty more will be written in the aftermath of the 1996–7 inter-governmental conference.

The Commission, for all its critics, has accomplished its central task of maintaining the drive towards European integration very successfully. Commissioners have succeeded in initiating new waves of integration, or marshalling the forces in favour of new moves in that direction. Roy Jenkins, as Commission president in the 1970s, set the ball rolling again for economic and monetary union, after the drive towards Emu had been thwarted by the currency turbulence of that decade. His suggestion, taken up enthusiastically by France and Germany, led directly to the setting-up of the European Monetary System in 1979. The Commission pushed through the Single Market programme with vigour and, thanks to the energy of Jacques Delors, secured a new consensus on Emu and broad agreement on the provisions of the Maastricht treaty in 1991. The Commission, despite its reputation for bureaucracy and over-regulation, has in recent years pursued global free trade more enthusiastically than many EU members.

For the future, the Commission could develop in a number of ways. There are those who see its current, relatively powerful position as a symptom of the political immaturity of the EU. Thus, the Commission has moved into the vacuum created by a Parliament which has limited power and a Council whose members have to concern themselves with national as well as European policy matters. By increasing the Parliament's powers the Commission could then revert to its intended role as a secretariat for the Council, and the conduit – a true European civil service – for the passage of legislation agreed by the Council through the Parliament. Others see the Commission developing its powers. For Jacques Attali, as we have seen, the Commission would become home to a European Treasury, managing the much greater fiscal policy responsibilities, including greatly enhanced resource transfers, of a Europe under Emu. Karl Lamers, of Germany's CDU/CSU, sees the Commission becoming, in essence, Europe's government, with its president elected by the Parliament, who would then have the right to choose his own 'cabinet' of 10 or 12 senior Commissioners, unconstrained by the need to select, by quota, representatives from each member state.

'*Plus ça change*' is the name of one of the scenarios in this book. This is likely to be the watchword for Europe's institutions. They will evolve only gradually from their present state, held back by traditional concerns about allowing supranational bodies to accrue too much power and, in the case of the Parliament, the feared loss of autonomy for national parliaments. The power and influence of the Commission will ebb and flow, according to the energy and enthusiasm of its president – Delors gave it a new lease of life in the mid-1980s. If Emu survives, the pressure for greater centralisation of fiscal policy should mean an increase in the EU budget and the powers of the Commission. The Parliament will continue to struggle to overcome public apathy. Europe's institutions will muddle along.

■ Russia

Winston Churchill's 'riddle wrapped in a mystery inside an enigma' remains more or less that as far as predicting its course in the 21st century is concerned. While it is perfectly possible to be optimistic about Russia's economic potential, the political outlook is a minefield of potential disaster. In 1997, the fate of Russia and its relations with the rest of the world seemed too obviously dependent on the survival of an obviously very sick man, Boris Yeltsin, for comfort. Michael Emerson, in his LSE lecture 'Re-drawing the Map of Europe', cited a Russian view of four possible scenarios for Russia, which were: full integration or a formal alliance with Europe, perhaps with Russia joining the European Economic Area; an attempt by a new, more aggressive Russian leadership to, in essence, re-create the old USSR, 'leading to serious tensions in all or any of the border areas from the Baltic to the Ukraine, Caucasus and central Asia'; partnership but not full integration with the EU and Nato; and a 'cold peace' with limited co-operation between Russia, on one side, and the EU and Nato on the other. Of these, the third and fourth scenarios were considered more likely, the difference between them being harmonious and mutually beneficial relations in the event of a partnership, and mutual distrust in the case of a cold peace.

Just as Nato has had to tread carefully when it comes to enlargement to the east, so this will have to be for the EU. The biggest danger would lie in giving Russia the impression that its old allies are being gradually picked off, leaving it isolated and ignored, a bear which, while its teeth and claws are not as sharp as they were, is still capable of inflicting some nasty damage. The position of the **Ukraine**, stuck between the expanding EU and an angry Russia, would be particularly dangerous. The most optimistic vision is that of eventual Russian membership of a successful and dynamic EU. It could happen, well before the end of the 21st century, but it cannot be rushed. Providing Russia with membership of the European Economic Area would be a highly significant step. Taking it further, as Emerson points out, cannot yet be on the agenda:

> The EU and Russia could not reasonably aim at an even more integrationist agenda for the time being, not simply because Russia is so big but because the two parties are such mirror-image opposites in the following sense. The EU is a set of countries with advanced economies and rather stable civic societies, whose collective system of governance or constitution however is highly immature. Russia is a country with a strongly structured democratic, presidential and federal constitution but with a shattered economy and little as yet of a modern civic society. These are the objective facts which mean that, without any offence being intended, the redrawing of the map of Europe would not for a long time embrace Russian membership of the EU, although the question might be discussed again in years to come. (p. 38)

Whether Russia will thus miss out on enormous benefits, like the boy pressing his nose against the sweetshop window, or whether it will be better off out of a declining economic bloc, and thus better able to foster productive relationships elsewhere, remains to be seen.

■ The United States

America's attitude towards European integration has always been positive, sometimes unquestioningly so. The Marshall Plan and the establishment of the Organisation for European Economic Co-operation (OEEC), the OECD's predecessor, were seen as not merely providing for the rebuilding of Europe but, in addition, fostering closer integration, including as a first step free trade, between its component countries. American attitudes have partly been a question of scale – if the United States can be a single economy, why cannot

Europe? – and partly a question of political convenience. If Europe spoke with one voice, Washington would know, rather more easily, where it stood. Economically, America was always attracted by the idea that a successful European economy would be better able to shoulder the burden of its own defence against the cold war threat from the east. Some of this support has had to be discreet – France, in particular, has always been hostile to any suggestion that, in pursuing integration, Europe has been following a US foreign policy line. But America supported the Six in their creation of the ECSC, EEC and Euratom. And Washington has given its implicit backing to Emu, again largely on the grounds that if it is possible for America to have a single currency, why should the EU have fourteen? Only latterly have their been subtle hints from across the Atlantic that the process of getting to that European single currency looks to involve too much fiscal masochism, to the detriment of the world economy (and thus America).

There is a sense in the American attitude of a 'Goldilocks' approach to Europe – wanting it to be successful, but not too successful. Henry Kissinger once wrote: 'American policy has been extremely ambivalent: wanting European unity while recoiling before its probable consequences.' Thus, if there was a genuine, lasting economic renaissance in Europe, and if the euro came to replace the dollar as the world's most important currency, America could begin to rue its earlier backing for European integration. There is a sense too in which, while Washington has been critical of Europe for its foreign policy indecisiveness – in the 1990s over Bosnia and Iraq – it might not welcome a new European superpower, throwing its weight around on the international stage. America, on the other hand, does not want political instability or economic failure in Europe in the 21st century. One clear possibility if Europe's Single Market is seen to be successful is the development of transatlantic free trade, even a formal transatlantic free trade area (Tafta), effectively providing a single market linking the EU and the members of Nafta (the North American Free Trade Agreement) – America, Canada and Mexico. According to Bruce Stokes of the Council on Foreign Relations:

> A transatlantic economic initiative is a logical complement to US efforts to create free trade areas in the Pacific Basin and in the Western Hemisphere. With a transatlantic undertaking the United States would be at the hub of a global effort to reduce

trade barriers. The Asia Pacific Economic Co-operation (Apec) forum, the Free Trade in the Americas initiative, and a transatlantic initiative would be spokes in that wheel. A US–European initiative would create regional competition to see which area of the world will be the first to derive the greatest benefits from trade and investment liberalisation. It would also send a signal to foot-draggers in Asia and Latin America that the United States has other options if the recently established free trade goals for Asia and Latin America are not met. Similarly, drawing Europe into this web of trade-liberalising efforts will encourage Brussels to pursue its own initiatives with Asia and Latin America, helping keep Washington honest. ('Open for Business', p. 5)

■ *Japan*

Japan's relations with the EU have often been characterised by tensions over trade. Latterly, however, Japan is seen to be less of a competitive threat than the emerging economies of Asia. Indeed, in the 1990s, the bursting of the 'bubble' economy of the late 1980s appears to have made Japan more sclerotic than many of Europe's slow-growing economies. Japan, even more so than America, has had a straightforward attitude to European integration – if it means a larger open market in which Japanese companies can freely trade, then it is a good thing. Britain, in particular, has worked hard to attract inward investment from Japan, stressing that such investment can service the much larger 'home' market of the EU. In this it has been successful. Inward investment projects from Nissan, Toyota and Honda have transformed the ailing British motor industry. There has also been large-scale investment, and not just in Britain, in consumer electronics and other industries. Part of the motivation, undoubtedly, was the fear of a protectionist backlash against Japanese imports. Japanese attitudes towards Emu have been harder to discern. The president of Toyota, Hiroshi Okuda, created controversy in 1997 when he suggested that future investment in Europe would probably be directed towards those countries inside the single currency (and thus probably not Britain). Other Japanese firms, however, said that Emu participation was only one of many factors affecting location decisions.

This may, in any case, be a side issue. Corporate Japan appears to have decided that the world's future growth hub will be on its doorstep in Asia. Most decisions that involve shifting investment overseas settle, in response to the high yen or for strategic reasons, on projects elsewhere in Asia. The European market is important to Japan but, unsurprisingly, its firms see bigger prizes (and more cost-efficient production locations) closer to home. According to Jim Rohwer:

> Decade-old fears in Japan that its manufacturing base is being 'hollowed out' by the migration of its factories are much exaggerated. But the process of moving offshore does seem sure to help push Japanese business in the direction it ought anyway to be going at home – towards higher-value-added production. And the modest uprooting of Japanese small and midsize manufacturers will have a bigger impact, in terms of technology transfer and the balance of trade in capital goods and parts, on the places the factories are being transferred to. Those places are overwhelmingly in Asia: the destination for more than three-quarters of the smallish companies that moved factories out of Japan in 1993. (*Asia Rising*, pp. 221–2)

■ China

No look into the 21st century can ignore the potential role of China, with more than 20% of the world's population and a virtual guarantee that, in the next two decades, it will once more become the world's biggest economy. Even allowing for the likelihood that Chinese economic growth will slow from its rapid late 20th-century pace, with growth projected by the OECD at 10% a year over the 1995–8 period, China is bound to overhaul both Europe and the United States. The calculations are straightforward enough. When per capita GDP in China exceeds about 22% of the US level, China overhauls America. To overtake the EU, China needs a per capita GDP level of 29% or more of European levels. There is, on the face of it, a long way to go – the average Chinese has a per capita GDP level, on a purchasing power parity basis, of just over $2,000, compared with more than $25,000 for Americans. But the power of compound numbers suggests that catch-up will be rapid. If Chinese economic growth is, on average,

5% faster than America's, China will become the world's biggest economy between 2015 and 2020.

Such a prospect does not, of course, mean that Europe is necessarily facing economic eclipse. European companies can benefit from China's continued emergence, although the evidence is that they start some way behind the rest of Asia and America in exploiting the opening-up of the Chinese economy. Deng Xiaoping, for two decades China's paramount leader, and architect of the economic reform process, died in February 1997 at the age of 92. Most observers believe reform is sufficiently ingrained for there to be no serious prospect of a fundamental reversal of the process. Nearly 20 years of reform have brought a more than sixfold increase in living standards. China has, however, taken unpredictable courses of action before, and could do so again.

This applies to China's conduct on the world stage as much as it does to the way it runs the economy at home, although the two are plainly related, for example in official attitudes to foreign investment in China. Combining economic freedom with a continued lack of political freedom looks to be a fundamental contradiction which cannot survive, for long, the country's continued, and rapid, economic emergence. Which of the two forces wins out will be critical. China could become a 'rough neighbour' or could become the increasingly liberal hub of a dynamic Asian economy. Which course it chooses is a question of fundamental importance, and not just to Europe.

Conclusion

Readers will judge which of the scenarios outlined in this book they consider most likely. My choice of *'Plus ça change'* as the most probable scenario for Europe in the 21st century is, on the face of it, optimistic. Adding up the probabilities of the three gloomy scenarios – Les Etrangers, The Dark Ages and The Apocalypse – gives, however, 55%, against 45% for the combined probability of the two more upbeat versions of Europe's future. These things can, quite obviously, never be precise. It seems to me that, on balance, a degree of pessimism is justified at this stage, if only as a warning against complacency.

The number of possible different futures for Europe is, of course, infinite. Combinations of these scenarios are quite possible. For example, my stylised approach has been to take the view that there is a trade-off between the extent of Asian economic emergence and Europe's economic prosperity. This is not necessarily true, as I touched on in scenario two – world trade is not a zero-sum game. It would be possible, rejecting this trade-off, to have a super-optimistic economic vision for the 21st century, with Asia, the Americas and Europe all enjoying a sustained boom at once or, equally, all suffering from some global economic sclerosis.

■ *Postscript*

This is a book which has looked forward into the 21st century and has, of necessity, made certain assumptions about the state of Europe as it moves into that century. There is also a risk, even about relatively short-term assumptions. In particular, a central assumption, underlying all the scenarios, has been that the final stage of Emu begins more or less on time during 1999. But what happens if Europe does not even get to that first base – if economic conditions or a waning of political will cause a postponement, possibly indefinitely, of Emu? It could happen, some say it will happen. In many ways it could be a much more desirable outcome than pressing on with Emu when the circumstances are not right. Even so, the underlying economic forces that will affect Europe in the 21st century do not rest solely on whether the single currency happens or not. There is, plainly, a vigorous debate over whether the Maastricht process has forced fiscal consolidation which would, in any event, have been needed and will force other measures to make European economies more competitive or, in fact, has complicated the process of making Europe ready for the challenges that lie ahead. That debate will continue.

References

Albert, Michel (1993), *Capitalism Against Capitalism*, Whurr Publishers.

Attali, Jacques (1996), 'For a New Political Order', *Time* Golden Anniversary Issue on Europe.

Bainbridge, Timothy, and Teasdale, Anthony (1996), *The Penguin Companion to the European Union*, Penguin.

Berners-Lee, Tim (1996), 'Europe and the Info Age', *Time* Golden Anniversary Issue on Europe.

Booker, Christopher, and North, Richard (1996), *The Castle of Lies*, Duckworth.

Borchardt, Klaus-Dieter (1995), *European Integration: the Origins and Growth of the European Union*, European Commission.

Burkitt, Brian, Baimbridge, Mark, and Whyman, Philip (1996), 'There *is* an Alternative', Campaign for an Independent Britain.

Callaghan, James (1988), *Time and Chance*, Fontana/Collins.

Callow, Julian (1996), *Life after Emu*, Kleinwort Benson, December.

The Chatham House Forum (1996), *Unsettled Times,* Royal Institute of International Affairs.

Cockfield, Lord (1996), 'Why the Single Market Must Remain a Priority', in *Is the Single Market Working?*, Philip Morris Institute, November.

Confederation of British Industry (1996), National Conference Session Papers, November.

Connolly, Bernard (1995), *The Rotten Heart of Europe*, Faber and Faber.

Crawford, Malcolm (1993), *One Money for Europe?*, Macmillan.

De Charette, Hervé (1996), Interview with RTL, September 29, 1996.

Denman, Roy (1996), *Missed Chances – Britain and Europe in the 20th Century*, Cassell.

Dornbusch, Rudiger (1997), quoted in 'Emu: A Political Perspective', Nomura Research Institute, January.

The Economist (1995), *The World in 1996.*

Ehrhart, Hans-Georg (1996), 'Kohl's Dream to Take the War Out of Europe', Parliamentary Brief, March.

Emerson, Michael (1996), *Redrawing the Map of Europe*, LSE Public Lecture, November 19, 1996.

Emerson, Michael, and Huhne, Christopher (1991), *The Ecu Report*, Pan.

Engels, Friedrich (1973), *The Condition of the Working Class in England in 1844*, Lawrence and Wishart, first published 1845.

Englander, Steven (1996), 'Europe's Unemployment Problem – Lessons from the German Labour Market', European Policy Forum.

European Commission (1990), 'One Market, One Money', European Economy, September 1990.

European Commission (1994), *Freedom of Movement.*

European Commission (1996), 'The Impact and Effectiveness of the Single Market', October 30.

European Movement (1996), 'The Other Side of the Coin'.

Fernández-Armesto, Felipe (1995), *The Times Illustrated History of Europe*, Times Books.

Fontaine, Pascal (1995), *Europe in Ten Points*, European Commission.

Fukuyama, Francis (1996), 'Social Capital', speech at Merrill Lynch seminar on European Restructuring, November 15, 1996.

Gentle, Christopher (1996), *After Liberalisation: A Vision of Europe in the Global Economy of the 21st Century*, Macmillan.

Goldman Sachs (1996), 'The Dublin Summit – Stability Pact, Euro and ERM2', December 13, 1996.

Grant, Charles (1994), *Delors: Inside the House that Jacques Built*, Nicholas Brealey Publishing.

Hall, Jeremy (1996), *Real Lives, Half Lives*, Penguin.

Hampden-Turner, Charles, and Trompenaars, Fons (1994), *The Seven Cultures of Capitalism*, Piatkus Books.

Hindley, Brian, and Howe, Martin (1996), *Better Off Out? The Benefits and Costs of EU Membership*, Institute of Economic Affairs.

Hirsch, Seev, and Almor, Tamar (1996), *Outsiders' Responses to European Integration*, Handelshojskolens Forlag, Copenhagen.

Hogg, Sarah, and Hill, Jonathan (1995), *Too Close to Call*, Little, Brown.

Holmes, Martin (ed.) (1996), *The Eurosceptical Reader*, Macmillan.

Hornik, Richard (1996), 'Special Report on Central Europe', *Time*, November 25, 1996.

House of Commons Social Security Committee (1996), 'Unfunded Pension Liabilities in the European Union'.

Huntington, Samuel (1997), 'The West and the Rest', *Prospect*, February.

Hutton, Ray (1996), Review of the Skoda Octavia, *The Sunday Times*, September 22, 1996.

Jay, Peter (1995), 'Employment, Regions and Currencies', The Darlington Economics Lecture.

Jenkins, Lindsay (1996), *Godfather of the European Union – Altiero Spinelli*, Bruges Group.

Jenkins, Roy (1989), *European Diary, 1977–81*, Macmillan.

Johnson, Christopher (1996), *In with the Euro, Out with the Pound*, Penguin.

Kenen, Peter (1995), *Economic and Monetary Union in Europe: Moving Beyond Maastricht*, Cambridge University Press.

King, Stephen (1996), *Emu, Four Endings and a Funeral*, James Capel.

Klaus, Vaclav (1997), 'Europe in 2007', speech to the Davos World Economic Forum, February.

Lamers, Karl (1994), 'Where Does Europe Go From Here?', *The European*, November 18, 1994.

Lascelles, David (1996), *The Crash of 2003: An Emu Fairy Tale*, Centre for the Study of Financial Innovation.

Lawson, Nigel (1992), *The View from No. 11*, Bantam Press.

Layard, Richard, and Parker, John (1996), *The Coming Russian Boom*, The Free Press.

Lindsey, Lawrence (1996), Evidence to the House of Commons Treasury and Civil Service Committee, May.

Llewellyn, John (1996), 'Tackling Europe's Uncompetitiveness', *Oxford Review of Economic Policy*, Autumn 1996.

Lynch, Peter (1996), *Minority Nationalism and European Integration*, University of Wales Press.

Magnus, George, and Donovan, Paul (1996), *Labour Markets and Emu*, Global Economic Themes, July/August, UBS.

Marjolin, Robert (1989), *Memoirs, 1911–86*, Weidenfeld & Nicolson.

McKay, David (1996), *Rush to Union: Understanding the European Federal Bargain*, Clarendon Press, Oxford.

Middlemas, Keith (1995), *Orchestrating Europe: The Informal Politics of the European Union, 1973–95*, Fontana Press.

Miles, David (1996), 'The Future of Savings and Wealth Accumulation: The Differences Within the Developed Economies', Merrill Lynch.

Miles, David, and Patel, Binit (1996), 'Savings and Wealth Accumulation in Europe: The Outlook into the Next Century', Merrill Lynch.

Monnet, Jean (1976), *Memoires*, Fayard.

Monti, Mario (1995), 'The State of the Single Market', European Commission, September 27, 1995.

Naisbitt, John (1996), *Megatrends Asia*, Nicholas Brealey Publishing.

National Institute of Economic and Social Research (1996), October 1996 Review.

Organisation for Economic Co-operation and Development (1994), *The OECD Jobs Study*.

Organisation for Economic Co-operation and Development (1996a), *The OECD Jobs Strategy: Pushing Ahead with the Strategy*, May.

Organisation for Economic Co-operation and Development (1996b), *The OECD Economic Outlook*, June.

Organisation for Economic Co-operation and Development (1996c), *OECD Economic Survey: The Slovak Republic*.

Organisation for Economic Co-operation and Development (1996d), *The OECD Economic Outlook*, December.

Organisation for Economic Co-operation and Development (1997), *OECD Economic Survey: Poland*.

Owen, David (1996), *Balkan Odyssey*, Victor Gollancz.

Padio-Schioppa, Tommaso (ed.) (1987), *Efficiency, Stability and Equity*, Oxford.

Panic, Mica (1992), *European Monetary Union: Lessons from the Classical Gold Standard*, St Martin's Press.

Philip Morris Institute (1996a), *In a Larger EU, Can All Member States be Equal?*, April.

Philip Morris Institute (1996b), *Does Europe Need a Constitution?*, June.

Philip Morris Institute (1996c), *Is the Single Market Working?*, November.

Reading, Brian (1995), *The Fourth Reich*, Weidenfeld & Nicolson.

Roberts, J.M. (1995), *The Penguin History of the World*, Penguin.

Rohwer, Jim (1996), *Asia Rising*, Nicholas Brealey Publishing.

Royal Institute of International Affairs (1996), *The 1996 IGC – National Debates, Germany, Spain, Sweden and the UK*.

Sassoon, Donald (1996), *Social Democracy at the Heart of Europe*, Institute for Public Policy Research.

Smith, David, *From Boom to Bust*, Penguin.

Stokes, Bruce (1996), *Open for Business*, Council on Foreign Relations.

Swann, Dennis (1995), *The Economics of the Common Market*, 8th edition, Penguin.

Taylor, Christopher (1996), *Emu 2000? Prospects for European Monetary Union*, Royal Institute for International Affairs.

Thurow, Lester (1996), *The Future of Capitalism*, Nicholas Brealey Publishing.

Trent, Bill (1996), 'The Outlook for Industrial Restructuring in Continental Europe', Merrill Lynch seminar, November 15, 1996.

Valladão, Alfredo (1996), *The 21st Century Will be American*, Verso.

Walsh, Brendan (1996), 'Stabilisation and Adjustment in a Small Open Economy: Ireland 1979–95', *Oxford Review of Economic Policy*, Autumn 1996.

Watson, Alan (1992), *The Germans: Who Are They Now?*, Thames Methuen.

Welsh, Michael (1996), *Europe United?*, Macmillan.

World Economic Forum (1996), *The Global Competitiveness Report*.

Index

Adenaeur, Konrad 14
Adonnino committee 25
ageing populations 164–7
Albert, Michel 50–1
American system 50–1
Andreatta, Beniamino 130
Anglo-Saxon model 50, 107–8
apocalypse scenario: business apocalypse 210; capitalist reversal 202–4; crash 196–9; dangerous nationalism 188–9; dirty Europe 204–6; divided and unstable 199–200; end of politics 209; euro nightmare 190–2; European tribalism 186–7; fifty years on 210–11; loose nukes 206–9; probability of 218–19; role of EMU 190; rough neighbours 200–1; shock treatment 192–5; splitting the axis 195–6; war and peace 185–6; when? 210
Asia 101–2, 120–1, 203; economic development 86–9; turbulence in 90–2
Asian tigers 42, 68, 72, 102
Asian-Pacific Economic Co-operation (Apec) 119, 244
Association of South East Asian Nations (Asean) 118
Attali, Jacques 178, 240
Attlee, Clement 18
Austria 232–3

Bainbridge, Timothy and Teasdale, Anthony 115

banking system *see* finance and banking systems
Barre, Raymond 23
Barrell, Ray and Pain, Nigel 140
Basayev, Shamil 208
Belgium–Luxembourg Economic Union 128
Berners-Lee, Tim 169
bicycle theory 117, 186
black market 105
'Black Wednesday' 79
Booker, Christopher and North, Richard 54
Borchardt, Klaus-Dieter 115, 185
Bossi, Umberto 142, 230
Bretton Woods system 22, 23
Briand, Aristide 34
Britain 127, 144–6, 149, 227–9; extra-European links 173–4; labour market in 160–1; as member of Common Market 19; non-participation of 17–19
Brittan, Sir Leon 118
Bretherton, Russell 18
Brussels 127; as Tower of Babel 129
Bulgaria 238
Burkitt, Brian *et al.* 59
business: apocalypse 210; bonanza in 84–5; improvement in 113–14; struggle and retrenchment 176; uncertain environment for 148–9

Callaghan, James 29, 30
Callow, Julian 157–8
Campaign for Independent Britain 59

capitalism: divergent systems 50–1; failure of 202–4
Cecchini, Paolo 78
Centre for the Study of Financial Innovation 196
Charette, Hervé de 82
Chatham House Forum 120, 200–1, 206
Chelyabinsk 207
Chernobyl 206–7
China 87–8, 90–1, 102, 119, 120–1, 200–1, 202, 205, 245–6
Chirac, Jacques 197, 198
Christian Democrat Union/Christian Social Union (CDU/CSU) 132
Churchill, Winston 13, 17, 241
city states 209
'Club Med' countries 27, 143
Cockfield, Lord 27, 109, 111–12, 228
Committee for a People's Europe (Adonnino committee) 25
Common Agricultural Policy (Cap) 17, 20, 22, 72
Common Market *see* European Economic Community (EEC)
Communism 70, 203
competitiveness 103–6, 149, 192, 217, 226; and restructuring 106–8; and specialisation 108–9
Confederation of British Industry 40
conflicts 194, 199
Connolly, Bernard 92, 194
convergence criteria 43–5; disagreement between economists and monetarists 45–6
core countries *see* 'the Six'
corporate sector 107–8
Court of auditors 127
'The Crash of 2003 – An Emu Fairy Tale' (Lascelles) 196–7, 198
Croatia 238
Cyprus 52, 144, 237
Czech Republic 238

dark ages scenario: American century 168–70; burden of ageing population 164–7; business suffers 176; EMU irrelevance 167–8; EMU stultifies Europe 156–9; European labour markets don't work 159–63; extra-European links 173–5; faded glories 155–6; fifty years on 179; little fortresses 171–3; a living museum 176–8; nationalism rules 175–6; no escape from slow growth's grip 163–4; no United States of Europe 170–1; probability of 217–18
Davos World Economic Forum (1997) 239
de Gaulle, Charles 19, 22, 173–4, 199
defence spending 201
Delors; committee 31, 44; report 134
Delors, Jacques 30, 37, 75, 92, 114, 241
Denman, Sir Roy 16
Denmark 233–4
d'Estaing, Valéry Giscard 29, 134
Dooge committee 26
Dooge, James 26
Dounreay 207
Dublin summits, (1990) 32; (1996) 136, 196

eastern Europe 105–6, 133, 143–4, 149, 203, 205, 238–9; economic growth 71–3; links with Germany 174–5; problems 69–70
'Economic Outlook'(OECD) 165
'Efficiency, Stability and Equity' (EC) report 75–6
elections 55
Emerson, Michael 119
employment 68–9, 81, 113, 144, 179, 189, 191, 194, 198, 200, 214, 219; and ageing population 165–7; cost of 42–3, 103; labour mobility 159–62; problems of 41–2; structural variations 48; and working time directive 162–3
'empty chair' policy 199
Engels, Friedrich 204
environment 204–6
Erhart, Hans-George 174
Estonia 238

Index

euro 31, 81–3, 111, 140–1; design of 56; nightmare of 190–2; in search of 43–5

Europe: brotherly tensions in 56–8; composed of little fortresses 171–3; cultural diversity in 147; cultural exchanges in 121; cultural identity in 24–6, 92; cultural renaissance in 92–3; decline in 155–6; defined 57; disunion in 136–40; economic benefits in 83–4; economic size 67–9; effect of single currency in 80–5; enlargement of 51–3; future of 1–2, *see also named* scenarios; growth in 112–13; inequality in 149; as a museum 176–8; place in the world 118–20; politics in 53–5, 85, 115–17; progress of 37–8; stability in 89–90; tribalism in 186–7

European Atomic Energy Community (Euratom) 16, 17, 127

European Bank for Reconstruction and Development 73

European Central Bank (ECB) 31, 44, 45, 114, 118, 156, 158, 191, 197

European Coal and Steel Community (ECSC) 14, 15, 18, 90, 127, 135–6

European Commission 45–6, 239–40

European Council 239, 240

European Council of Finance Ministers (Ecofin) 23, 111

European Court of Justice 127, 162

European Defence Community Treaty (1952) 15

European Economic Community (EEC) 16, 16–17, 127; establishment of 19–21; move to single market 26–8

European Free Trade Area (Efta) 19, 128

European Investment Bank 127

European Monetary Co-operation Fund 29

European Monetary Institute (EMI) 31, 45, 56

European Monetary System (EMS) 29, 30, 79, 240

European Monetary Union (EMU) 30–1, 59–60; averaging down 80–1; convergence criteria 43–5; core countries 132–4; crash of 196–9; creates divisions 136–40; criticisms and concerns 47–8; decline of 167–8, 170; disagreement between economists and monetarists 45–6; economic benefits and advantages 83–5; exclusions from 141–6; and foreign exchange markets 81–3; Franco-German project 134–6; goes ahead 46–7; and interest rates 49–50, 80–1; mark I 21–4; mark II 28–32; muddling through 111–12; pessimistic models for 190; probabilities of scenarios 213–19; slow-growth outlook 163–4; and stultification of Europe 156–9; two-tier approach 133

European Parliament 239, 240

European Regional Development Fund 28

European Reserve Fund (ERF) 23

European Union (EU) 31, 116; criticism of 53–5; eastern applicants 238–9; founding fathers 13–15; historical sequence of events 5–10; as lasting process 58–60; multi-speed approach to 59, 118, 216; new entrants 237; north v. south 141–3; Treaty of 32–3; west v. east 143–4; widening and deepening of 74–5, 147

Eurosceptics 34–6, 59, 145–6, 147, 227, 233

Eurosclerosis 68

exchange rate mechanism (ERM) 28, 29, 30, 43–5, 79, 195

Far East 70, 71, 84; pricking of the bubble 86–9

Fernández-Armesto, Felipe 57, 189

finance and banking systems 49–50, 81–3, 85, 144, 171–2
Finland 234
flags 24
foreign policy 53–5
Fortress Europe 140–1, 149
franc fort strategy 29, 135, 195
France 225–7; *see also* Franco-German axis
Franco-German axis 134–6, 141, 145, 186, 211, 225, 229; consequences of split 199–200; split 195–6; *see also* France; Germany
French-Spanish model 50
Fukuyama, Francis 106

Garel-Jones, Tristan 33
General Agreement on Tariffs and Trade (Gatt) 21, 111; Uruguay round 118
Gentle, Christopher 103, 114
George, Eddie 46
German (Rhine) model 50–1
Germany 83–4, 223–5; eastern European links 174–5; unification of 69–70, 74–5, 117, 135, 185–6; *see also* Franco-German axis
Giroday, Frédéric Boyer de la 23
'Global Competitiveness Report' (WEF) 42–3
Goldman Sachs 137
Goldsmith, Sir James 36
Gorbachev, Mikhail 69
Greece 234–5
Greenland 58–9
Group of Seven (G7) 83–4, 200
Group of Three (G3) 83–4

Hague, summit meeting (1969) 23
Haider, Joerg 232
Hall, Jeremy 208
Hindley, Brian 172
Hiroshima 206
Hirsch, Seev and Almor, Tamar 140
Hogg, Sarah and Hill, Jonathan 32, 33
Holmes, Martin 145
Hong Kong 202
Hungary 238

Huntington, Samuel 202
Hutton, Ray 71

India 205
insider–outsider effects 140, 146–8, 175
Institute for Peace Research and Security Policy (Hamburg University) 174
Institute for Public Policy Research 185
institutions 55–6, 239–41; as unwieldy 129–31
Integrated Mediterranean Programmes 234
Inter-Governmental Conference (IGC) (1996–7) 55, 114, 130
interest rates 49–50, 80–1
International Institute for Strategic Studies (IISS) 86
International Monetary Fund (IMF) 73, 167
Ireland 104, 235
Italian model 50
Italy 138–9, 142, 146, 229–31

Japan 83–4, 90, 102, 119, 120–1, 201, 244–5
Japanese model 51
Jay, Peter 191
Jenkins, Roy 14, 28, 134, 240
'Job's Study' (OECD) 41–2, 159–60
Johnson, Christopher 77
Juppé, Alain 135, 197, 226

Kalergi, Coudenhove 34
Kenen, Peter 81–2
King, Stephen 193
Kissinger, Henry 243
Klaus, Vaclav 239
Kohl, Helmut 33, 37, 43, 75, 85, 90, 185, 186, 197, 199, 223–5
Kornik, Richard 72
Krugman, Paul 86

Lamers, Karl 132, 150, 216, 217, 240
Lamfalussy, Alexandre 156
Lamont, Norman 33
language 170

Lascelles, David 196–7, 198
Latvia 238
Lawson, Nigel 22, 28
Layard, Richard and Parker, John 73–4, 207–8
Le Pen, Jean-Marie 197
Lebrun, Albert 13
Leigh-Pemberton, Robin 31
Les Etrangers scenario: British schizophrenia 144–6; building a fortress 140–1; core monetary union 132–4; core success 139–40; dangerous inequality 149; EMU divides the Union 136–8; explosive political cocktail 148; fifty years on 150; Franco-German axis 134–6; insiders/outsiders 146–8; Italian question 138–9; north v. south 141–3; probability of 216–17; Schengenland 131–2; the six are special 127–9; Tower of Babel 129–31; uncertain business environment 148–9; west v. east 143–4
Levy, Paul 24
Lindsey, Lawrence 160
Lithuania 238
Llewellyn, John 162
Louvre accord (1987) 83
Luxembourg 127–9, 235; compromise 27
Lynch, Peter 188

Maastricht, Treaty of (1992) 32–3, 44, 111, 117, 135; rejection of 34–5
McKay, David 55, 60, 136, 141
Madelin, Alain 197
Madrid summit (1989) 32
Magnus, George and Donovan, Paul 161
Major, John 33, 35
Malta 52, 144, 237
Mansholt plan 20
Mansholt, Sicco 20
markets, opening up of 76
Marshall Plan 242
Messina, meeting at 16–17, 18

Middlemas, Keith 54, 128, 188
Miles, David 166
Mitterand, François 29, 33, 37, 75, 85, 185, 186
Mohamad, Mahathir 203
Monnet, Jean 13, 34, 85, 89–90, 115
Monti, Mario 40, 78
Morrison, Herbert 18
Movimento Federalista Europeo 15

Naisbitt, John 205
nationalism 175–6, 185, 188–9, 194, 225
Netherlands 235–6
North American Free Trade Area (Nafta) 173, 243
North Atlantic Treaty Organisation (Nato) 14, 15, 18
Northern League 142, 230
nuclear accidents 206–9

O'Donnell, Gus 33
'One Market, One Money' (EC) 79
opt-outs 33, 163
Organisation for Economic Co-operation and Development (OECD) 41–2, 67, 72, 101–2, 143, 144, 159–60, 165–6, 242
Organisation for European Economic Co-operation (OEEC) 242
Organisation of Petroleum Exporting Countries (Opec) 23, 41, 68
Owen, David 187

Padoa-Schioppa, Tommaso 75–6
Pan-European Movement 34
Panic, Mica 133
passports 25
'peace dividend' 91–2
pension schemes 165–7
'People's Europe' 25, 27
Pétain, Phillippe 13
Philip Morris Institute 110, 143
Plaza agreement (1985) 83
plus ça change scenario 99–100: Asian question 120–21; bicycles can be ridden slowly 117–18; business regains its edge 113–14; competitiveness and other myths

103–4; declining but prospering 101–3; edging to closer union 114–17; Europe in the world 118–20; European restructuring 106–8; European specialisation 108–9; Europe's low-cost economies 104–5; Europe's low-cost producers 105–6; fifty years on 122; muddling through on single currency 111–12; muddling through in the Single Market 109–11; no need for growth miracle 112–13; not a zero-sum game 100–1; probability of 214–15; sailing along 121
Poland 238
politics 85, 114–17; end of 209; maintaining the middle ground 115–17
popular culture 170–1
population; ageing 164–7; migration 191–2
Portugal 231–2
Prodi, Romano 137
production, low-cost 105–6
'Public Pension Systems: The Challenge Ahead' 165

Radaelli, Giorgio and Shea, Ryan 164–5
Rapallo, Treaty of (1922) 174
Rassemblement pour la République (RPR) 130
Reading, Brian 70
renaissance scenario 67: Asian turbulence 90–2; business bonanza 84–5; cultural renaissance 92–3; eastern illusion 69–70; eastern promise 71–3; Europe as Rip van Winkle 67–9; European stability 89–90; Europe's potential 75–80; fifty years on 93; from G7 to G3 83–4; new political mood 85; once currency, biggest currency 81–3; one currency, cheap money 80–1; pricking the Asian bubble 86–9;

probability of 213–14; Russian boom 73–4; wider and deeper 74–5
resource transfers 193–4, 238
restructuring programmes 106–8, 149
Rhine (German) model 50–1, 203
Roberts, J.M. 88
Rohwer, Jim 88
Romania 238
Rome, Treaty of (1957) 17, 26, 31, 48, 141
'Rough Neighbours' 200–1
Royal Institute of International Affairs 120, 200
Russia 119–20, 200, 241–2; economic boom 73–4

Sachs, Jeffrey 42
Santer, Jacques 81
Sassoon, Donald 185
Schengen agreement 49, 131–2, 216, 233
Schmidt, Helmut 28, 134
Schuman plan 14
Schuman, Robert 13–14, 18
Segal, Gerard 86, 91
Séguin, Philippe 197
shocks 192–4
single currency, effects of *see* European Monetary Union (Emu)
Single European Act (1986) 26–8, 49, 78, 131
Single Market ('1992' programme); assessment of 38–41; and growth 112–13; growth and success of 76–80; muddling through 109–11 'the Six' 148; divisions among 139–40; as special 127–9
Slovak Republic 238
Slovenia 238
'Social Democracy at the Heart of Europe' (IPPR) 185
Spaak committee 16–17, 18
Spaak, Paul-Henri 14, 16
Spain 231–2
specialisation 108–9
Spinelli, Altiero 14–15, 26
'Stability and Growth Pact' 136–8

Stoiber, Edmund 197
Stokes, Bruce 243
Sumitomo Finance International 49
Swann, Dennis 89
Sweden 236
Switzerland 233, 237–8

Taiwan 91
Taylor, Christopher 49, 81, 134
Tebbit, Norman 160
Thatcher, Margaret 22, 28, 31, 104, 128, 186, 227
Thorn, Gaston 30
Three Mile Island 207
Thurow, Lester 203
Tindemans, Leo 25
trade 100–1; barriers to 109–11, 213; decline in 101–3; liberalisation of 171–3; and protectionism 110; specialisation 108–9
trans-European networks (TENs) 108
Transatlantic Free Trade Area (Tafta) 243
Trent, Bill 107
tribalism 186–7
Turkey 238

Ukraine 241–2
unemployment *see* employment

United Nations High Commissioner for Refugees (UNHCR) 187
United States 83–4, 121, 201, 242–4; economic dominance of 168–70; labour market in 160; trade links 173
United States of Europe 170–1
Uri, Pierre 17

Valladao, Alfredo 168–9
voting procedures 129–31, 142

Walsh, Brendan 104
war, effect of 99–100
welfare 106–7
Welsh, Michael 116
Western European Union (WEU) 15, 18
Windscale (Sellafield) 207
World Economic Forum (WEF) 42
World Trade Organisation (WTO) 118, 143
World Wide Web 169

Young, Lord 27
Yugoslavia 54, 58, 186–7

zero-sum game 100–1
Zwickauer Mulde valley 207